THE PROTESTANT CHURCHES

of America

The

Protestant Churches

of America

by **JOHN A. HARDON, S.J.**

Professor of Dogmatic Theology
The Jesuit Theologate
West Baden College
West Baden Springs, Indiana

THE NEWMAN PRESS

WESTMINSTER, MARYLAND

1957

First published, 1956
Second printing, 1957

Imprimi Potest: WILLIAM J. SCHMIDT, S.J.
Provincial of the Chicago Province
July 17, 1956

Nihil Obstat: EDWARD A. CERNY, S.S., D.D.
Censor Librorum

Imprimatur: FRANCIS P. KEOUGH, D.D.
Archbishop of Baltimore

October 29, 1956

The *Nihil Obstat* and *Imprimatur* are official declarations that a book or pamphlet is free of doctrinal and moral error. No implication is contained therein that those who have granted the *Nihil Obstat* and *Imprimatur* agree with the opinions expressed.

Acknowledgments

THE AUTHOR and publishers are gratefully indebted to about fifty copyright holders for permission to use quotations from their books and periodicals. Special gratitude is due to the National Council of the Churches of Christ for its generous cooperation in furnishing the statistical data on the religious bodies in the United States.

Where publishers requested a certain wording in the acknowledgment, this has been followed in each case. However specific permission was received for the use of quotations from all the publications here listed.

Necessarily the quoted material is adapted to Catholic readers. At the same time, the author's avowed intention was to do full justice to every denomination treated in the following pages. When persons and institutions are sometimes criticized, the motive has been a sincere desire to have the truth appear, and not to make invidious comparisons among the various churches.

ABINGDON PRESS, New York and Nashville:
William K. Anderson (editor), *Methodism*, 1947; *Protestantism, A Symposium*, 1945.
Elmer T. Clark, *The Small Sects in America*, 1949.
Doctrines and Discipline of the Methodist Church, 1952.
General Minutes of the Annual Conferences of the Methodist Church, 1954.

Frank S. Mead, *Handbook of Denominations in the United States,* 1951.

Charles C. Selecman, *The Methodist Primer,* 1953.

William M. Sweet, *Methodism in American History,* 1933.

BAKER BOOK HOUSE, Grand Rapids, Michigan:

The Twentieth Century Encyclopedia of Religious Knowledge, Vol. II, 1955.

BEACON PRESS, INC., Boston:

Ralph L. Roy, *Apostles of Discord,* 1953.

Harry B. Scholefield, *Pocket Guide to Unitarianism,* 1955.

Services of Religion, 1953.

Earl M. Wilbur, *Our Unitarian Heritage,* 1954.

THE BETHANY PRESS, St. Louis:

B. A. Abbott, *The Disciples, An Interpretation,* 1926.

Alonzo W. Fortune, *Origin and Development of the Disciples,* 1953.

Winfred E. Garrison and Alfred T. DeGroot, *The Disciples of Christ, A History,* 1954.

Benjamin L. Smith, *Minister's Manual,* 1951.

LEROY BROWNLOW PUBLICATIONS, Fort Worth, Texas:

Leroy Brownlow, *Why I Am a Member of the Church of Christ,* 1945.

The author was requested by Mr. Brownlow to add the following clarification: "One of the basic and fundamental teachings of the church of Christ is that she is neither Roman Catholic nor Protestant, but Christian only, believing that such was true of the church in the first century. Yet, permission is granted to quote from the book, *Why I Am a Member of the Church of Christ,* in this volume on *The Protestant Churches of America,* understanding that the purpose of the volume is to acquaint Roman Catholics with the views and convictions of non-Roman Catholics."

CAMBRIDGE UNIVERSITY PRESS, New York:

John L. Nickalls, *Journal of George Fox,* 1952.

CHRISTIAN BOARD OF PUBLICATION, St. Louis. (See THE BETHANY PRESS.)

THE CHRISTIAN CENTURY, Chicago:

Issues of Dec. 16, 1953; Sept. 1, 1954; July 6, Nov. 23, Dec. 14, 1955; Feb. 8, 1956. Copyrighted by the Christian Century Foundation and reprinted by permission from The Christian Century.

CHRISTIAN EDUCATION PRESS, Philadelphia:

Oscar J. Rumpf, *Christian Faith and Life,* 1952.

The Constitution and By-Laws of the Evangelical and Reformed Church.

My Confirmation, 1955.

THE CHRISTIAN SCIENCE PUBLISHING SOCIETY, Boston:
  The Christian Science Journal, passages reprinted from Dec.
  1954 issue.
THE CHURCH OF JESUS CHRIST OF LATTER-DAY SAINTS, Salt Lake City:
  Book of Mormon, 1921.
  Joseph F. Smith, *Essentials in Church History,* 1950.
  James E. Talmage, *Articles of Faith,* 1952.
CONCORDIA PUBLISHING HOUSE, St. Louis:
  Walter A. Baepler, *A Century of Grace,* 1947.
  John H. C. Fritz, *Pastoral Theology,* 1945.
  F. E. Mayer, *The Religious Bodies of America,* 1954.
  John T. Mueller, *My Church and Others,* 1945.
  J. L. Neve and Willard D. Allbeck, *History of the Lutheran
  Church in America.*
  Francis Pieper, *Christian Dogmatics,* Vols. II, III, 1953.
  Arthur G. Piepkorn, *What the Symbolical Books have to say
  about Worship and the Sacraments,* 1952.
  E. G. Schwiebert, *Luther and His Times,* 1950.
  Doctrinal Declarations.
  Dr. Martin Luther's Small Catechism, 1943.
  The Lutheran Agenda.
  The Lutheran Hymnal, 1941.
  The Lutheran Witness, Aug. 2, 1955.
CONGREGATIONAL CHRISTIAN CHURCHES, New York:
  A Book of Worship for Free Churches, Copyright 1948 by The
  Board of Home Missions of The Congregational and Chris-
  tian Churches. All rights reserved.
  The Congregational Christian Ministry, 1953, Quoted with per-
  mission from the Department of the Ministry.
COWLES MAGAZINES, INC., New York:
  Leo Rosten (editor), *A Guide to the Religions of America,* 1955.
DUELL, SLOAN AND PEARCE, INC., New York:
  Norman Beasley, *The Cross and the Crown,* 1952, by permission
  of Duell, Sloan and Pearce, Inc.
EDEN—HEIDELBERG BOOKSTORES, St. Louis:
  James I. Good, *Aid to the Heidelberg Catechism.*
  J. H. Horstmann and H. H. Wernecke, *Through Four Cen-
  turies,* 1938.
  Book of Worship, 1947.
  Evangelical Catechism, 1929.
THE EVANGELICAL PRESS, Harrisburg, Pennsylvania:
  Paul H. Eller, *These Evangelical United Brethren,* 1950.
  Paul W. Milhouse, *Christian Worship in Symbol and Ritual,*
  1953.
  The Discipline of the Evangelical United Brethren, 1947 and
  1955.

GENERAL CONVENTION OF THE NEW JERUSALEM, Boston:
  Official Book of Worship, 1912.
GOSPEL ADVOCATE COMPANY, Nashville:
  Leslie G. Thomas, *Restoration Handbook,* 1954.
GOSPEL TRACTS UNLIMITED, Hayward, California:
  J. M. Stowell, *Background and History of the General Association of Regular Baptist Churches,* 1949.
HALF MOON PRESS, Grand Rapids, Michigan:
  Howard G. Hageman, *Our Reformed Church,* 1952.
  Constitution of the Reformed Church in America, 1950.
HARPER AND BROTHERS, New York:
  Harry E. Fosdick, *The Man from Nazareth,* 1949.
  Winfred E. Garrison, *Religion Follows the Frontier,* 1931.
  Rufus M. Jones, *The Faith and Practice of the Quakers,* 1927.
  Charles S. Morrison, *The Unfinished Reformation,* 1953.
  Anson P. Stokes, *Church and State in the United States,* Vols. II, III, 1950.
  Mark Twain, *Christian Science,* 1907.
  J. Paul Williams, *What Americans Believe and How They Worship,* 1952.
W. L. JENKINS, Philadelphia:
  Presbyterian Law for the Local Church, edited by Eugene Carson Blake, Copyright, 1954, by W. L. Jenkins. Used by permission.
THE JUDSON PRESS, Philadelphia:
  Edward T. Hiscox, *The New Directory for Baptist Churches,* 1954.
  J. M. Pendleton, *Baptist Church Manual,* 1955.
  Robert G. Torbet, *A History of the Baptists.* Copyright 1950 by The Judson Press.
JOHN KNOX PRESS, Richmond, Virginia:
  Walter Lingle, *Presbyterians, Their History and Beliefs.* Copyright, 1950, by John Knox Press, Richmond, Virginia. Used by permission.
THE LIVING CHURCH, Milwaukee:
  Editorials from the issues of Apr. 29, 1951; Aug. 30, 1953; Nov. 6, 1955.
LONGMANS, GREEN AND CO., INC., New York:
  Ernest W. Barnes, *The Rise of Christianity,* 1947.
  William James, *The Varieties of Religious Experience,* 1902.
THE McBRIDE CO., INC., New York:
  E. Katherine Bates, *Do the Dead Depart?,* 1929.
THE MACMILLAN COMPANY, New York:
  Vergilius Ferm, *What Is Lutheranism?,* 1930.
  Rufus M. Jones, *A Call to What is Vital,* 1948.
  William A. Linn, *The Story of the Mormons,* 1923.

MENNONITE PUBLISHING HOUSE, Scottdale, Pennsylvania:
Mennonite Church Policy, 1952.

MOREHOUSE-GORHAM CO., INC., New York:
George P. Atwater, *The Episcopal Church, Its Message for Men of Today,* pages 83-84. Copyright 1953 by Marie Carey Atwater. Used by permission of Morehouse-Gorham Co., New York.

George E. De Mille, *The Episcopal Church Since 1900,* pages 67, 74-5, 83, 85-6, 118, 147, 152, 155. Copyright 1955 by Morehouse-Gorham Co.

F. S. B. Gavin, *Liberal Catholicism and the Modern World,* Vol. I, page vii. Copyright 1934 by Morehouse-Gorham Co.

NATIONAL COUNCIL OF THE CHURCHES OF CHRIST, New York:
John L. Cowan, *Christian Day Schools under Protestant Auspices,* 1955. Report used with permission.

Yearbook of American Churches 1957. Copyright 1956 by The National Council of Churches. Used with permission.

OUTLOOK PUBLISHERS, Richmond, Virginia:
Kenneth J. Foreman, *God's Will and Ours,* 1954.

OXFORD UNIVERSITY PRESS, INC., New York:
The Book of Common Prayer, 1944. Quotations used through the courtesy of Rev. John W. Suter, D.D., Custodian of the Standard Book of Common Prayer.

PACIFIC PRESS PUBLISHING ASSOCIATION, Mountain View, California:
Uriah Smith, *The Prophecies of Daniel and the Revelation,* 1951.

Ellen G. White, *The Desire of the Ages,* 1955; *The Great Controversy between Christ and Satan,* 1953.

PHILADELPHIA YEARLY MEETING OF THE RELIGIOUS SOCIETY OF FRIENDS:
Faith and Practice of the Philadelphia Yearly Meeting, 1955.

PHILOSOPHICAL LIBRARY, INC., New York:
Vergilius Ferm (editor), *The American Church,* 1953.

Henry W. Steiger, *Christian Science and Philosophy,* 1948.

PILGRIM PRESS, Boston:
G. G. Atkins and F. L. Fagley, *History of American Congregationalism,* 1941.

Richard H. Bennet, *Christian Faith and Purpose, A Catechism.*

L. Wendell Fifield, *What It Means to be a Member of the Congregational Church.*

Oscar Maurer (editor), *Manual of the Congregational Christian Churches,* 1951.

Roy L. Minich, *What the Church Has to Offer.*

Albert W. Palmer, *I Believe in Baptism.*

Christian Teachings: A Manual for those Preparing for Church Membership.

Manual for Church Members, 1952.

My Church: Pastor's Manual, 1944.
The Congregational Christian Churches, For What They Stand.
We Believe.
PRESBYTERIAN CHURCH IN THE U.S.A., Philadelphia:
   The Book of Common Worship. Copyright, 1946, by the Board
   of Christian Education of the Presbyterian Church in the
   U.S.A. Used by permission.
   The Constitution of the Presbyterian Church in the U.S.A.,
   Revised Edition. Copyright, 1955, by the Board of Christian
   Education of the Presbyterian Church in the U.S.A. Used by
   permission.
   C. McAfee and E. Porter, *Why A Presbyterian Church.* Copy-
   right, 1930, by the Board of Christian Education of the
   Presbyterian Church in the U.S.A. Used by permission.
FLEMING H. REVELL COMPANY, Westwood, New Jersey:
   Gaius G. Atkins, *Modern Religious Cults and Movements*, 1923.
REVIEW AND HERALD PUBLISHING ASSOCIATION, Washington, D. C.:
   Leroy E. Froom, *The Prophetic Faith of Our Fathers*, Vol. IV,
   1954.
   Emma E. Howell, *The Great Advent Movement*, 1952.
   James White, *Sketches of the Christian Life and Public Labors
   of William Miller*, 1875.
   Manual for Ministers, 1954.
   Seventh-Day Adventist Yearbook, 1955.
SALVATIONIST PUBLISHING AND SUPPLIES, LTD., London:
   William Booth, *In Darkest England and the Way Out*, 1942.
   M. L. Carpenter, *Salvationists and the Sacraments*, 1945.
   Alfred J. Gilliard, *The Faith of the Salvationist.*
   Orders and Regulations for Officers of the Salvation Army, 1950.
   Salvation Army Ceremonies, 1947.
   Salvation Army Handbook of Doctrine, 1955.
   Salvation Army Yearbook, 1956.
SCIENTIFIC AMERICAN, New York:
   Issues of February and May, 1952.
CHARLES SCRIBNER'S SONS, New York:
   James T. Addison, *The Episcopal Church in the United States*,
   1951.
   William A. Brown, *Toward A United Church*, 1946.
   Edwin F. Dakin, *Mrs. Eddy*, 1930.
   Reinhold Niebuhr, *Beyond Tragedy*, 1937; *Human Destiny*,
   1935.
THE SEABURY PRESS, INC., Greenwich, Connecticut:
   Powel Mills Dawley, *The Episcopal Church and Its Work*, 1955.
   Greenwich: The Seabury Press. Used by permission of the
   publisher.

Contents

Part One

MAJOR PROTESTANT DENOMINATIONS

Part Two

MINOR PROTESTANT DENOMINATIONS

Part Three

STATISTICS ON RELIGIOUS BODIES
IN THE UNITED STATES

Introduction

THIS VOLUME is intended primarily for Catholic readers,
to give them an up-to-date manual of information on
the Protestant churches in the United States. The need for
such a manual is obvious. Catholics deal with Protestants
on every level of human relationship, from the intimacy
of family life to the less personal but very important associations in the professional and business world. Yet they
often have only the vaguest notion of what Protestants believe, how they worship, and what their religion means to
them. There is no lack of books written by non-Catholics
on the churches and sects in the United States. At least
ten have been published in the last decade: *They Have
Found a Faith* by Marcus Bach, *These Also Believe* by
Charles Braden, *The Small Sects in America* by Elmer
Clark, *The Story of American Protestantism* by Andrew
Drummond, *Religion in the Twentieth Century* by Ver-
gilius Ferm, *The Religious Bodies of America* by F. E.
Mayer, *Handbook of Denominations* by Frank Meade, *A
Guide to the Religions of America* by Leo Rosten, *Re-
ligion in America* by Willard Sperry, and *What Americans
Believe and How They Worship* by J. Paul Williams.
From the Catholic standpoint there is not a single volume,
if we except *Christian Denominations* by Krull, first pub-

lished in 1911, and the same title by Algermissen, written for German readers.

Instead of trying to cover all two hundred denominations in the country, and as a consequence saying little about any one of them, it seemed preferable to separate the churches into two classes, the major and minor, and treat the individual sects in greater detail. The fifteen churches in the first class were chosen on the basis of their size or because of their recognized influence in American sectarian life. They include every denomination with a half million or more members, and smaller groups like the Unitarians and Quakers because of their historic impact on our pluralistic society. By actual count, these fifteen bodies represent ninety per cent of the current total of fifty-seven million Protestants in the United States. The other ten per cent, scattered through a bewildering variety of sects, were conveniently grouped into distinctive families to make their treatment more intelligible. The major denominations are covered at greater length, going into the respective church histories, their doctrinal position, ritual practice and organizational structure. But in every case, even for the smallest sect, the aim was to concentrate a maximum of significant detail in order to give the reader a concise picture of American Protestantism in the present day.

The most serious problem that faces anyone who writes on Protestant beliefs and practices is where to find authentic information. When a cynic remarked that "trying to describe Protestantism is like trying to describe the United States, one can say almost anything about it," he was exaggerating. But the fact remains that Protestants have "no united voice with which to give authoritative answers" on what they believe and how their people worship. They are disunited as denominations, and further disunited as sects, and still further as churches within the sectarian divisions. The practical solution which the writer adopted was to limit his source of information in doctrinal and ritual matters to official publications of the various bodies and to writings by leaders within the denominations. It was assumed that in spite of the freedom of thought in American Protestantism, whatever common elements the churches profess, may be found in these two sources. Moreover, even for historical data, only Protestant authorities were used in order to give as objective a presentation as the resources of time (several years) and material (over a hundred books and tracts) would allow.

There is an obvious risk in reading about so many different sects with such a variety of religious persuasions. It may be impossible to recognize the forest for the trees. Yet Protestantism in America is not only a glomeration of conflicting opinions. It has features that are quite different from those of other religious bodies in the country, and even distinct from Protestantism outside the United States. The first may easily be traced to its Reformation ancestry. The second is more subtle, and may be partially explained as a transfer of American love of liberty to the sphere of religion, with consequent fragmentation of churches, and more recently with a growing ecumenical consciousness that is trying to correct this "wild sectarianism."

Reformation Ancestry. With rare exception, the Protestant churches in America owe their beginning to the religious upheaval in the sixteenth century when Luther, Calvin, and their followers broke with Roman unity and began religious institutions of their own. Few of the sects will admit this, of course. They claim to be the original Church of Christ which goes back to apostolic times. But when they try to prove their claim, they fall back on one of two expedients: either they deny that Catholicism was ever the true Church and trace their genealogy through the gallery of heretics from Marcion and Arius to Luther,

Calvin and Zwingli; or they admit that Catholics formed the true Church up to the Reformation but, contrary to the promise of Christ, were overcome by the gates of hell so that a new church had to be founded. Certain denominations, like the Lutherans, emphasize the second method. Others, like the Baptists and Episcopalians, prefer the first. Sometimes the lineage from Reformation times is not very clear historically; but there is never any doubt about the transmission of ideas from the original Reformers to modern sectarians. When Orestes Brownson charged that Protestantism has "no fixed and permanent character except hatred of Catholicism," and "no principles, doctrines, or forms which, in order to be itself, it must always and everywhere maintain," he oversimplified the case.[1] But substantially it is true to say that Protestantism as a form of Christianity is essentially changeable and unstable. Whatever religious stability individual sects may show, they owe to whatever doctrines or practices they still share in common with the Catholic Church. The instability of Protestantism is due to the strange concept of human autonomy which the Reformers injected into the body of Christian tradition.

Church historians correctly say there were two fundamental principles of the Reformation: the supreme authority of Scripture and the doctrine of justification by faith. Against these the Catholic position is that Scripture alone is not sufficient, but tradition is also needed; and that a man is justified or made pleasing to God not only by faith but also by the good works he performs. However, beneath these two Reformation issues lay a deeper error from which they are both derived. This was the assertion of man's independence of any society as the final arbiter in questions of faith and morals. It was "the Protestant belief in the inspiration of the individual and the consequent right of private judgment."[2] So basic is this principle that by it we may explain not only the Protestant imperviousness to history and argument which is so incredible to Catholics, but also the resistance among Protestants themselves to any attempt on the part of their leaders to unite the churches under "authoritarian domination." By this standard the Catholic Church is accused of being the worst pretender in history. She has "usurped the majesty of God," according to Reinhold Niebuhr, because her priests claim to be "in control of God's redemptive powers and purposes and in possession of the keys of heaven." [3]

Sectarianism and the Ecumenical Movement. Protestants deplore the multiplicity of their sects in the United States. They confess that "denominationalism is scandalously wasteful of Protestant resources," by it "the missionary expansion of the Christian faith is seriously handicapped," it "robs Protestantism of its inherent strength in its inescapable competition with a formidable and aggressive Roman Catholicism," it "provincializes Protestant mentality" and "breeds a subtle and perilous moral insincerity among Protestant Christians." [4] The ecumenical movement is an effort to check this rampant sectarianism, and to join a divided Protestantism into some semblance of religious unity.

While the beginnings of the ecumenical movement in America go back more than a century, large-scale mergers of Protestant denominations have all taken place since 1900. During this time, thirty religious bodies have merged into thirteen, and these by remerger have been reduced to nine. At least three large-size reunions are expected to take place in the near future. In May, 1954, three major Presbyterian denominations brought merger negotiations, begun in 1937, to the decisive stage. Final approval is also expected for a union plan that will bring into being a 1,800,000 member Lutheran Church two years from now.

There were once eighty-five Lutheran sects in the United States. Today there are nineteen. A more radical merger plan involves the prospective union of the Congregational Christian with the Evangelical and Reformed Church, to become the United Church of Christ, with an aggregate membership of over three million. A minority of Congregationalists is trying to block the merger by every possible means, including several court proceedings. Unless they succeed, the union will take place in June, 1957.

Besides denominational mergers in which the uniting elements fused into a new society or one element absorbed the others, there have been three other coalitions on a wider but less intensive scale, in which the product was not a new church but a cooperative organization. The three federations are closely related.

In 1908 came the Federal Council of Churches of Christ in America, when twenty-eight Reformed Churches were organized along structural lines which duplicated the federal union of the United States. It was difficult at first for the churches of the Federal Council to believe that their autonomy would not be jeopardized. This suspicion kept many sects from joining the union. Actually they had nothing to fear because the federation was most careful not to encroach on the independence of the member churches. One incident in the forty-year existence of the Federal Council may illustrate its character. For years the Unitarians had asked to be admitted and were always refused. Their creedal position was too liberal. They deny the Trinity and their concept of God is not far removed from monism. Ostensibly, therefore, the motive for refusing them admission was based on principle. But when the president of the Council was directly questioned, he admitted it was a matter of expediency. "If we let in the Unitarians, we let out the Lutherans." [5]

The second stage in federated unionism came in 1941,

when ultra-conservative Protestants, called Fundamentalists, formed an organization of their own in protest against
the libertarian Federal Council. While the latter would
have been happy to admit the Fundamentalists, "provided
they came in a cooperative spirit," their opponents claimed
that the leaders of the Federal Council were promoting a
new denominational effort independently of the Word of
God. The American Council of Christian Churches is
therefore a rival organization, comprising fifteen national
constituent bodies together with independent congregations. However, because Fundamentalists are generally
found among the poorer and less privileged classes, in
rural areas and small towns, educated sectarians do not
take them seriously. Their aggressive dogmatism is said to
be antiquarian, "frozen in the crudest form of orthodoxy
known in Protestant history." [6]

Finally, in 1950 the Federal Council of Churches en-
larged its scope of activities and changed its name to the
National Council of the Churches of Christ, to become
the largest federated union of Protestants in American
history. At the present writing, it numbers twenty-five
Protestant denominations and five Eastern Orthodox
bodies, representing over thirty-five million church communicants. Structurally the National Council is the same
as its predecessor, with a notable difference. Three new
agencies were added for cooperative effort: Christian Education, and the Home, and Foreign Missions. "Their inclusion in the National Council marks an appreciable
deepening of the feeling of Protestant unity. For these
three functions come nearer to being ecclesiastical than
any which the denominations had ever committed to a
federal responsibility." [7]

However, the National Council is not a union of denominations; it is a merger of their common, external interests. Its avowed purpose is to accelerate the growth of

"unity within diversity," to reduce the supervisory expenses and needless duplication of buildings and personnel, to become a clearing house for the exchange of ideas and views aimed at the development of a "sound Protestant strategy." In a word, it is an attempt to retrieve some of the loss in prestige and influence which American Protestants have suffered through more than three centuries of sectarianism.

There is a permanent tension in American Protestantism which it is hoped the following pages will clarify: a tension between the "Protestant" and "Catholic" elements in the denominations; between the spirit of independence and a respect for Christian tradition; or, in Paul Tillich's phrase, between the autonomy which asserts that "man as the bearer of universal reason is the source and measure of culture and religion—that he is his own law," and the heteronomy which holds that man requires help from the outside, ultimately from God, but proximately "subjects the forms and laws of thinking and acting to authoritative criteria of an ecclesiastical religion." [8]

Certain denominations like the Episcopalians and Lutherans will be seen to emphasize the heteronomous side of Protestantism; others, like the Congregationalists, to stress autonomous self-sufficiency—but in every case the conflict is somehow there. Once recognized, it becomes a frame of reference for making a proper estimate of any religious body.[9] It helps to explain the ebb and flow of Protestant orthodoxy, the rise and disappearance of various sects, the constant struggle between liberals and conservatives in every denomination, and the growing sense of guilt that has produced the ecumenical movement. It affords an insight into what seem to be contradictions, but which Protestants prefer to call "an inclusive Christianity." Above all, it gives those who possess the fulness of revelation a sympathetic understanding and a desire to share the true faith with those who are still searching for the truth.

JOHN A. HARDON, S.J.
The Jesuit Theologate
West Baden College

REFERENCES

1. *The Works of Orestes A. Brownson*, Vol. XIII, Detroit, H. F. Brownson, 1905, p. 163.
2. Albert C. Knudson, "Cardinal Principles of Protestantism," *Protestantism: A Symposium* (William K. Anderson, ed.), Nashville, Parthenon Press, 1945, p. 126.
3. Reinhold Niebuhr, "Our Dependence Is on God," *The Christian Century*, LXXI, September 1, 1954, p. 1035.
4. Charles C. Morrison, *The Unfinished Reformation*, New York, Harper, 1953, pp. 29-35.
5. J. Paul Williams, *What Americans Believe and How They Worship*, New York, Harper, 1952, p. 130.
6. Morrison, *op. cit.*, p. 190.
7. *Ibid.*, p. 12.
8. Paul Tillich, *The Protestant Era*, Chicago, University of Chicago Press, 1948, pp. 56-57.
9. Among Protestants, the terms "church," "denomination," and "sect" are often used indiscriminately. But technically there is a distinction which official writings are careful to observe. "Church" is used to refer either to the whole body of Christians, or (usually in small letters) to all the members of a given body, like the Baptists, Methodists, and Lutherans. When the religious group is described in terms of its peculiar spirit or ancestry, instead of "church," the term "denomination" is preferred, except that it has a slightly unwelcome connotation. Within the larger churches, except the Episcopalians, there are smaller units into which the denominations have split. These are properly called "sects" (from *secare*, to cut). The Baptist Church (or denomination), for example, has 27 sects. To be emphasized is that the real ecclesiastical units of Protestantism are the sects. They are juridically self-governing, doctrinally autonomous and legally erected religious bodies which are entirely distinct not only from other denominations but even from other sects within the same denominational "family."

Part One

MAJOR PROTESTANT DENOMINATIONS

1. Adventists

THE LARGEST Adventist body in the United States, the Seventh-Day Adventists, epitomizes practically all the main characteristics of Protestant Christianity. Its emphasis on Old Testament practices as a corrective of the New Law has led to the adoption of the Jewish Sabbath in place of the Christian Sunday, and the acceptance of a rigid code of abstinence from forbidden food and drink. Its desire for release from the evils of this world has become crystallized in the doctrine of an early second coming of Christ and the consequent millenium. Its insistence on private interpretation of the Bible has developed into a theory of private inspiration independently of the Scriptures, with visions and prophecies which amplify the Christian revelation.

At the same time, the Seventh-Day Adventists have gained a reputation as the most generous church-givers in America. An annual per capita contribution of almost 200 dollars amounts to an aggregate total of 50 million dollars for less than a third-million members. The tangible result has been "a globe-encircling chain of publishing houses . . . a world-wide chain of sanatoriums," and an educational system of about 3,000 institutions that reaches every nation, including Soviet Russia.

HISTORY

While Adventism as a religious phenomenon has been found in every period of Christian history, the existing Adventist churches in America trace their origin to the preaching of William Miller, a Baptist minister, who predicted the end of the world in the early 1840's. Miller was a farmer whose studies of the Book of Daniel convinced him that the second coming of Christ to the earth would take place between March 21, 1843, and March 21, 1844. He preached his first Adventist sermon in 1831, and by 1844 an estimated 50,000 followers anxiously awaited the imminent parousia. When March 21, 1844, passed without anything happening, the Adventists were dismayed and Miller wrote, "I confess my error and acknowledge my disappointment." But he added, "I still believe that the day of the Lord is near, even at the door."[1] One of his disciples discovered that Miller had miscalculated by seven months. The real date was October 21, 1844. Enthusiasm flared up again; men planted no crops, gave away their money and settled their debts in anticipation of the fateful day. When nothing happened a second time, the Millerite movement split into three main divisions. A small group remained faithful to Miller and organized as the American Millenial Association (later the Evangelical Adventists), but through internal dissensions was finally (1926) dissolved as a separate denomination. Another segment was rallied by Jonathan Cummings, who advanced the coming of Christ to 1854. When nothing materialized, the society was reorganized along congregational lines, minus the specific millenium, and came to be known as the Advent Christian Church, which today numbers about 30,000 members.

The most important offshoot of the Millerites, the present Seventh-Day Adventists, owes its inception and remarkable development to the reputed mystical experiences

of a woman disciple of William Miller, Ellen Harmon,
later Mrs. James White. Her family joined the Miller
followers in 1840. In December, 1844, at the age of 17,
she reported her first heavenly vision, predicting the
growth of Adventism, to be followed by other communications which directed the disillusioned Millerites to organize into an evangelistic sect. After years of struggle
along with encouragement from Ellen White, the Adventists held their first General Conference, May 20-23, 1863,
at Battle Creek, Michigan. They elected Mrs. White's
husband, James, as president, but he declined in favor of
John Byington; although White later served three full
terms as head of the Seventh-Day Adventists. Meantime
his wife became the mainstay and guide of the young denomination, alternating between messages from God and
communication to the Adventists by word of mouth and
in published writings. Though she had never studied theology, her output of religious literature was monumental:
20 full-length volumes and upwards of 3,000 articles, dealing with every phase of Scripture exegesis, dogmatics,
morals, and church organization and government. "Of
myself," she wrote in 1905, "I could not have brought out
the truths in these books, but the Lord has given me the
help of His Holy Spirit. These books, giving instruction
that the Lord has given me during the past sixty years,
contain light from heaven, and will bear the test of in-
vestigation." [2]

Under her direction, the Adventists entered the publishing business on a scale unparalleled in any other denomination of like size. "You must begin to print a little
paper," a vision told her. "From this small beginning it
was shown to me to be like streams of light that went clear
around the world." [3] At present, the Adventists have 39
publishing houses in 35 countries, printing literature in
198 languages and dialects, with Braille for the blind, and

including 348 periodicals. "These simple facts," the Adventists claim, "speak for themselves. The test of prediction (by Ellen White) seems fully met in this . . . literary production." [4]

In 1872 Mrs. White published a work on *Proper Education,* after "God had shown her . . . the plan upon which our denominational schools should be founded." [5] She urged the building of church schools, with special emphasis on combining mental training with physical exercise and the learning of mechanical skills. From a single academy in 1872, the Adventists now operate several thousand institutions, in addition to so-called Sabbath Schools, numbering about 18,000, with more than a million pupils.

Early in the beginnings of Adventism, some leaders urged the Scriptural obligation of keeping the Sabbath instead of Sunday as the Lord's Day. The controversy which arose was finally settled by a vision of Mrs. White, in which she saw the tables of the Law and "the fourth (Catholic third) commandment with a soft halo of light encircling it." She was told by the angel in the vision that, "It is the only one of the ten which defines the living God." And "if the true Sabbath had been kept, there would never have been an infidel or an atheist." [6] Further publicity insured acceptance of the doctrine as co-essential with the imminent second coming of Christ. The name, "Seventh-Day Adventists," was officially adopted in 1860.

Another divine communication from Mrs. White confirmed the Adventists in the elaborate health program which is now part of their denominational character. First came "a message which pointed out the dangers of the use of such poisonous articles as tobacco, tea and coffee. A little later, further instruction was given on the importance of cleanliness, both of the person and of the surroundings." Finally, "there was opened up to Mrs. White, in a very comprehensive vision, the important relationship

which exists between good health and godliness and efficiency in service. The causes of disease, its treatment
through aiding nature in its work, and other phases of the
health message, such as diet, rest, exercise and cleanliness,
were all opened up to Mrs. White in this vision." [7] In response to these revelations, the Adventists went into the
manufacture and distribution of vegetarian, non-stimu-
lant, non-intoxicating foods. There are 58 such food com-
panies in various countries, 3 in the United States with
branches in 16 cities. They also began the construction of
hospitals, sanatoria, and rest homes, numbering 212 in
1954, with a concentration in the foreign mission field; for
example, there are 11 hospitals and 30 dispensaries directly
controlled by the Seventh-Day Adventists in South Africa.
The American Health and Temperance Association was
formed in 1879, requiring its members to abstain from
intoxicating beverages, tobacco and all stimulants, including coffee and tea. During the presidential campaign of
1932, the American Temperance Society was organized "to
preserve the cause of temperance," by education and
propaganda.

Under pressure from their environment, the Adventists
founded the National Religious Liberty Association, now
a department of the General Conference. Its establishment
in 1888 was occasioned by the introduction into Congress
of a bill which provided for the proper observance of Sunday as a day of rest. Adventists opposed the bill in public
congressional hearings because they considered "the whole
principle of (civil) legislation in behalf of a religious institution as fundamentally wrong." [8] Twenty years later a
series of similar bills was proposed for the District of
Columbia, but defeated when the Adventists presented to
Congress a lengthy memorial which has since become a
classic statement of protest against Sunday legislation in
America. The passage of such laws, it declared, "would

mark the first step on the part of the national government
in the path of religious legislation—a path which leads inevitably to religious persecution." [9] In practice, the Religious Liberty Department is mainly concerned with
protecting the Adventists' right to observe the Sabbath
instead of Sunday as the Lord's Day. Behind this agitation
lies a principle delivered to the sect by Mrs. White, foretelling that "there would arise in the United States a
hierarchy similar to the Papacy of the Middle Ages, which
would use the civil power of the government to accom-
plish its own ends." [10] By its insistence on the observance
of Sunday, Adventists are told, the United States is promoting the world domination by Rome which changed
the Sabbath Day of Scripture in opposition to the law of
God.

Evangelism outside the States began in 1874, when an
American Adventist "responded to a call" from a small
group of "Sabbath-keepers" in Switzerland. A year later
the movement spread to Germany, and then through all
the countries of Europe. Spearheading the work on the
continent was an apostate priest, M. B. Czechowski, who
"believed in the second coming of Christ and in the
seventh-day Sabbath," after proper indoctrination in
America. Currently 63 Adventist periodicals are published
in Europe, exclusive of England, in 16 languages, including Icelandic, Spanish, and Italian. Oceania was opened
to the Adventist apostolate in 1885, after Mrs. White had
a vision which specified Australia as the next object of
evangelization. A newspaper criticism of the Adventists
read by a man in Argentina led to the introduction of the
sect into South America in 1890, which has since become
the principal field of missionary activity, where over 70
radio stations are broadcasting Adventist propaganda.
Missions in Asia and Africa are operating in all the major

countries, especially India and South Africa. No matter how thinly spread, the Adventists want to be represented in as many nations as possible, on the conviction that even a handful of zealous workers can affect a whole country because of the promised help of the Holy Spirit. According to their own calculation, they are established in 197 countries, whose combined population is 98.5 per cent of the world total.

DOCTRINE AND RITUAL

The Seventh-Day Adventists have no formally adopted creed. They consider the Scriptures "all sufficient" and "the only unerring rule of faith and practice." [11] Jesus Christ is accepted as "very God, being of the same nature and essence as the Eternal Father." While remaining God, "He took upon Himself the nature of the human family, lived on earth as a man, exemplified in His life as our Example the principles of righteousness, attested His relationship to God by many mighty miracles, died for our sins on the cross, was raised from the dead, and ascended to the Father, where He lives to make intercession for us." [12]

As a church system, the Adventists refuse to "consider themselves . . . simply another in the maze of denominations, but rather are in the line of those dissentients of the centuries (like) the Waldenses, Wycliffites, Hussites, Reformers, Baptists and Wesleyans." [13] They claim that many innovations alien to apostolic Christianity were introduced, first by Rome and then by modernist Protestants. Above all, two principles of the ancient Church need to be recovered: adventism and sabbatarianism, from whose emphasis the Seventh-Day Adventists receive their distinctive name. As Adventists, they believe in "the imminent, personal, visible, and pre-millenial return of Jesus Christ to redeem His followers"; as Sabbatarians, they hold "the

observance of the seventh day as the Sabbath in obedience
to the changeless obligation of the moral law and the express example of Christ." [14] Both elements call for explanation.

Second Coming. Adventist teaching on the parousia
is based on a singular interpretation of the prophetic text
in Daniel 8:14, foretelling that: "Unto evening and morning, 2,300 days: and the sanctuary shall be cleansed." William Miller explained the text to mean that 2,300 years
from 457 B.C. (the reputed date of Daniel's vision), Christ
would come to cleanse the sanctuary (earth) in final judgment at the end of the world. He projected 2,300 years
from 457 B.C. and concluded that the end of the world
would come in 1843-1844 A.D. When the prediction failed,
the Adventists reinterpreted the prophecy, retaining 1844
as a key date, but explaining that what actually happened
in that year was not a purification of the earthly sanctuary
but a cleansing of the sanctuary of heaven. Really the
cleansing process only began in 1844 and "its completion
will close human probation." It is "a time of investigative
judgment, first with reference to the dead, and secondly
with reference to the living. This investigative judgment
determines who of the myriads sleeping in the dust of the
earth are worthy of a part of the first resurrection and who
of its living multitudes are worthy of translation." [15] To
be stressed is the brevity of this investigative judgment,
which is the present age. Once completed, there will be
the second coming of Christ, accompanied by the resurrection of the just, to be followed by a thousand years
(millenium) which are closed with the resurrection of the
wicked. At the end of the millenium, "the finally impeni-
tent, including Satan, the author of sin, will, by the fires
of the last day be reduced to a state of non-existence, becoming as though they had not been, thus purging God's
universe of sin and sinners." [16]

Seventh-Day Sabbath. Reverting to the Jewish custom of keeping Saturday as the day of rest, the Adventists acquired a logical basis for their opposition to the Catholic Church, which they accuse of corrupting the Scriptures and usurping the place of God. They argue that since the decalog is unalterable, "the fourth commandment of this unchangeable law requires the observance of the seventh-day Sabbath." [17] No other pertinent argument is offered, except the immutability of God and His commandments. Ignoring the Acts of the Apostles, where the early Church is described as keeping holy the first day of the week, Adventists claim the change was made by the Roman papacy, through centuries of gradual innovation. "The arch-deceiver," wrote Mrs. White, "was resolved . . . to exercise his power through his vicegerent, the proud pontiff, who claimed to be the representative of Christ . . . In nearly every council (of the Catholic Church) the Sabbath which God had instituted was pressed down a little lower, while the Sunday was correspondingly exalted. Thus the pagan festival (of Sunday) came finally to be honored as a divine institution, while the Bible Sabbath was pronounced a relic of Judaism." [18]

In common with most Protestants, the Adventists recognize only two sacraments, baptism and the Lord's Supper, but they have added ceremonies and interpretations which considerably modify both of these "ordinances of the Church."

Baptismal Service. No provision is made for the baptism of infants, since this ordinance "should follow repentance and forgiveness of sins. By its observance faith is shown in the death, burial and resurrection of Christ." [19] Before the administration of baptism, the candidate must answer a series of questions in the presence of the whole congregation, or at least of the local church board. He is asked about his belief in God, the atonement of Christ, the renunciation of Satan, the Bible as the only rule of faith, and the keeping of the Sabbath on the seventh day. Then more specifically:

> Do you believe that your body is the temple of the Holy Spirit and that you are to honor God by caring for your body in abstaining from such things as alcoholic beverages, tobacco in all its forms, and from unclean foods?
>
> Do you accept the doctrine of spiritual gifts, and do you believe that the Spirit of prophecy is one of the identifying marks of the remnant church?
>
> Is the soon coming of Jesus the blessed hope in your heart, and is it your settled determination to prepare to meet Him in peace, as well as to help others to get ready for His glorious appearing?
>
> Do you believe in church organization, and is it your purpose to support the church by your tithes and offerings, your personal effort, and your influence? [20]

After satisfactorily answering these questions, the candidate is baptized by immersion. But *"before* the immersion takes place, the minister should raise his right hand and solemnly utter one of the following declarations:

> 'My brother, upon the profession of your faith in Jesus Christ as your personal Saviour, I now baptize you into the name of the Father, and of the Son, and of the Holy Spirit. Amen.'
>
> 'In harmony with the commandment of our Lord and Saviour, Jesus Christ, I now baptize you into the name of the Father, and of the Son, and of the Holy Spirit. Amen.' " [21]

Communion Service. The Seventh-Day Adventist Communion Service begins with the ritual of foot washing. After an appropriate sermon, the men and women in the congregation go into separate rooms or cubicles where basins of water and towels have been prepared. "It is the practice, based on the example of Jesus, to wash both feet of those who participate." [22] Deacons and deaconnesses assist in the process, which may be accompanied by hymns, "and such conversation as may be carried on is of a devotional and religious character and in a subdued voice." [23] According to Adventist belief, the washing of feet is a kind of sacrament of penance. "As baptism symbolizes the cleansing from sin at the beginning of the Christian experience, so the ordinance of foot washing represents the efficacy of the blood of Christ in washing away sin from the stained heart of one who, although a church member, has either knowingly or unintentionally committed sin after baptism." [24]

Following the washing of feet, the men and women reassemble for the celebration of the Lord's Supper. While the people are seated, the minister stands at the communion table where he uncovers the plate on which unleavened bread has been placed. After the words of institution from St. Paul and other prayers are recited, the bread is broken into small pieces, during which time "the one officiating may repeat suitable Scriptures or make timely remarks, or the organist may play suitable soft music." [25] Deacons distribute the bread to the people, who hold it in their hands until the minister is served. Then all partake together. A brief interlude of silent prayer introduces the same ritual for the wine, which is received in individual glass cups. Like the Methodists, the Adventists require that "only the unfermented juice of the grape . . . should be used in the Lord's Supper." [26] They also practice open communion, allowing anyone who attends the service to communicate. "Christ's example (in favor of Judas) forbids exclusiveness at the Lord's Supper . . . There may come into the company persons who are not in

heart servants of truth and holiness, but who may wish to
take part in the service. They should not be forbidden." [27]
This directive is taken verbally from a communication of
Mrs. White.

Although the Eucharist is considered as only "symbol-
izing Christ's broken body and spilled blood," [28] the ritual
demands that great reverence be shown for the elements
after the public Communion Service is over. The deacons
are instructed to "see that any unused bread that remains
is disposed of by burning. Any unused wine should be
poured out on the ground. In no case should either bread
or wine be distributed or consumed in private or at home."
Moreover, "if sickness has prevented members from attending the ordinances, either the minister or the elder
may take a small portion of the emblems to these sick ones
and thus share with them the rich blessing of fellowship." [29]

GOVERNMENT AND ORGANIZATION

The Seventh-Day Adventist Church is at once hierarchical and highly representative. On the global level, the
General (World) Conference meets every four years and
has authority to amend, repeal, or enact provisions which
affect the whole denomination. A two-thirds vote is required. Below the General Conference are Divisions (13
in 1956) with their own subordinate Conferences, which
are "to operate within a specified territory, for example,
North America, in harmony with the policy of the General
Conference." [30] Next in authority, on an intra-continental
basis, are Union Conferences which, at least in America,
are further divided into State Conferences, with immediate jurisdiction over the local churches. It was Mrs.
White's desire to have a thoroughly democratic society.
"Every member of the church," she declared, "has a voice
in choosing officers of the church. The church chooses the

officers of the State [or local] conferences. Delegates chosen
by the State conferences choose the officers of the union
conferences; and delegates chosen by the union conferences choose the officers of the General Conference. By
this arrangement, every conference, every institution, every
church, and every individual, either directly or through
representatives, has a voice in the election of the men who
bear the chief responsibilities of the General Conference." [31]

In practice, however, the Adventist is fundamentally
congregational. Each local body is largely independent in
its government, although subject to the State Conference
of which it is a member. Churches are started, as among
the Congregationalists, when a group of believers "desires
to unite in fellowship." Under the leadership of a minister, they are duly baptized, elect officers and become incorporated in the larger Adventist denomination. There
is not the same degree of "independency" among the local
churches that is found in other congregational sects like
the Baptists. This is precluded by the two doctrinal "foci"
of Adventism: the imminent second coming and the Saturday Sabbath, along with a uniform code of abstinence
from tobacco and every kind of stimulant. What unites
the Seventh-Day Adventists more than any other factor,
however, is the common acceptance of their foundress as
a messenger from God. "The spirit of prophecy as manifested through Mrs. White" is held to be "woven so in-
tricately into the progress of our denominational history
that the story of no work can be told without the feature
of divine leadership standing out clearly and unmistaka-
bly." [32] More than any pontiff, whom they identify with
the beast of the Apocalypse,[33] Mrs. White was the visible
head of the Adventists for sixty years, and after death still
consolidates their organization.

STATISTICS

International

Church Members	924,822
Churches	11,158
Countries in which Seventh-Day Adventists are Working	197
Radio Stations Carrying Weekly Adventist Programs	1,067
Sanatoriums and Hospitals	129
Food Companies	58
Students in Educational Institutions	233,950

United States

Church Members	270,079
Churches	2,845
Ordained Clergy	1,628
Radio and T.V. Stations Carrying Weekly Adventist Programs	661
Sabbath School Enrollment	265,443
Day School Enrollment (919 Institutions)	29,724

REFERENCES

1. James White, *Sketches of the Christian Life and Public Labors of William Miller,* Battle Creek, Seventh-Day Adventist Publishing Association, 1875, p. 279.
2. LeRoy E. Froom, *The Prophetic Faith of Our Fathers,* Vol. IV, Washington, Review and Herald, 1954, p. 992.
3. *Ibid.,* p. 997.
4. *Ibid.,* pp. 1000-1001.
5. Emma E. Howell, *The Great Advent Movement,* Washington, Review and Herald, 1951, p. 82.
6. *Ibid.,* p. 43.
7. *Ibid.,* pp. 97-98.
8. *Ibid.,* p. 108.
9. Anson P. Stokes, *Church and State in the United States,* Vol. III, New York, Harper, 1950, p. 164.
10. Howell, *op. cit.,* p. 109.
11. *Seventh-Day Adventist Yearbook, 1955,* Washington, Review and Herald, 1955, p. 4.
12. *Loc. cit.*
13. LeRoy E. Froom, "Seventh-Day Adventists," *The American Church* (Virgilius Ferm, ed.), New York, Philosophical Library, 1953, p. 380.
14. *Ibid.,* pp. 377-378.
15. *Yearbook,* pp. 4-5.
16. *Ibid.,* p. 4.
17. *Loc. cit.*
18. Ellen G. White, *The Great Controversy between Christ and Satan,* Mountain View, Calif., Pacific Press, 1953, p. 53.
19. *Yearbook,* p. 4.

20. *Manual for Ministers,* Washington, General Conference of Seventh-Day Adventists, 1954, p. 86.
21. *Ibid.,* p. 88.
22. *Ibid.,* p. 91.
23. *Loc. cit.*
24. *Ibid.,* p. 90.
25. *Ibid.,* p. 93.
26. *Ibid.,* p. 95.
27. *Loc. cit.*
28. Ellen G. White, *The Desire of the Ages,* Mountain View, Calif., Pacific Press, 1955, p. 661.
29. *Manual for Ministers,* pp. 94-95.
30. *Yearbook,* p. 7.
31. Howell, *op. cit.,* p. 59.
32. *Ibid.,* p. 36.
33. Uriah Smith, *The Prophecies of Daniel and the Revelation,* Mountain View, Calif., Pacific Press, 1951, p. 619. The pope is identified as the beast of the Apocalypse by a naive interpretation of chapter 13, verse 18: "He who has understanding, let him calculate the number of the beast, for it is the number of a man; and its number is six hundred and sixty-six." One of the titles of the pope is *Vicarius Filii Dei* (Vicar of the Son of God). "Taking the letters out of this title which are used as Roman numerals, we have V, 5; I, 1; C, 100; I, 1; U (formerly the same as V), 5; I, 1; L, 50; I, 1; I, 1; D, 500; I, 1. Adding these numbers together, we have 666." *Loc. cit.*

2. Baptists

THE BAPTISTS exemplify in a striking way the importance of a name in the genesis and development of a religious movement. It was a mere accident of history that they came to be called Baptists, as a term of opprobrium to describe their insistence on immersion and profession of believer's baptism. They accepted the title and capitalized on it as a synthesis of fifteen centuries of controversy over the sacrament of regeneration, and a mark of their ancestry from apostolic times. In common with the Donatists they hold that baptism is invalid unless conferred by one of their own sect; with the Arians they deny that baptism removes the stain of original or actual sin; with the Waldenses and Albigenses they reject infant baptism as superstition and against the words of the Bible; with the Anabaptists they claim that no one can be validly baptized until after a personal confession of faith in Christ as his Savior, and consequently demand a rebaptism (anabaptism) of all those baptized in infancy; with the English Separatists they require immersion in water as the only mode of baptism allowed by the Sacred Scriptures.

Centering their specific difference as a religious society around these various phases of the first sacrament, the Baptists have acquired a spirit of unity that is difficult to reconcile with a denomination which is nominally the

largest Protestant group in the country, but is also the
most fragmented. Whatever their differences, however, in
doctrine, ritual and church organization, they are still
united in a common preoccupation with the place of baptism in the Christian economy. It is the key to an understanding of this people, bound together by only "a rope of
sand," yet the most flourishing non-Catholic organization
in the United States.

HISTORY

There are two views as to the origin of the Baptists:
the domestic viewpoint of certain Baptist apologists, and
the objective data of religious history. Among themselves,
Baptists do not hesitate to trace their beginning to Christ
Himself. "No man can put his finger," they claim, "upon
any person or date this side of Jesus Christ and truthfully
say, 'here is where and when Baptists began.' " [1] They appeal to the spirit of independence as a distinguishing mark
of the church in apostolic times. Since "the New Testament shows that each church at that time was a free independent body, directing its own affairs, and that its officers
were servants and not masters," any organization, like the
Baptists, which has remained "loyal to this type, trusting
the Holy Spirit," must go back to early Christianity.[2] Although their church was founded by Christ, the name
"Baptist" is said to have "originated with John the Baptist, who was divinely sent to be the forerunner of Our
Lord." [3] No serious effort, however, is made to defend this
origin of the title. In tracing the church's lineage, some
Baptist writers developed the theory of spiritual kinship
with successive anti-Romanists like the Novatians, Donatists, Waldenses, and the continental Anabaptists. But
this theory is rejected by moderate Baptist scholars as
violating "the principles of historical accuracy." [4]

As a matter of history, commonly recognized by Protestant writers, the Baptists were started by John Smyth, Cambridge graduate and ordained Anglican minister (1570-1612), who "approved himself a factitious man" by his non-conformism and had to flee to Holland.[5] At Amsterdam he organized the first Separatist Church, with some eighty parishioners. Technically he was not yet a Baptist, until about a year later, when he came under the influence of the Waterlander Mennonites and decided that "infants ought not to be baptized" because there is no precept or example of infant baptism in the New Testament, and because Christ told His disciples first to preach and only then to baptize.[6] Some of Smyth's followers returned to England and started another church in London. The English branch soon divided into three conflicting groups: the General Baptists who believed in a general redemption of all men; the Particular Baptists who followed Calvin's doctrine of selective predestination; and Immersion Baptists who required baptism by immersion as of divine precept.

The Baptists migrated to America "to escape the restrictions which had been placed upon their religious practice and faith in the Old World." [7] Under the leadership of Roger Williams, founder of Rhode Island, the first Baptist Church in the colonies was established at Providence in 1639, and two years later the first Baptist Church of Newport was started by John Clarke. Both were Particular or Calvinist Baptists, and to this day their basic theology is the doctrinal standard of most Baptists in the country.

During the next century and a half, American Baptists split into a number of factions that were temporarily united under the common foreign-missions crusade. The first Protestant Mission Society in America, the *American Board,* was originally made up of Baptists, Reformed, Congregationalists and Presbyterians. In 1814, the Bap-

tists withdrew to form a society of their own, the General
Missionary Convention, which "marked the first real denominational consciousness of American Baptists." [8] Other
organizations soon followed along national lines, but the
unity was only transient. Between 1810 and 1830, Alexander Campbell initiated the defection which formed the
Disciples of Christ; in 1845 William Miller, preacher in
New York, was voted out of the Baptist ministry and took
with him a group of followers who became the Adventists.
The most serious schism in Baptist ranks, however, was
provoked by the slavery question. Two parties, the north
and south, could not agree on whether slaves should be
kept or not. "The southerners did not attempt to defend
the evils of the slavery system, but described the institution as an inherited disease to be healed slowly; many
justified its continuance on biblical grounds, pointing out
that the Negroes' contacts with white masters brought
them in touch with the gospel. Northern abolitionists also
argued from the Scriptures, holding that they taught the
inherent dignity and worth of every individual in the
sight of God and the moral wrong of the enslavement of
men by their fellows." [9] Unable to conciliate the two
parties, leaders on both sides decided to effect a division—
with the southern slave-holding Baptists taking the initiative. In April, 1845, the separation was voted on favorably
by the American Baptist Home Missionary Society, and
in the following month was born the Southern Baptist
Convention, "a new type of Baptist organization, being
a firmly centralized denominational body functioning
through various boards," as it has remained substantially
to this day.[10] At the time of the division, there were approximately 325,000 Baptists below, and 250,000 above
the Mason-Dixon line.

Further dissension over doctrinal and ritual questions

created a medley of sects, usually with names that expressed their characteristic differences. But the most deep-rooted division, besides the cleavage of the Northern and Southern Baptists, occurred along racial lines. With the Emancipation Declaration arose a desire among the Negroes to establish their own churches, independently of the non-colored Baptist organizations. In 1895, therefore, the Negroes founded their own National Baptist Convention of America, which was to function through a Foreign Mission Board, a Board of Education and a Board of Missions. Twenty years later a dispute arose over the control of property and publications, resulting in court action and a new schism. The larger segment became incorporated as the National Baptist Convention of the U.S.A., Inc., with a current membership of 4,500,000; the smaller section kept the original name and had a membership of 2,600,000 in 1956. The two Conventions account for about one half the negro population in the United States.

After the defection of the Southern Baptists in 1845, the northerners were hard put to maintain their home and foreign mission work. So in 1907 they united in a loose corporation which absorbed the Free Baptists in two mergers, one in 1911, and another in 1950, when the expanded body changed its name to the American Baptist Convention. It is now fourth among the major Baptist associations in America, with a current enrollment of 1,-500,000. The nearest competitor among the remaining Baptist bodies has less than half a million members.

Since American Baptists have long represented about nine-tenths of the world total, they were the logical prime movers in organizing the Baptist World Alliance. Founded in London, England, in 1905, its object is "the more fully to show the essential oneness of the Baptist people in the Lord Jesus Christ, to impart inspiration to the brotherhood, and to promote the spirit of fellowship, service, and cooperation among its members, and serve as the nerve center and corporate will of Baptists throughout the world." [11] Headquarters are in Washington, D. C.

DOCTRINAL POSITION

I. *Major Baptist Confessions of Faith*

Since there are twenty-seven autonomous Baptist sects in present-day America, it is clearly beyond the scope of this study to analyze their doctrinal positions in detail. However a close approximation is possible if we first survey the basic points of faith which Baptists hold in common, and then review the principal differences among the larger sectarian bodies. The common doctrinal element is agreed to exist in two great Baptist Confessions of faith: the Philadelphia Confession of 1688, and the New Hampshire Confession of 1833. The first is practically a redaction of the Presbyterian Westminster Confession, and strongly Calvinistic. Though always referred to in Baptist histories, it has been largely supplanted by the New Hampshire Confession, which is accepted, at least nominally, by all American Baptist communions.

Among the doctrines held in common with the Catholic Church are the Trinity, the divinity of Christ, original sin and the need of redemption, salvation through Christ, everlasting heaven and hell. But the divergences are numerous.

Scripture is declared to be "divinely inspired, and is a perfect treasure of heavenly instruction." At the same time, tradition is implicitly outlawed, since the Bible alone is held to be "the supreme standard by which all human conduct, creeds and opinions should be tried." [12]

The Fall of Man is described in the tradition of the Reformers. As a consequence of Adam's sin, "all mankind are now sinners . . . being by nature utterly void of that holiness required by the law of God, positively inclined to evil and therefore under just condemnation to eternal ruin." [13]

Justification is a restatement of Luther's *sola fide,* since "it is bestowed, not in consideration of any works of righteousness which we have done, but solely through faith in the Redeemer's blood." [14] Correlative to this is the doctrine of distinction between the "truly regenerate" and the "superficial professors." The former alone, once converted, "will not utterly fall away and finally perish, but will endure unto the end;" whereas the latter fall back into sin and so are considered as never having been truly justified. [15]

The Church is nowhere described, explicitly, as invisible; which is a departure from the Philadelphia creed where the "Catholic or Universal Church" is called "invisible," and said to consist of "the whole number of the elect, that have been, are, or shall be gathered into one, under Christ." [16] In the more recent doctrinal formula, "a visible Church of Christ is a congregation of baptized believers, associated by a covenant in faith and fellowship of the Gospel; observing the ordinances of Christ; governed by His laws; and exercising the gifts, rights and privileges invested in them by His word." [17] Several items are worth noting: Since Baptist churches are built along Congregational lines, what constitutes a church in the visible order is the single local organization called a parish. The term "baptized believers" is technical. Mere baptism does not make a person a member of the church; faith plus baptism are required. Association by covenant is also redolent of Congregational polity, where a church is organized by the

consent of a group of people, who agree to worship together under a common pastor of their choice. "The ordinances of Christ" are Baptist parlance for the sacraments,
only two of which are admitted: baptism and the Lord's
Supper.

Ecclesiastical Authority and Ministry are limited to
two categories, as the Church's "only scriptural officers are
bishops or pastors, and deacons, whose qualifications,
claims and duties are defined in the Epistles to Timothy
and Titus." [18] Baptists lay great stress on the identity of
bishop, presbyter and elder in the New Testament, in
order to eliminate the episcopate as a distinct hierarchical
office. "Only two orders of officers," it is claimed, "are
known in the Church until near the close of the second
century. Those of the first are styled either bishops or
presbyters; of the second, deacons." [19] In defending this
position, they rest their case on the textual interchange of
episcopos and *presbyteros* in St. Paul, while ignoring the
context which shows an exercise of episcopal authority
superior to the presbyterate. Clement of Rome and Ig-
natius of Antioch (c. 100 A.D.) who regarded the episcopate as essential, are naively described as "defenders of
prelatical—as against episcopal—supremacy," but without
quotation.[20]

Baptism is called an ordinance, not a sacrament, and
defined as "the immersion in water of a believer in Christ,
into the name of the Father, and Son, and Holy Ghost,
to show forth, in a solemn and beautiful emblem, our
faith in the crucified, buried and risen Savior, with its
effect, in our death to sin and resurrection to a new life."
It is considered "prerequisite to the privileges of a Church
relation, and to the Lord's Supper." [21] Baptists are generally agreed that, "Baptism does not provide salvation, or
produce salvation, or procure salvation, or even perfect
salvation." Their contention is that, "no external physical

act can produce a spiritual blessing upon the soul." [22]
And more warmly:

> We protest vigorously against assigning a virtue to the
> act of baptism that it does not possess . . . It is not the
> act of baptism, submitted to by one person and ad-
> ministered by another that brings about the remission
> of sins or provides salvation. It is a symbol and only a
> symbol of the blessed truths upon which remission of
> sins, salvation, and eternal life depend. When one ac-
> cepts Jesus Christ by faith he is saved with all that sal-
> vation means. Therefore, nothing that comes after
> faith is essential to one's salvation. [23]

Baptist writers arrive at this conclusion by ignoring the
constant tradition of Christianity up to the Reformation,
and attributing orthodoxy to those heretics who denied
the necessity of baptism for salvation. Also no provision
is made for the destiny of infants who die without either
faith or baptism, except an appeal to the theory of absolute predestination, which negatives the need not only of
baptism but also of faith as a condition for salvation.

With rare exception, immersion is regarded as essential for valid baptism; although not a few northern Baptist congregations no longer insist upon the baptism of
their members, hence equally dispense from the need of
immersion. Such liberties, however, are comparatively
rare, and promptly branded as modernistic. [24]

As taught by the Baptists, the efficacy of baptism is a
denial of the Catholic doctrine on infusion of sanctifying
grace, *ex opere operato.* "Baptism," they say, "does not
produce faith and a new heart . . . Regeneration is by
the Holy Ghost alone and should precede Baptism." [25]
Consequently infants are not baptized.

The Lord's Supper is conceived in the Zwinglian sense
of a mere external sign, and declared to be "a provision of

bread and wine as symbols of Christ's body and blood, partaken of by the members of the Church, in commemoration of the suffering and death of their Lord." [26] While denying the real presence, Baptists generally are rigid in their practice of "closed communion," which prohibits any but "immersed believers" from partaking of the Lord's Supper. Lengthy prescriptions are formulated to exclude the non-baptized, those baptized only in infancy, and those baptized as adults but not by immersion.

Faith was added as a new item to the original New Hampshire Confession, and is defined in modern Baptist creeds as "an evangelical grace wrought by the Spirit . . . It is an assent of the mind and a consent of the heart, consisting mainly of belief and trust." [27] The intellectual element is a late innovation, likely introduced to answer those who criticized Baptists as a "creedless body," principally concerned with religious feelings and emotions.

II. *Differences in Doctrine Among Baptist Sects*

Among the Baptist confessions of faith, "none are binding on the conscience of any, and members are not required to subscribe to any." The New Testament alone is respected as authoritative. At most, these Confessions "help to hold the minds of the people to the radical forms of evangelical truth." [28] Consequent on this freedom, Baptist churches have, on their own initiative, added to the basic New Hampshire creed other doctrines and statements of religious principle. Thus the powerful Southern Baptist Convention has an article on religious liberty which declares that, "Church and state should be separate . . . The Church should not resort to the civil power to carry on its work. The gospel of Christ contemplates spiritual means alone for the pursuit of its ends . . . The state has no right to impose taxes for the support of any form of religion." [29] Consistent with this principle, Louie D. Newton, then president of the Southern Baptist Convention, helped to found in 1948 the society of Protestants and Other Americans United for Separation of Church and State (P.O.A.U.), in order "to assure the maintenance of the American principle of separation of church and state upon which the Federal Constitution guarantees religious liberty to all people and all churches of this republic." [30] Inconsistently, though perhaps with an implied distinction between Catholic and Protestant churches, the Southern Baptist Confession insists that "the state owes the church protection . . . in the pursuit of its spiritual ends." [31]

More serious than addition, is the option of giving verbal approval to a confession of faith and then acting as though the confession did not exist. A striking example is the General Association of Regular Baptist Churches which was formed in 1932, as a protest against the prevailing modernism in the policies and program of the Northern Baptist Convention. Beginning with twenty-two churches, the Association in 1956 had about 600 member congregations. In a published indictment of the parent denomination, leaders of the new association summarized the charges against the Northern Baptists. The latter, they said, praise and reward persons who profess modernistic doctrines: that the Bible is only a human record of the best thoughts of men and not an inspired revelation from God; that Jesus Christ is a son of God like other men and not God Himself in human form; that Christ died as a martyr to give us an example, not to redeem us from sin, and that after death He did not rise from the grave in a physical body but only seemed to be risen as a sign that His spirit is immortal.[32]

Comparable to the doctrinal liberties indulged by groups of Baptist churches is the liberalism of individual ministers in good standing in their denomination. In the mid-twenties, Harry Emerson Fosdick was accused of modernism by fundamental Baptists and his case was tried by church leaders. He was acquitted, and until his retirement in 1946 remained at the Riverside Church in New York City, as "America's most popular preacher." His thirty volumes of sermons, reflections, and essays are literary models built around the concept of an ethical religion whose founder, Jesus Christ, was just "The Man from Nazareth," with no such divine sonship "as Hellenistic Christianity later put into the Nicene Creed." [33] In 1955, Fosdick's successor in the pastorate was a guest lecturer at the Southern Baptist Theological Seminary in Louisville. Conservative Baptist journals deplored this evident compromise on traditional Christianity, observing that, "immense harm may be done by giving encouragement, directly or indirectly, to the teachers of error. The propagation of false doctrines should receive no countenance." [34]

RITUAL AND WORSHIP

Their ordinary religious service is criticized by Baptist writers as "too often limited to the monotonously regular use of only three items—hymns, Scripture and prayer." [35] Under suasion from liturgical reformers, a variety of changes are being introduced in order to make "an arresting and impressive worship service." One recommended sequence includes five items, out of which the elder may choose what he wants. Commentary explanations are given in the pastor's manual:

1. The opening is a *Call to Worship,* which usually follows a quiet musical prelude and is designed to remind the congregation of the presence of God and their purpose in assembling for worship. The "Call" may consist of passages from the Psalms or a stanza of poetry, like Christina Rosetti's, "Trembling before Thee, we fall down to

adore Thee . . ." Among the recommended poems is Dante's *Divina Commedia*.

2. The minister then offers an *Invocation*, followed by one or more hymns. Nothing is more important for worship, pastors are told, than "a good hymn-book," in accordance with Luther's declaration that, "I am strongly persuaded that after theology there is no art that can be placed on a level with music; for, besides theology, music is the only art capable of affording peace and joy to the heart, like that induced by the study of the science of divinity." [36] Anglican and Methodist hymns are especially popular.

3. The *Scripture Reading* is varied, in content and mode of presentation. It may be introduced with a bit of poetry, like Whittier's, "We search the world for Truth . . . ," and is rendered either by the preacher alone, or by a group of trained readers, "selected for the quality and blend of their voices." On occasion, the reading is dramatized by means of a tableau or biblical play; more often with the room dimmed, a strong light is focused on a scripture painting, or a biblical scene is projected on a movie screen.

4. Following the reading is a period of *Prayer,* which may be vocal or silent, extempore or according to set formula, alone by the elder or alternating, litany-fashion, between the leader and the people, or the men and women in the congregation. When an individual worshiper spontaneously or on invitation prays aloud, "the perennial danger to be avoided . . . is 'much speaking and vain repetition.' " Hence the need of "thoughtful preparation," by previous selection of "specific objects of prayer" to be used in public worship.[37]

5. *Religious Stories,* along with prayer, are an integral part of the Baptist service. Worship leaders are told to

"keep a file or book in which to record discovered sources of great stories." [38] These may be religious or merely ethical, and may be drawn from any quarter, e.g., novels, biographies, news items, magazine articles, private letters or personal experience.

As further evidence of departure from their Calvinist origins, modern Baptists are urging the use of pictures and symbols as aids to devotion in worship services. Symbols, they are told, have played an important role in the history of Christian liturgy. "The cross," for example, "has become to all the world a symbol of the Christian faith." Consequently, "while recognizing that the use of symbols may become too dominant a feature of worship, we nevertheless emphasize the values to be derived from an intelligent use of them." [39] Among the symbols suggested are IHS, incorrectly interpreted to stand for the Latin, *Iesus Hominum Salvator*; the triangle, signifying the Trinity; a seven-pointed star to represent the seven gifts of the Holy Spirit; a six-pointed star "to remind us of God, the Creator"; a single circle depicting eternity; and a triple circle representing the Trinity. The same five liturgical colors as in Catholic services are admitted and similarly explained, with the addition of blue as a symbol of loyalty, faith, heaven, and eternity. Object symbolism is practically limited to six items: the cross representing Christ, the Bible standing for the word of God, an anchor for hope, a banner for victory, a globe for authority, and a gate for protection and freedom. Religious pictures are used, but restricted to "heightening the spirit of worshipful devotion" during actual services.

The most solemn ritual among Baptists is the ordination of a pastor or elder, and the administration of the Lord's Supper. Ordination is basically congregational. The initiative comes from a local church requesting some person to become their pastor. If he is not yet ordained, but otherwise prepared by study in a seminary and approved by a committee drawn from several churches, the rite of ordination is duly performed by one of two bodies, a council or the presbytery. In the South, ordinations are generally done only by a presbytery, i.e., a group of ordained ministers under the authority of the Baptist denomination; elsewhere the laying on of hands is usually performed by a simple council, composed of ministers and unordained laymen. The ordination ceremony is very plain. There is a sermon, preceded by Scripture reading, song and prayer, and followed by the laying on of hands. "After the sermon has been preached, the candidate is asked to kneel, and some brother chosen for the purpose prays the ordination prayer; when the prayer is completed, the candidate remains on his knees while the members of the presbytery or council lay their hands on his head as a token of his full ordination to the Baptist ministry." [40] No formula of prayers or method of imposition is prescribed. The effect of ordination, whether to eldership or the diaconate, is purely external and juridical. It does not endow the candidate "with any intellectual, moral or spiritual grace which he did not before possess." [41]

There is wide divergency among Baptists on the frequency of celebrating the Lord's Supper. "Some churches celebrate it the first Sunday in each month, others the first Sunday in each quarter, others semi-annually and still others but once a year." [42] The rite of administration follows the general plan of an ordinary Baptist service, except for the addition of the Eucharistic ritual which includes, in order, reading the account of the institution from Luke 22:7-22, pronouncing the words: "This is my body," breaking the bread and giving it to the deacons for distribution to the people, and the same for the wine. The communion service is closed with a hymn and a collection taken up by the deacons.

ORGANIZATION AND GOVERNMENT

While details of operation differ widely, Baptists are
fairly agreed on certain principles of church government.
These may be reduced to three:

1. The governing power of the church is vested ultimately in the people. "It resides with the people in con-
tradistinction from bishops or elders—that is to say,
bishops or elders can do nothing, strictly and properly
ecclesiastic, without the concurrence of the people." [43]

2. Majority rule prevails in Baptist church polity, "in
accordance with the law of Christ." So that, "the will of
the majority having been expressed, it becomes the minority to submit." [44]

3. Local church authority is inalienable and final in all
matters of ecclesiastical law and doctrine. Thus "the
power of a church cannot be delegated. There may be
messengers of a church, but there cannot be delegates in
the ordinary sense of the term." [45] Even Baptists have to
be reminded occasionally that "in their letters to associations and councils," the church should "say messengers,
not delegates," since "no church can empower any man,
or body of men, to do anything which will impair its independency." [46]

Against the background of these principles, it is easy to
see why Baptists, with notable exceptions, have stayed
aloof from the ecumenical movement. They are afraid to
compromise the autonomy of the individual congregations;
where cooperation with other churches is practiced and
effective, it is at the sacrifice of Baptist ecclesiology. This
is also the radical explanation of the fragmented status of
Baptist denominations, since the idea of local church independence is inherent in their constitution, with consequent sectarian differences among the churches, often
united only by the semantic ties of a common name.

BAPTIST SECTARIAN DIVISIONS

In 1956, there were twenty-seven Baptist bodies in the United States, ranging in membership from the multimillion Southern Convention to the Independent Baptist Church of America with barely ten listed adherents. All have an official status in the *Yearbook of American Churches,* but only the larger denominations with significantly distinctive features will be considered here:

1. *Southern Baptist Convention.* Founded in 1845, when the Southern Baptists withdrew from the General Missionary Convention over the question of slavery. It is the fastest growing Protestant body in the States, with a net increase of 300,000 in the past year. Originally confined to the southeastern states, the Southern Convention is rapidly developing in the north by the absorption of conservative groups who are dissatisfied with the liberalizing tendency of northern Baptist organizations. Inclusive membership is over eight million, with 30,000 churches and a Sunday-school enrollment of six million. Southern Baptists operate fifty colleges and universities, thirty-three hospitals, and are very active in publication and missionary work. In 1956, they reported fifty national and twenty-three state periodicals, including ten weeklies with circulations over 50,000 and one with 300,000 subscribers. One thousand missionaries are laboring in twenty-one countries, with concentration in Brazil, Nigeria, and Japan.

2. *National Baptist Convention, U.S.A., Inc.* and *National Baptist Convention of America.* Organized in 1895 and 1915, these two Conventions have a combined all-negro membership of approximately seven million. Substantially alike in organization and doctrinal profession, the old enmities between the two bodies seem to be waning, but there is no immediate prospect of union. Generally more Calvinistic than white Baptists, the negro

churches are only poorly known outside their own denomination. All the evidence points to an undeveloped condition. The large number of churches (36,739) gives an average of less than two hundred persons to a congregation. Only a single monthly periodical is listed officially for both Conventions. Alone of all the Baptist bodies, no data is available on the negro Conventions' annual church contributions, except $.05 per capita for the missions as compared with $6.48 in the white Southern Convention. Similarly, only one of the two sects, the National Baptist Convention, U.S.A., Inc., gives information on the relative number of ordained and active clergy: 30,251 to 18,-964, which is the highest disproportion in any Protestant denomination. Foreign mission work is emphasized by the two Conventions, with Nigeria, Liberia, and South Africa as the principal outposts. Since 1937, an evangelical group, formerly part of the National Baptist Convention of America, has become an independent sect. Under the title, National Baptist Evangelical Life and Soul-Saving Assembly of the U.S.A., its main efforts are devoted to revival and relief activity. The Assembly operates an Automatic Correspondence School, with courses in "evangelology, deaconology, missionology, pastorology, and laymanology," conferring degrees in sixty to one hundred and twenty days. There are 260 churches with 60,000 members.

3. *American Baptist Convention.* This competitor to the Southern Convention for Baptist leadership in America began as the Northern Baptist Convention in 1907, changing its name to the present form in 1950. "As we adopt the name American Baptist Convention," the delegates affirmed, "we hold the name in trust for all Christians of like faith and mind who desire to bear witness to the historic Baptist convictions in a framework of cooperative Protestantism." [47] While adhering to the historic Baptist Confessions, the A.B.C. stands for a more liberal concept

of Scripture and theology. It is also more ecumenical-minded, officially participating in the National and World Council of Churches, with delegates playing a leading role in the Assemblies at Edinburgh, Utrecht, and Evanston. The A.B.C. is actively promoting the union of all major Baptist bodies; in 1911 it was joined by the Free Baptists. But its free-lancing modernism has resulted in numerous defections, the most serious being the exodus of the General Association of Regular Baptists in 1932. Highly organized and socially conscious, the American Baptist Convention is widely accepted as the most representative Baptist organization in the States, although its total membership is less than two million. Besides maintaining twenty-seven colleges and universities, twelve theological seminaries, and upwards of fifty hospitals and welfare homes, it supports about six hundred foreign missionaries, mostly in Latin America and the Far East. The A.B.C. has formed a cooperative union with the General Baptists, originally an anti-Calvinist segment which emigrated from England and Holland. Like the A.B.C., the Association of General Baptists professes to exist in order "to effect better relations and closer cooperation between various bodies of liberal Baptists."[48] There are 50,000 members in 700 churches.

4. *Free-Will Baptists.* Of Welsh origin, they were founded in 1780 by Benjamin Randall, son of a ship captain in New Hampshire. Randall's kindly nature rebelled against the harsh Calvinism of the Baptists of his time. In a reported mystical experience, he discovered "the universal love of God to man, the universal atonement in the work of redemption by Jesus Christ . . . the universal appearance of Grace to all men, and . . . the universal call of the Gospel."[49] True to the spirit of their founder, the Free-Will Baptists represent the right-wing opposition to Calvinist predestinarianism still prevalent among many

Baptists. Since their partial absorption by the American
Baptist Convention in the north, the Free-Will Baptists
are now practically confined to the south. Their doctrinal
position is Arminian.[50] They hold that all may be saved,
and are one of the few Baptist sects which practice open
Communion, i.e., giving the Lord's Supper to those baptized in infancy, or not by immersion, or in a non-Baptist
church. Besides baptism and the Lord's Supper, they observe the rite of foot-washing as an ordinance of Christ.

While numerically inferior (4,000 churches and 40,000
members), by their fidelity to Randall's universalism the
Free-Will Baptists are credited with providing "a corrective which has influenced Baptists favorably by causing
them to combine with their traditional point of view a
warm evangelism." Their principles of "free grace, free
salvation, free will and free communion have become increasingly acceptable to numerous Baptists, particularly in
the Northern States." [51]

The negro counterpart of the Free Baptists is organized as the United American Free-Will Baptist Church,
with 100,000 communicants in 800 churches. Doctrinally
similar to the white denomination, the U.A.F.B.C. separated from the parent body in 1910 for racial reasons. Its
governmental structure gives less autonomy to the local
church and is more hierarchical. Special provisions are
made for presenting the settlement of doctrinal disputes
up to the General Conference; District Conferences have
the right to exclude unworthy members from fellowship—
both of which practices are somewhat unique in Baptist
church policy.

5. *American Baptist Association.* Also called Land-
markers, members of the American Baptist Association
deny that other Baptists are faithful to the Scriptures.
They profess a strict fundamentalism: the verbal inspiration of the Bible, the Trinity, Virgin-Birth, divinity of

Christ and His substitutionary passion, the bodily resurrection of Christ and of all the saints. They also believe in a second coming of Christ, "physical and personal," which is to be premillenial.[52] Like the Southern Baptists, they are strongly opposed to any kind of union of church and state. Current membership is about 300,000, divided among 2,500 churches. Originally rural, the Association is rapidly shifting to an urban status. Because of their insistence on perfectly equal rights among local churches, adherents of the A.B.A. are sometimes called Church-Equality Baptists.

In May, 1950, a schism in the A.B.A. produced an independent faction, legally entitled the North American Baptist Association, which withdrew over doctrinal differences. Militantly fundamentalist, the new society now has 250,000 members and about 1,600 churches. Organized at Little Rock, Arkansas, the denomination is still limited to the midwestern and southern states, but gradually expanding elsewhere. Titles of periodicals like *The Baptist Trumpet* and *The Advancer* illustrate the uncompromising character of this latest addition to the Baptist family.

6. *The General Association of Regular Baptist Churches.* This group severed connections with the Northern Baptist Convention in 1932 because the latter had become modernist. A dozen years before the final break, conservatives drew up a protest resolution that was to become the doctrinal basis of the new denomination. "Within our own fold," they complained, "we hail as leaders men who deny the miraculous birth of Christ, the vicarious death of Christ, the triumphant resurrection of Christ, and the promised second coming of Christ. If one dares to raise his voice in protest, some one immediately hauls up the banner of Christian charity and seeks to cover with its folds the teaching that denies our Lord, meanwhile say-

ing, 'Yes, we have radical differences among us, but surely the Baptist denomination is big enough, generous enough, charitable enough to include men of all shades of opinion.' . . . This subtle appeal put forth in the name of tolerance and charity is utterly at variance with the admonition that we 'contend earnestly for the faith.' " [53] In 1932, when this protest crystallized into an autonomous sect, its first avowed purpose was "to maintain a testimony to the supernaturalism of Christianity as opposed to the anti-supernaturalism of modernism." [54] Interestingly, the conservatives referred to the action of Rome which "put down the (modernist) views extended by the Abbé Loisy . . . by the Encyclical of Pius X," as a precedent for its condemnation of like errors in the Baptist communion.[55] Beginning with only 25 congregations, the Association has grown through new aggregation to 700 churches with a total membership exceeding 100,000.

7. *Primitive Baptists.* They are concentrated in two denominations, the white, simply called Primitive Baptists, and the colored, organized in the National Primitive Baptist Convention of the U.S.A. More popular names for these sects are: Old School, Regular, Antimission, and Hard-Shell Baptists, which correspond to their reputation for being the most strictly orthodox of Baptist churches. Strongly predestinarian, they believe that Adam's fall completely vitiated human nature. All church societies are regarded as human inventions. Ministers must have a special call from God, which, even in the absence of theological training is considered sufficient for ordination to the clergy. Most Primitive Baptists are opposed to the use of instrumental music in churches as unscriptural. Admission to a local church is conditioned on a doctrinal examination and favorable vote by the congregation. Primitive Baptists have about 2,000 churches and 150,000 members, equally divided between the white and the colored denominations.

STATISTICS

Baptist World Membership	20,680,478
Baptists in Europe	1,107,611
U.S.S.R.	512,000
England	202,361
Asia	642,157
India	349,849
Burma	142,499
Africa	220,385
Belgian Congo	94,998
Nigeria	44,355
South America	132,345
Brazil	109,241
Argentina	11,545
Central America and West Indies	98,437
Haiti	28,457
Jamaica	23,617
Australasia and Oceania	45,345
North America	18,434,198
Canada	144,353
United States (27 Bodies)	18,274,088

REFERENCES

1. James E. Dillard, *We Southern Baptists,* Nashville, Executive Committee Southern Baptist Convention, 1949, p. 5.
2. *Loc. cit.*
3. *Ibid.,* p. 6.
4. Robert G. Torbet, *A History of the Baptists,* Philadelphia, Judson Press, 1952, p. 62.
5. *Ibid.,* p. 63.
6. *Ibid.,* p. 64.
7. *Ibid.,* p. 219.
8. Frank S. Meade, *Handbook of Denominations in the United States,* New York-Nashville, Abingdon Press, 1951, p. 27.
9. Torbet, *op. cit.,* p. 309.
10. *Loc. cit.*
11. Dillard, *op. cit.,* p. 40.
12. Edward T. Hiscox, *The New Directory for Baptist Churches,* Philadelphia, Judson Press, 1954, p. 543.
13. *Ibid.,* p. 544.
14. *Ibid.,* p. 552.
15. *Ibid.,* p. 554.
16. Philip Schaff, *The Creeds of the Evangelical Protestant Churches,* London, Hodder and Stoughton, 1877, p. 738.
17. Hiscox, *op. cit.,* p. 556. The Catholic Church teaches that Scripture is not the only source of revelation; it must be supplemented by tradition, which is the oral transmission of the revealed word of God. In both cases, Scripture and tradition, the Church holds that God's revelation to the human race

was completed at the death of the last Apostle (c. 100 A.D.). The necessity of tradition is clear from the fact that otherwise we should not know which are the inspired books of the Bible. In other words, without tradition there would be no certitude about the Scriptures.

18. *Loc. cit.*
19. *Ibid.*, p. 87.
20. *Ibid.*, p. 88.
21. *Ibid.*, p. 557.
22. Austin Crouch, *Is Baptism Essential to Salvation?*, Nashville, Broadman Press, 1953, p. 73.
23. *Ibid.*, pp. 73-74.
24. Robert T. Ketcham, *The Answer*, Chicago, General Association of Regular Baptist Churches, 1951, p. 6.
25. Hiscox, *op. cit.*, pp. 125-126. Catholic teaching on the effects of baptism is unequivocal. By this sacrament, all the guilt and punishment of original and actual sin are removed; a permanent supernatural character is imprinted on the soul; the recipient becomes a member of the Catholic Church, the Mystical Body of Christ; sanctifying grace is infused into the soul, together with the virtues of faith, hope and charity; the one baptized becomes a child of God and heir of heaven.
26. *Ibid.*, p. 558.
27. *Ibid.*, p. 550.
28. *Ibid.*, p. 536.
29. *The Baptist Faith and Message,* "A Statement Adopted by the Southern Baptist Convention," Nashville, n.d., p. 14.
30. Ralph L. Roy, *Apostles of Discord,* Boston, Beacon Press, 1953, p. 146. Co-founders with Newton of the P.O.A.U. were John A. Mackay, president of Princeton Theological Seminary; G. Bromley Oxnam,

bishop of the New York area of the Methodist Church; Edwin McNeill, president of Colgate-Rochester Divinity School; and Charles C. Morrison, former editor of the *Christian Century.*

31. *The Baptist Faith and Message,* p. 14.
32. Ketcham, *op. cit.,* pp. 42-43.
33. Harry E. Fosdick, *The Man from Nazareth,* New York, Harper, 1949, p. 180.
34. Clarence Walker, *Ashland Avenue Baptist,* March 11, 1955, Lexington, Ky.
35. Thomas B. McDormand, *The Art of Building Worship Services,* Nashville, Broadman Press, 1946, p. 13.
36. *Ibid.*, p. 25.
37. *Ibid.*, p. 85.
38. *Ibid.*, p. 87.
39. *Ibid.*, p. 101.
40. James R. Hobbs, *The Pastor's Manual,* Nashville, Broadman Press, 1954, p. 189. The ordination of deacons is the same as that of elders, including imposition of hands.
41. Hiscox, *op. cit.,* p. 273.
42. Hobbs, *op. cit.,* p. 224.
43. J. M. Pendleton, *Baptist Church Manual,* Nashville, Convention Press, 1955, p. 101.
44. *Ibid.*, p. 102.
45. *Loc. cit.*
46. *Loc. cit.*
47. Benson Y. Landis, *Yearbook of American Churches, 1956,* New York, National Council of the Churches of Christ, 1955, p. 16.
48. Meade, *op. cit.,* p. 35.
49. Torbet, *op. cit.,* p. 275.
50. Arminianism is opposed to Calvinism, chiefly as holding a less rigorous view of the divine sovereignty. It owes its name to Jacobus Arminius (1560-1609), a Dutch Protestant theologian.
51. Torbet, *op. cit.,* p. 276.

52. Millenialism is now associated only with the minor sects of Protestantism. But it has an impressive history which goes back to the Old Testament hopes of the Jews for a temporal Messias. As understood by Christian writers, it is a belief in the second coming of Christ before (premillenialism) or after (postmillenialism) a thousand-year period of the highest spiritual and material blessings on earth, as a prelude to the end of the world. Among the ancients, Papias, Justin, and Tertullian professed the doctrine. Even St. Augustine for a while believed in a spiritual sort of millenium. By the Middle Ages, millenialism had practically died out among Catholic writers, until revived by the 16th century Protestant radicals who believed in a golden age under the sceptre of Christ after the overthrow of the papacy and secular empires. Fortunately for the main body of Protestantism, this messianic complex led to such doctrinal excesses that millenialism was repudiated by the Lutheran and Reformed theologies.

53. Joseph M. Stowell, *Background and History of the General Association of Regular Baptist Churches,* Hayward, California, J. F. May Press, 1949, p. 13.

54. *Ibid.,* p. 36.

55. *Ibid.,* p. 3.

3. Christian Scientists

FIFTY YEARS AGO, Mark Twain wrote a volume on Christian Science, in which he described it as "a sovereignty more absolute than the Roman Papacy, more absolute than the Russian Czarship; it has not a single power, not a shred of authority, legislative or executive, which is not lodged in the sovereign; all its dreams, its functions, its energies, have a single object—to build the glory of the sovereign, and keep it bright to the end of time. Mrs. Eddy is the sovereign; she devised that great place for herself, she occupies that throne." [1]

Twain's description is substantially accurate even today. If ever a religious sect was authoritarian and has remained faithful to the teaching of its founder, that sect is Christian Science. Both factors should be kept in mind in order to make a just appraisal of the Church of Christ, Scientist, as an ecclesiastical system whose influence on religious thought in America and elsewhere is greater than commonly supposed. A single organ of its principles, *The Christian Science Monitor,* is a daily newspaper with a circulation of 200,000 scattered over all the continents, and rated so highly that since 1915 it has won more than sixty awards for journalistic excellence in city, national and world competition.

HISTORY

The history of Christian Science is the history of its founder, Mary Baker, born at Bow, New Hampshire, July 16, 1821. Her early life was marked by long periods of sickness, owing to her naturally delicate temperament and nervous disposition. At the age of twenty-two, she married George Washington Glover, a bricklayer, who died six months later, leaving his widow practically destitute among strangers. When her only child was born, posthumously, she named him after his father.

In 1853 Mrs. Glover married a traveling dentist, Daniel Patterson. But by 1866 he declared that living with her was unbearable. His periodic sojourns at home were "made dreary . . . by the ills of a neurotic wife whose strange spells and fierce tempers became a byword over the whole neighborhood." [2] Meantime she had been visiting a Dr. Quimby, mesmerist faith healer, from whose notes she copied the principles and technique and later re-edited as her own. The gist of Quimby's teaching, still operative in Christian Science, was a simple rule of auto-suggestion: Disease is a matter of faith, and so is its cure.

Not coincidentally, less than a month after Quimby died, Mrs. Glover-Patterson initiated Christian Science. On January 30, 1866, she fell at her home and suffered an injury that required medical care. There are two versions of the accident and its sequel: Mrs. Patterson's and the doctor's who treated her. According to Mrs. Patterson, the physician said she was injured beyond recovery. Awaiting a clergyman who was to prepare her for death, she began to read the Bible and came upon the words of Christ in St. Matthew's Gospel, addressed to the man sick with palsy. As she read, "Arise, take up thy bed," she realized that death is only a figment of the mind, based on the error of duality in human nature. "This moment marked the end of any belief she might have had that God created man into parts—a body that rots and a soul that lives." [3] She was instantly cured. But this story is contradicted by the doctor's testimony, as witnessed by an affidavit, stating, "I did not at any time declare, or believe, that there was no hope for Mrs. Patterson's recovery, or that she was in a critical condition." [4]

Mrs. Patterson now divided her time between organizing the practice of healing, usually done by others, and teaching the principles of her new-found science. In 1875 she published the first edition of *Science and Health,* which she kept revising and practically rewriting till the end of her life. Each new edition had to be bought by faithful Christian Scientists, although the change might be as little as a single sentence. Each volume sold for three dollars, the greater part going as royalty to the authoress. Two years after the first printing of *Science and Health,* Mrs. Patterson married a student, Asa Gilbert Eddy, who died five years later. She had divorced Patterson on grounds of infidelity.

In 1879, Mrs. Glover-Patterson-Eddy founded the Church of Christ, Scientist; the State charter authorizing the new organization was dated August 23. In 1881, at the age of sixty, she founded the Massachusetts Metaphysical College, with herself as the entire faculty for most of the eight years of the school's existence. Courses were offered in "pathology, ontology, therapeutics, moral science, metaphysics, and their application to the treatment of diseases." On her own testimony, 4,000 students took the twelve-lesson course, later reduced to seven lectures. Tuition was three hundred dollars for the elementary course, with an occasional charity student admitted; there were no discounts or scholarships in the higher courses.

As the number of her followers grew, dissatisfaction increased over the way Mrs. Eddy treated her disciples. She would give the lessons in Christian Science, but they

had the burden of demonstrating it before the public,
sometimes with tragic consequences. The most celebrated
case was the unexpected death of mother and child when
practitioner Mrs. Corner of Chicago attended her own
daughter in childbirth. Instead of being defended, Mrs.
Corner was denounced by her former teacher as a quack.
A large percentage of Mrs. Eddy's disciples rebelled and
were finally dismissed, which occasioned a complete ecclesiastical reorganization. The foundress conceived the idea
of making the society in Boston the Mother Church of
Christian Science. She stipulated that branch churches in
other cities or even countries must be not only affiliated
with the Boston church but entirely dependent on its
jurisdiction. Only members of the Mother Church could
receive a degree C.S.B. (Bachelor of Christian Science) or
C.S.D. (Doctor of Christian Science); only such members
could teach and only they could be Readers in branch
churches. Mrs. Eddy then placed herself as head of the
Mother Church, with detailed provisions to exclude any
interference with her monopoly. No conference of churches
was permitted; officers in the church, from the president
and board of directors down to local church managers,
were to be chosen only with her approval; she abolished
the office of pastors, substituting instead the Readers, who
were allowed only to read from *Science and Health* and
forbidden even to make explanatory remarks on the text;
any Reader could be removed from office at the foundress'
pleasure.

Evidence abounds for the high esteem in which Mrs.
Eddy was held by her followers. Her deposed pastors submitted without complaint, like one who attributed his
demotion to a divine communication received by Mrs.
Eddy. "Did anyone suspect such a revelation," he wrote
in the *Christian Science Journal*, "such a new departure
would be given? No . . . Such disclosures are too high

for us to receive. To One alone did the message come." [5] Not only were pronouns referring to Mrs. Eddy frequently capitalized, but, on occasion, the Mother of Christian Science herself encouraged such adulation. When, for example, in 1903 the question arose of dedicating a new million dollar church in New York, she was given a choice of two inscriptions. One read, "To the glory of God;" the other, "A tribute of love to our Leader and Teacher, Mary Eddy Baker." After careful consideration, Mrs. Eddy decided against the dedication to God.

While consolidating her church, she met opposition on all sides. The worst was a phobia of her own making: Malicious Animal Magnetism, by which absent enemies could mentally project their hatred and injure her. Out of this fear grew the attempted-murder charge against her husband, Asa Eddy, that he wished to dispose of one such mental tormentor of his wife. The case was later dismissed for want of evidence. More real, if less distressing, were the court proceedings by which her son and other prospective heirs tried, but failed, to get a legal declaration of her insanity. And only a year before her death, the whole control of Christian Science was in danger of falling into the hands of her rival, Mrs. Augusta Stetson—until the latter humbly submitted to being excommunicated from the church she helped to found.

In spite of her protestations against the reality of death, Mrs. Eddy Baker died of pneumonia, December 3, 1910. Unimpeachable testimony indicates that she freely used drugs all through life to quiet her nerves, and later on for physical pain, to the point of developing a "morphine habit." [6] When she died, her followers decided, "There will be no 'Leader' named to take the place of Mrs. Eddy. There is no need for any leader." [7]

During the past forty years, this prediction has been fairly verified because of the loyalty to her person which

still unifies Christian Science, and because of the absolute
control over every member exercised by the Mother
Church of Boston. In a true sense, the Church of Christ,
Scientist, has not changed since the death of its foundress.
The numbers have increased, from 100,000 to about 300,-
000 in the United States; but the organizational structure,
doctrine and method of procedure are practically the same
as when Mrs. Eddy wrote that, "Exegesis on the prophetic
Scriptures cites 1875 as the year of the second coming of
Christ. In that year the Christian Science textbook, *Science and Health with Key to the Scriptures,* was first published." [8]

DOCTRINE AND PRINCIPLES

The principles of Christian Science are the teaching
of Mrs. Eddy Baker, as found in her published books (17
volumes) and her contributions over a period of 27 years
to the four periodicals she founded, especially *The Christian Science Journal* (1883) and *The Christian Science
Sentinel* (1898). In spite of an arbitrary use of language
that often seems like pure jargon to the uninitiated, there
is enough intelligibility in Mrs. Eddy's writings to recon-
struct the main outline of her teaching.

God. Although Mrs. Eddy wrote a short treatise in self-
defence, *Christian Science vs. Pantheism,* it is certain that
the deity of Christian Science is pantheistic. According to
the author of *Science and Health,* we may speak of God
as all substance, so that whatever is substantial is divine.[9]
We may also describe Him as all real being, so that nothing is real except God.[10] Given these premises, the basic
doctrine of Eddyism is the identification of God with all
substance and reality. "Christian Science," says its founder,
"reveals incontrovertibly that Mind is All-in-all, that
the only realities are the divine Mind and idea." [11] If she
seems to object to speaking of God as a person, it is only

when the word "person" implies a real distinction between God and the human race. "As the word *person* and *personal* are commonly and ignorantly employed, they often lead, when applied to Deity, to confused and erroneous conceptions of divinity, and its distinction from humanity." [12] Provided no such distinction is inferred, God may be called a person.

When Mrs. Eddy denied that Christian Science was pantheistic, it was because she arbitrarily defined pantheism as a kind of animism which claims that matter can think. [14] Hers was rather "a spiritual pantheism, which holds that God is all in all, but that matter is only an appearance and not reality." [15] One of her favorite expressions in speaking of God was the compound term, "Father-Mother," which meant that as "Father (is) Eternal Life; the one Mind; the divine Principle, commonly called God," [16] so "Mother (is) God; divine and eternal Principle; Life, Truth and Love." [17] As understood by one of her followers, "Mrs. Eddy Baker . . . has set forth clearly the idea of God not only as the wise Father, but also as the tender Mother." [18]

Man. Christian Science describes man in terms of God. He is "the compound idea of infinite Spirit; the spiritual image and likeness of God; the full representation of Mind." [19] Man's body is non-existent. Accordingly, "matter (is) mythology; mortality; another name for mortal mind; illusion"; it is often mistaken for "intelligence, substance, and life in non-intelligence and mortality; life resulting in death, and death in life"; but really it is "sensation in the sensationless; mind originating in matter; the opposite of Truth; the opposite of Spirit; the opposite of God; that of which immortal Mind takes no cognizance; that which mortal mind sees, feels, hears, tastes, and smells only in belief." [20] The human spirit is indeed real, but identical with God. We may not speak therefore of a mul-

tiplicity of souls. "The term *souls* or spirits is as improper
as the term *gods*. Soul or Spirit signifies Deity and nothing
else. There is no finite soul nor spirit. Soul or Spirit means
only one Mind, and cannot be rendered in the plural." [21]

Sickness and Death. Logically there can be no sickness
or pain if there is no body in which they can occur; and
no death, because there is no body from which the divine
Soul can be separated to make a person die. Thus "man
is never sick, for Mind is not sick and matter cannot be
(exist) . . . It is well to be calm in sickness; to be hopeful
is still better; but to understand that sickness is not real
and that Truth can destroy its seeming reality, is best of
all, for this understanding is the universal and perfect
remedy." [22] Moreover since God is the only life, and He
is immortal, death is an illusion.[23] The erroneous "belief
that matter has life results, by the universal law of mortal
mind, in a belief in death. So man, tree, and flower are
supposed to die; but the fact remains that God's universe
is spiritual and immortal." [24] Contrary to appearances,
however, "In reality, man never dies." [25]

Christ and Christianity. Mrs. Eddy distinguishes between Christ and Jesus. The former is spiritual and divine; the latter is corporeal and human.[26] She explains
that "the invisible Christ was imperceptible to the so-
called personal senses, whereas Jesus appeared as a bodily
existence. This dual personality of the unseen and the
seen, the spiritual and material, the eternal Christ and the
corporeal Jesus manifest in flesh, continued until the Master's ascension, when the human, material concept, or
Jesus, disappeared, while the spiritual self, or Christ, continues to exist in the eternal order of divine Science, taking away the sins of the world, as the Christ has always
done, even before the human Jesus was incarnate to mortal
eyes." [27]

According to Mrs. Eddy, "The Church is that institution which affords proof of its utility, and is found elevating the race, rousing the dormant understanding from material beliefs to the apprehension of spiritual ideas and the demonstration of divine Science, thereby casting out devils, or error, and healing the sick." [28] There is no question of a Church founded by Christ, no place for mysteries or creeds, no priesthood or sacraments; only a society of like-minded people who band together to be undeceived about the existence of matter, suffering and death.

Essence of Christian Science. It was in 1866, Mrs. Eddy wrote, that "I discovered the Christ Science or divine laws of Life, Truth and Love, and named my discovery Christian Science. God had been graciously preparing me during many years for the reception of this final revelation of the absolute divine Principle or scientific mental healing." [29] Her discovery is called *Christian* because Christ first "demonstrated the power of Christian Science to heal mortal minds and bodies." [30] It was a *discovery*, because "this power was lost sight of, and must again be spiritually discerned, taught and demonstrated according to Christ's command, with 'signs following.' " [31] It is a *Science* in opposition to mere belief. In Mrs. Eddy's vocabulary, science is synonymous with understanding, as against belief which means ignorance. The object of belief is the visible corporeal world and an apparent distinction among persons and things. The object of science is Spirit and Mind, or God, which alone has real existence, animating the world of ostensible reality as the Soul of the Universe. "Science," then, "so reverses the evidence before the corporeal human senses as to make this Scriptural testimony true in our hearts, 'The last shall be first, and the first last,' so that God and His idea may be to us what divinity really is and must of necessity be—all inclusive." [32] It is a practical science, however; its purpose is not prayer or contemplation but the shedding of sickness, death and sin by driving out

the devil of belief in their existence.[33] Another name for
this exorcism is Christian Science healing.

PRACTICE OF HEALING

The healing process of Christian Science covers three
principal types of activities sponsored by the Church.
Every Sunday and Thanksgiving Day, public services are
held, which consist substantially of reading alternately
from the Bible and from *Science and Health,* done by professional Readers, one man and one woman. The main
part of the function is a Lesson-Sermon prepared by a
committee from the Mother Church in Boston and issued
quarterly by the Christian Science Publishing Society. On
Wednesday evenings, the First Reader reads select passages
from the Bible along with correlative sections from *Science and Health,* but the feature of these Midweek Services is the public testimonies from the congregation. telling about their healing from sickness and sin.

Besides public services, there is an elaborate system of
private healing, performed by certified practitioners who
are listed as such in the official catalogue of the Mother
Church. A practitioner who had class instruction from an
authorized teacher is indicated with a C.S. (Christian Scientist) after his name; if he took a course at the Massachusetts Metaphysical College or in the Christian Science
Board of Education, he is designated as C.S.B. (Bachelor
of Christian Science.)

Practitioners are allowed to engage in healing on request from clients, whether members of the Church or
not. Phone numbers and in some cases, office hours, are
listed for all practitioners; up to 100 and more in a single
city like Chicago or New York.

In the early days, Mrs. Eddy favored manipulation as
part of the practice of healing. She described this mes-

merism in detail, explaining how her students should treat
their patients:

> Wetting your hand in water, rise and rub their
> head. This rubbing has no virtue; only as we believe
> and others believe, we get nearer to them by contact,
> and now you would rub out a belief, and this belief is
> located in the brain. Therefore, as an M.D. lays a
> poultice where the pain is, so you lay your hands where
> the belief is, to rub it out forever.[34]

But in 1872, when one of her students (Richard Ken-
nedy) left her fold, to repudiate him she accused him of
pernicious mesmerism because he used manipulation. At
the same time she changed her own method, dispensing
with any physical handling of the subject. Current practice absolutely forbids manipulation; pure mental healing
of mind to mind is alone permitted.

As described in case histories, the actual healing process
is quite simple. The client listens to the practitioner, reading from Science literature or talking extempore, in order
to undeceive the patient about his sickness by making him
lose himself in the conviction of his identity with the infinite Mind which is God. If personal testimonies are to
be believed, the method works even with children, as recently witnessed by a mother:

> With the help of a practitioner our young son had
> a quick healing of enlarged tonsils. The public school
> authorities had said that he must have an operation
> because the tonsils were so large they feared the con-
> sequences should they become inflamed and addition-
> ally swollen. He was taken to a practitioner, who lov-
> ingly and firmly declared man's oneness, or unity, with
> his Father-Mother-God and the perfection of his being.
> The tonsils returned to their normal size after this
> one treatment.[35]

In most cases, however, the healing takes place without the help of a practitioner, and often involves the curing of a moral disease. A woman testified gratefully that she was estranged from a friend who had treated her, she felt, "most unjustly and cruelly." She began to reflect on Mrs. Eddy's words that, "In Science, Mind is *one,* including noumenon and phenomena, God and His thoughts." Suddenly came the cure:

> The absolute unity of divine Mind and its expression was revealed to me, and I saw that truth prohibits the misconception of two warring minds and the unpleasant results that go along with the belief. That realization wiped out the whole false picture, including the grief.
>
> My consciousness was filled with forgiveness and compassion for the other woman, for I saw that since we both had the same Mind, she in reality loved me as I loved her.[36]

The Christian Science Reading Rooms in every large city are intended to serve this purpose of "self-healing," where quiet reflection on the great truths of Eddyism dispels the error of mortal belief in physical sickness and mental pain.[37]

ORGANIZATION AND AGENCIES

The organization of Christian Science is rigidily centralized. At the head stands the Mother Church in Boston. Branch churches in other cities are completely dependent on the Mother Church; a prospective branch church is called a Christian Science Society. "When members of The Mother Church in a community believe the time has come for the organization of a Christian Science Society, or a branch Church of Christ, Scientist," they contact the Mother Church and request affiliation, conditioned on the observance of strict regulations laid down by Mrs. Eddy.

Among Protestant bodies, Christian Science is unique in having two kinds of members: those associated immediately and only with the Mother Church, and those who also belong to a branch church of the denomination. Heading the Mother Church is the Board of Directors, including a president, readers, a clerk and treasurer; comparable officers also direct the branch churches, which are called First, Second, etc., Church of Christ, Scientist, according to the order of erection in a given locality.

The proselytism of Christian Science is world-wide, and directed by a series of agencies, emanating from the Mother Church and outstanding for their efficiency.

The Christian Science Publishing Society publishes all the official writings of Mrs. Eddy and of the Mother Church of Boston. Five periodicals are printed: *The Christian Science Journal,* an English monthly; *Christian Science Sentinel,* an English weekly; *Herald of Christian Science,* monthly and quarterly, in French, German, Dutch, Danish, Norwegian, Swedish, Spanish, Portuguese, Italian, English, and Braille; *Christian Science Quarterly* in eight languages; and *The Christian Science Monitor,* daily except Sunday and holidays, in English, with a religious article in one of twelve different translations. To insure orthodox Scientism in its publications, "articles are accepted only from members of The Mother Church." Although "freshness, originality, naturalness, variety are prized," it is prescribed that "at least one quotation from the Bible and also one from our Leader's writings should be included." [38] In practice, the articles are either commentaries on Mrs. Eddy's doctrines, or personal testimonials (with appropriate quotations from the Leader), of how Christian Science has benefited the writer. Even a newspaper like the *Monitor* is written according to Christian Science prescription. For instance, the word "death" is never used when referring to persons, because, accord-

ing to editorial policy, "We don't believe this happens to
people; so we report the termination of the earthly residence of people in the news by saying that they have
'passed on,' which any Christian should admit is a more
accurate description of what has happened." [39]

The Board of Lectureship, consisting of some thirty
members, is appointed annually by the Board of Directors.
Its function is to accept invitations for giving free lectures
in branch churches throughout the world. In 1955 there
were branch churches in 40 countries besides the United
States. Western Germany, for example, had branches in
30 cities, France in 10 cities, England in more than 175.
London alone has 13 Churches of Christ, Scientist. Through
the lecture program, these disparate units are assured con-
formity of doctrine with the Mother Church of Boston.

The Board of Education instructs authorized teachers
of Christian Science. As prescribed in the *Church Manual,*
a certified teacher is limited to 30 in the number of pupils
he may instruct during any calendar year. Infraction of
this rule makes the teacher liable to dismissal from the
Church.

Less familiar is the Committee on Publication, whose
creation by Mrs. Eddy was occasioned by the repeated at-
tacks she suffered from newspapers and other molders of
public opinion. With a home office in Boston, state committees were appointed by the Mother Church with the
two-fold purpose of furnishing censored news and policy
releases to the press, and of watching the publications for
any statement unacceptable to the Church of Christ, Scientist. Under the duties of this agency Mrs. Eddy prescribed
a singular routine:

> This Committee on Publication shall be respon-
> sible for correcting or having corrected a false news-
> paper article which has not been replied to by other

Scientists, or which has been forwarded to this Committee for the purpose of having him reply to it. If the correction by the Committee on Publication is not promptly published by the periodical in which it is desirable that this correction shall appear, this Committee shall immediately apply for aid to the Committee on Business.[40]

Calling for aid from the Committee on Business meant to put pressure on the editor of the newspaper or periodical, e.g., through one of its advertisers, to avoid anything in the future which might offend the religious sentiments of Christian Scientists.

Proof of the Publication Committee's effectiveness is the practical absence of any controversial articles on Christian Science in American magazines, popular or scientific. During the ten year period, 1945-1954, the writer could find only two full-length articles in the 120 magazines listed in the *Readers' Guide to Periodical Literature* that were critical of Christian Science. Both were later answered in the same publications. Moreover, the Church's vigilance extends into other areas. Early in 1952 the *Scientific American* reported that the New York State Department of Education dropped all questions relating to bacteria and infection from the Regents' Examinations in biology. This was in accordance with a law which "the State Legislature, at the request of the Christian Science Church, had quietly passed . . . providing that 'a pupil may be excused from such study of health and hygiene as conflicts with the religion of his parents or guardian.' "[41] Three months later this news item was rebutted by a representative of the Mother Church, pointing out that "the Christian Science Committee on Publication for New York specifically asked that changes not be made in the examination questions because of certain legal exemptions available to Christian Scientists." [42] There was no suggestion, however, that these "exemptions" might have influenced the changes in the biology tests in order to avoid further conflict with the Scientists.

STATISTICS

N.B. One of the by-laws of the Church of Christ, Scientist, written by Mrs. Eddy, forbids publication of membership figures. "Christian Scientists," it states, "shall not report for publication the number of members of The Mother Church, nor that of the branch churches. According to the Scripture they shall turn away from personality and numbering the people." *Manual*, VIII, 28. Certain data, however, are available, as follows:

Members of the Church of Christ, Scientist, U.S.A., according to 1936 U.S. Census, but claimed to be far below the total number of adherents	268,915
Christian Science branch churches and societies in world (approx.)	4,300
Churches and Societies, U.S.A. (approx.)	3,100
Christian Science practitioners in world (approx.)	9,600
Practitioners in England (approx.)	1,000
Practitioners and Teachers, U.S.A. (approx.)	7,600
Christian Science Nurses, U.S.A. (approx.)	500
Christian Science Units in Colleges and Universities Number of Institutions, U.S.A. (approx.)	124

REFERENCES

1. Mark Twain, *Christian Science*, New York, Harper, 1907, p. 343.
2. Edwin F. Dakin, *Mrs. Eddy*, New York, Charles Scribners, 1930, p. 31.
3. Norman Beasley, *The Cross and the Crown*, New York, Duell, Sloan and Pearce, 1952, p. 5.
4. Georgine Milmine, *The Life of Mary Baker G. Eddy, and the History of Christian Science*, Garden City, N. Y., Doubleday, Page and Co., 1909, p. 87.
5. Dakin, *op. cit.*, p. 270.
6. *Ibid.*, p. 530.
7. *Ibid.*, p. 521.
8. Mary Baker Eddy, *Message to the Mother Church*, Boston, 1900, p. 6.
9. Mary Baker Eddy, *Science and Health with Key to the Scriptures*, Boston, First Church of Christ, Scientist, 1934, p. 587.

10. *Ibid.*, p. 108.
11. *Ibid.*, p. 109.
12. *Ibid.*, p. 116.
13. *Loc. cit.*
14. *Ibid.*, p. 129.
15. Henry W. Steiger, *Christian Science and Philosophy,* New York, Philosophical Library, 1948, p. 60.
16. *Science and Health*, p. 586.
17. *Ibid.*, p. 592.
18. *The Christian Science Journal,* December, 1954, LXXII, p. 636.
19. *Science and Health*, p. 591.
20. *Ibid.*, pp. 582, 591.
21. *Ibid.*, p. 466.
22. *Ibid.*, pp. 393-394.
23. *Ibid.*, p. 289.
24. *Loc. cit.*
25. *Ibid.*, p. 486.
26. *Ibid.*, p. 332.
27. *Ibid.*, p. 324. This is a species of Docetism (from *dokein,* to appear), familiar as a heresy from apostolic times. Considering matter as intrinsically evil, the Docetists held that Christ was not a man but only seemed to lead a human life. They were refuted by St. John in his Epistles, e.g., "Everyone that confesses not Jesus in the flesh is not of God" (I John 4:3).
28. *Ibid.*, p. 583.
29. *Ibid.*, p. 107.
30. *Ibid.*, p. 110.
31. *Loc. cit.*
32. *Ibid.*, p. 116. Pantheism (from *pan,* all, and *Theos,* God), which confounds the world with God, was already familiar to the ancient Greeks and Orientals. In modern times, one school of Pantheists claims that the world is absorbed by God (Spinoza); others teach that God is absorbed by the world of which He is the force and life (Goethe). Some look upon the world as a literal outpouring of the divine substance (Fichte); others, with Hegel, confound finite with infinite, being with nothing, the *ego* with *non-ego.* Christian Science is a type of Hegelianism. The absurdity of Pantheism is clear from its denial of a primary datum of consciousness, which is the individuality of the human person.
33. *Ibid.*, p. 584.
34. *McClure's Magazine,* May, 1907, XXXIX, p. 109.
35. *The Christian Science Journal,* p. 663.
36. *Ibid.*, p. 664.
37. The healings of Christian Science may be explained as cases in which psychotherapy has given relief in functional and nervous disorders. On occasion, the cures may be quite astounding. But they cannot be fairly compared to the healings at Lourdes or the miraculous cures accepted in the canonization of saints. Authentic medical records are not only incomplete, but, *ex hypothesi,* nonexistent; and all the devices of auto- (and hetero-) suggestion are used to induce new patterns of thought on impressionable personalities. Thus Christian Science anticipated the practice if not the theory of psychosomatic medicine by almost a century.
38. *Ibid.*, p. ii.
39. Quoted by Nathaniel M. Guptill, "The 'Monitor' Is Unique," *Christian Century,* September 7, 1955, LXXII, p. 1017.
40. *Manual of the Mother Church, the First Church of Christ, Scientist,* Boston, 1895, XXXIII, 2.
41. *Scientific American,* February, 1952, CLXXXVI, pp. 40-41.
42. *Ibid.*, May, 1952, p. 4.

4. Disciples and Christians

THE INITIAL difficulty to be cleared in any study of the Disciples and Christians is the matter of names. Are they one sect or two; and if two, how to distinguish between them when they seem to use each other's names interchangeably?

There are two sects, one called the Disciples, or Disciples of Christ, and the other Christians, or Churches of Christ. However the Disciples also call themselves collectively, the "Christian Church," especially in the Midwest and South, and local congregations with rare exception are named "Christian." The rival group, listed in the federal census as the "Churches of Christ," never speaks of itself as Disciples, but always uses the term "Christian" or "of Christ," either in denominating the whole body or when referring to a single congregation.

What further complicates the issue is the use of "Christian" to describe still other religious groups, whether existing or absorbed by another denomination. Among the defunct "Christian" bodies, the most important was an offshoot of the present-day Churches of Christ, which joined the Congregationalists in 1931. Among the still extant, but alien, Christian Churches the largest are the "Holiness Church of Christ," which is a Baptist derivative, and the "Christian and Missionary Alliance," specializing in evangelism.

A final source of confusion is the denominational status of the Disciples and Christians. Most Christians disclaim the title of denomination as unwarranted by reason of their amorphous ecclesiastical character; many Disciples also prefer to be considered interdenominational. Yet between them they number almost four million members, to constitute the largest purely indigenous religious movement in America.

HISTORY

The founder of the Disciples of Christ was Thomas Campbell, born in Ireland in 1763, of a Catholic father who renounced his faith. He began as an Anglican but withdrew from the English Church in protest against its ritualism. As a Presbyterian he worked for union in his own church and among other denominations. Discouraged by the opposition his efforts met in Ireland, he came to the States in 1807, beginning his ministry in Philadelphia as a Presbyterian. Within two years he was resisted by the presbyteries, especially after his now famous *Declaration and Address,* issued "to all that love our Lord Jesus Christ in all sincerity, throughout all the churches." Its main tenet was that the Church of Christ upon earth is one. It is "essentially, intentionally and constitutionally one," and consists "of all those in every place that profess their faith in Christ and obedience to him in all things according to the Scriptures." [1] The constitution of this Church of Christ, said Campbell, is not a creedal statement or confession of faith but the New Testament itself. Sectarian churches have no right to impose on their members as articles of faith anything not expressly taught in the Bible. Even inferences or deductions from the New Testament are not to be held binding on the conscience of individuals unless they are realized as true by the persons themselves. Just as in apostolic times "a manifest attachment to our Lord Jesus Christ in faith, holiness, and charity was the original criterion of Christian character," so in the united Church envisoned by Campbell, this alone should be "the foundation and cement of Christian unity." [2]

In the same year (1809), Thomas Campbell was joined by his son, Alexander, who came to America to share and later carry on the work of his father. Together they organized (1810) the Christian Association of Washington, Pa., the first local church of the new denomination. Soon after a crisis arose on the manner of administering baptism. Deciding that the ordinance must be by immersion, father and son had themselves rebaptized by the local Baptist minister. For seventeen years the Christian Association operated as a branch of the Baptists, until the younger Campbell's anti-creedalism aroused a storm of protest. The Baptists issued an eight-point manifesto, condemning the "reformers" for maintaining "that there is no promise of salvation without Baptism . . . that Baptism procures the remission of sins and the gift of the Holy Spirit . . . that no creed is necessary for the church but the Scriptures as they stand, and that all baptized persons have the right to administer the ordinance of Baptism." [3]

Three years after the Baptist ouster, the Campbellites were joined by Barton Stone, former Presbyterian minister who had formed a non-creedal group called the Christians. Excommunicated from the Presbyterians, Stone and his followers declared their "objections . . . to the Presbyterian Confession of Faith, and against all authoritative confessions and creeds formed by fallible men." They professed a "total abandonment of all authoritative creeds but the Bible alone as the only rule of faith and practice." [4] In 1832 a partial fusion of the Campbellites and Christians was effected at Lexington, Kentucky. When the question arose of a name for the merger, Stone insisted on "Christian," as the name given the followers of Christ "in the beginning by divine authority." Alexander Campbell and his friends preferred "Disciples" as less offensive to good people and quite as scriptural. The result was that no definite action was taken and to this day both names are used, the local organization being generally known as a "Christian Church" or a "Church of Christ," and rarely as a "Church of Disciples" or a "Disciples' Church."

The first national convention of the Disciples was held at Cincinnati in 1849, when 156 delegates from 11 States resolved on the formation of a Missionary Society "as a means to concentrate and dispense the wealth and benevolence of the brethren of this Reformation in an effort to convert the world." [5] Cincinnati was made the headquarters and Alexander Campbell was elected first president. A year later the first foreign missionary was sent "to engage in teaching, preaching and the practice of medicine among the Jews at Jerusalem." [6]

At the end of the nineteenth century, the Disciples counted more than a million members and were looking forward to the centennial celebration of the *Declaration and Address* when their ranks were split by a schism that was seventy years in the making. Alexander Campbell had been a Baptist from 1812 to 1829, during which time he advocated certain conservative policies, later abandoned by him but taken up and developed by a strong reactionary party among the Disciples. They were against open communion outside the denomination and the use of "Reverend" as a title for the clergy. But their chief objection was against the organization of missionary and other societies, which they construed as a form of denominationalism and a concession to authoritarianism. On the ritual their main grievance was the installation of organs in churches.

After years of controversy in the pulpit and religious press, the conservatives felt they had enough solidarity to separate from the main body and, as far as possible, form a new denomination. In the government census for 1906 they were listed for the first time as a distinct religious body, the Churches of Christ, numbering at the time about 200,000 adherents.

The schism of the Churches of Christ was not the only disruption among the Disciples. At least six "mutually hostile and exclusive groups" have been identified within the denomination: "the pro-music, pro-organized-missions group . . . the pro-music, anti-organized-missions group . . . the anti-music, anti-organized-missions group . . . the anti-music, anti-organized-missions, anti-church-school group . . . the anti-music, anti-organized-missions, anti-alien-immersion group . . . the anti-music, anti-organized-missions, anti-Sunday-school group," each with separate and rival publishing headquarters.[7]

Although, in effect, at least two opposing bodies exist within the framework of the Disciples, the liberals and fundamentalists, there is no prospect of a new schism for lack of sufficient unity among the different factions. One evidence of the increasing strength of the fundamentalists is the rising number of their missionaries, independently educated and supported, and the establishment of separate Bible Colleges (35 in 1953), generally small and non-accredited, but indicative of a growing dissatisfaction with the modernism that is rampant in the liberal half of the denomination.

Modernist Disciples have been outstanding in promoting the ecumenical movement. Though under fire from their co-religionists who call the National Council of Churches an "ecclesiastical monstrosity" by which "the Reformation has been set back several hundred years," the liberals have contributed more than a proportional share to the church unity efforts in America. Unique among the constituents of the N.C.C., the Disciples organized an administrative staff on a national scale, working through 164 state and regional board members and supported by generous financial aid, with the result that Protestant ecumenism in the country is taking on more and more the non-creedal aspect of the Disciples of Christ.

In contrast with the relative homogeneity among the Disciples, the Churches of Christ can scarcely be said to have a denominational history since the break of 1906. Protesting they are not a denomination, their principal source of unity in the past fifty years has been a steady resistance to the "human innovations" of other religious bodies, in the form of set creeds, church officials above the local congregation, and ritual requirements for membership. As distinct from the Disciples, they have been fairly consistent in opposing musical instruments in the churches, to such a degree that the Disciples commonly distinguish the Christians by describing them as the "non instrumental music" segment of the parent body. Their religious publications are carefully labeled "unofficial," their colleges and professional schools are "non-sectarian." While missionary societies are forbidden as having "no scriptural head, foundation, field or mission," foreign missionaries are privately sponsored by individuals or local Churches of Christ. In rare instances, "if a church is too weak to completely support a preacher in other fields, then two or three congregations (may) cooperate in the effort," since "this would be cooperation without creating an organization." [8]

DOCTRINE

Since both Disciples and Christians profess to be non-confessional, having no creed but Christ and no doctrines except those which are found in the New Testament, it would seem impossible to formulate their principal beliefs. In practice, however, they emphasize certain areas of faith which may be taken as representative of the two denominations.

The Scriptures. Disciples and Christians accept the Bible as the word of God, written by different persons at different times, somehow under the inspiration of the Holy Spirit. But even fundamentalists among them explain that "this revelation comes to us in many forms: in individual lives, in great epochs of history, in providence, in such organizations as the Church, in religious assemblies, but especially in men like the prophets, the apostles, the psalmists and the evangelists." [9] Allowance is therefore made for a difference of degree but not of essence between the "inspiration" of poetry or great genius and the supernatural inspiration of Sacred Scripture.

The Church. The Disciples and Christians are agreed in regarding the Church Universal as an essentially invisible "society of believers . . . instituted by Jesus Christ," and, by divine providence, indestructible.[10] "Single denominations and sects . . . after having served their purpose, may disappear and go the way of all flesh; but the Church Universal of Christ, in her divine life and substance, is too strong for the gates of hell." [11] Beyond this agreement on the existence of a world-wide spiritual society, the difference in concept of the visible Church of Christ is so radical between the Disciples and Christians that it practically constitutes the two religious groups. The Disciples frankly admit the existence and necessity of visible Christian sects like the Methodists, Baptists, and their own denomination. "To become a member of the Church (invisible) it is necessary to have (only) an inner experience," but to enter the visible church of, say, the Presbyterians, it is further required to have "an outward expression (and) a new social attachment." As distinct functions, "the inner experience is to hear and believe the gospel and to repent of sin . . . The new social alignment is to become a member of the visible organization." [12]

Against this concession that denominations are according to the will of God, the Christians range all their apologetic writings. First they defend their own claim to being non-denominational. "It is possible," they admit, "to sectarianize the name church of Christ or Christian, but that is what we endeavor studiously to avoid. We spell the word church with a small letter . . . We are not a part of any religious denomination for we refuse to divide up into parties." [13] Moreover, denominations in general are opposed to the Gospel teaching. Starting with the assumption that Catholicism is a corruption of apostolic Christianity, the origin of denominationalism is explained as an apostacy, when "the commandments and inventions of men led to the gradual development of the Roman Catholic Church." Luther, Calvin and others "tried to reform the Catholic Church, but their efforts only resulted in the establishment of more man-made churches. Their efforts gave birth to denominationalism with its hundreds of contradictory doctrines." [14] With minor differences, the Christians regard themselves as heirs of a new movement which began in the nineteenth century, "to restore the true church which had become lost to the multitudes because of the doctrines of Catholicism and denominationalism." [15] After the lapse of centuries, Thomas and Alexander Campbell rediscovered the fact that "faith in Jesus Christ as the Son of God (is) a sufficient profession to entitle a man or woman to become a member of the Church of Christ." [16]

A permanent tension among the Christians is how to operate their churches efficiently without some degree of unity beyond the local congregational level, and at the same time proclaim they are non-denominational in spite of their organization. They solve the problem by making concessions to cooperative effort among the churches, but always short of being on a national scale, assisted by books and periodicals from common publishing houses which serve to unite ostensibly independent congregations.

Sacraments. Two sacraments or ordinances are recognized by the Disciples and Christians: baptism and the Lord's Supper, Regarding baptism, Disciples are warned that, "We should neither overemphasize nor undervalue it." [17] Overemphasis would be to conceive it as efficacious independently of the active cooperation of the one baptized, e.g., a child, since "Baptism is (only) for all who understandingly, intentionally and sacrificially accept the Lordship of Jesus Christ, and want to declare that fact to the world." [18] Underestimation means a failure to realize that "Baptism is the experience that translates one from being a non-Christian to being a Christian," yet not "in any magical, commercial, formal or miraculous sense," as though sin is remitted or grace infused in virtue of the baptismal rite. At most, "it is the effort of the true Christian knight to honor Christ by the white flower of a stainless life. It is in this (promissory) sense that Baptism is for the remission of sins." [19]

Though variously described, the Lord's Supper for the Disciples and Christians is only "a sweet and simple memorial." Just "as we look at a flower from mother's grave in memory of man's truest earthly friend," or "we go to Washington's monument and stand with heads uncovered in memory of the father of our country, (so) also we gather around the Lord's table and take the Lord's supper in memory of Him who said, 'This do in remembrance of me.' " [20] Emphatically the Lord's Supper does not mean that "a real miracle, which changes the material elements into the actual body and blood of Christ, takes place in the elements." [21] That kind of miracle is unnecessary "to vitalize its power and enforce its influence over the soul." [22]

Whatever the Eucharistic presence means to Campbell's disciples, it is not determined by the words of the minister pronouncing the words of institution, but by the living faith of the communicants, since "to partake of it without thinking of Christ, to partake of it simply as a 'church ordinance,' to partake of it because it is a custom or is expected of us, is to miss its depth and to eat of nothing but bread, to drink of nothing but the blood of the grape." [23]

WORSHIP AND RITUAL

Separate minister's manuals are available for the Disciples and the Churches of Christ, but the differences are slight. Both are relative innovations, and presented to the clergy with an apology. "The Disciples of Christ," are told they "have always been a free people, including a freedom from ritualism," but "with an increasing culture there is a growing desire that all things be done decently and in good order." [24] Hence the need of a uniform ritual. Ministers of the Churches of Christ are also cautioned that the manual of worship "should not be slavishly used, either to the exclusion of heartfelt personal expression, or of loyalty to what is believed to be the teaching of God's Word." [25]

Baptism. Alexander Campbell's conviction that only baptism by immersion is valid was based, he said, on extensive study of the meaning of the word *baptizo* in the Greek New Testament. He found that "the ancient lexicons with one consent give *immersion* as the natural, common, and primary sense of this word." [26] Disciples and Christians have remained faithful to this tradition, directing that "every congregation should have a baptistry inside the church edifice," which should be of adequate dimensions, since "humiliating experiences can be related of shallow baptistries." Also "there should be an abundant supply of leaded robes for both sexes," and "the water in the baptistry should be heated in cold weather." It is suggested that "the baptistry should be surrounded by flowers" and that the baptismal service be approached "with songs and prayer." [27]

Ministers of the Church of Christ are given explicit directions:

> The ordinance of Christian baptism is best administered in a pool of water waist deep. The administrator stands to the left side and somewhat to the rear of the candidate. With his left hand he grasps the right wrist of the candidate, allowing the latter's hand to be free to hold a handkerchief to cover the nose and mouth. The candidate, with his left hand, grasps the minister's wrist. With the right upraised, the minister pronounces the charge, then placing the hand between the shoulders lowers the candidate gently backward until the head is completely under the water; he then lifts him up out of the water.[28]

In the administration of baptism, the Trinitarian formula is used, with special care to say, "I baptize you, N . . . , *into* the name of the Father and of the Son and of the Holy Spirit. Amen." [29]

Lord's Supper. There are two principal types of service among the Disciples and Christians, Morning Worship with the Lord's Supper, and Evening Worship without Communion. Ministers are told to "avoid elaborate worship programs . . . Emphasis should always be placed on simplicity." [30] A standard "Order for Morning Worship" in the Churches of Christ, substantially the same for the Disciples, begins with a hymn by the choir, during which the minister comes to the platform and takes charge of the function. Following the first hymn is the Doxology, an invocation, another hymn, Scripture reading and the Communion hymn which introduces the ceremony of the Lord's Supper.

Ministers have a choice of at least four "Orders of Observance" for the Communion service, in which elders and deacons participate. During the singing of the Communion hymn, the elders take their place at each end of a table on which are placed wide-rim metal plates covered with pieces of bread, and wooden or metal trays filled with small glasses of wine. The deacons take their places in front of the table, while the congregation stands. Without announcement, "the elder at the right returns thanks for the bread," always quoting the words of institution from the Last Supper. Immediately "the elder at the left returns thanks for the cup," again using the words of institution. After the congregation has been seated the elders "distribute the bread to the alternate deacons" who in turn give communion to the people. The remaining deacons close ranks and receive from the elders the trays of wine glasses to be served to the congregation. When the people have been served, the deacons give communion to the elders, after which "the elders then serve the deacons and close the service with a song of thanksgiving." [31] An essential difference in the ritual of the Christians is the recommendation that "unleavened bread and the unfermented juice of the grape should be used." [32] The Disciples do not specify unfermented bread and allow the use of wine; they also provide "Simultaneous Communion which is being observed in an increasing number of their churches." Bread is distributed to the people and held in the hands; then, as the minister recites the words: "And he gave to the disciples, and said, 'Take, eat; this is my body,' " all eat together, each his own portion. The wine is distributed and taken in the same way.

Following communion is the offertory, during which prayers of self-oblation are offered and contributions are made to the church as "a sacred and impressive part of divine worship." Then a sermon, which "should edify, inspire and secure decisive action on the part of the hearer." [33] After the sermon a benediction is invoked upon the congregation, with a choral response; and finally organ chimes are played to conclude the service.

Music in Public Worship. Historically the Churches of Christ differ from the Disciples by their opposition to the use of musical instruments in public worship. They agree that "music has a place in New Testament worship," and freely use hymns in their church services. They also permit musical instruments to accompany religious songs for private devotion, but not for public acts of worship. The argument is that since "the New Testament is silent concerning instrumental music in worship . . . it is evident that those who have it in the worship do so without scriptural authority. We should not presume to add to the divine pattern." [34] The argument is supported by an appeal to the Protestant Reformers. Among others, Calvin is quoted as saying that "Musical instruments in celebrating the praises of God would be no more suitable than the burning of incense, the lighting up of lamps, the restoration of the other shadows of the law. The Papists . . . have foolishly borrowed this . . . from the Jews." [35]

After this polemic from a Church of Christ publishing house in Texas, it comes as a surprise to find the *Christian Minister's Manual* (Cincinnati) not only tolerating instrumental music in public worship but providing a detailed consecration service for the installation of a church organ. The ceremony begins with an organ recital, and after suitable readings from Scripture, the people say, "We dedicate this organ." To which the minister adds, "To sum-

mon His people to the hour of worship and holy communion . . . to lift man's soul to communion with Christ
. . . and to bring to his life the comfort, peace and hope
which abide in him." [36]

ORGANIZATION AND GOVERNMENT

While ministerial associations have been organized for
mutual help and supervision, they have no authority
among the Disciples and Christians, which are strictly congregational in their form of government. Local churches
elect their own elders and deacons, "by voice, by show of
hands, by ballot or by rising," followed by the ceremony
of ordination if the officers are elected for a permanent
term, to be ended by death or resignation. However, many
congregations choose their ministers for a limited term
only, usually three years, and the list is so arranged that
one-third of the officers is elected each year.

In the early days, ordinations to the ministry were rare.
Even now the Disciples hold "there is no official distinction between the clergy and the laity . . . The real power
of a minister is personal, not official, power of a strong
compelling goodness of life and character." [37] This opinion
is shared by the Churches of Christ. Yet ordinations are
now a commonplace, and invested with considerable so-
lemnity, as "the formal setting apart of a man to the work
of the ministry." Essentially the ceremony consists in the
laying on of hands by one or more elders, accompanied by
the ordination prayer, for which there is no set formula
except that it be "fervent, personal and short, asking the
Lord to use the life now laid on His altar; to keep, guide
and bless by making him a blessing to the church and for
the saving of multitudes; and asking for him health of
body, mind and heart and that he may be fully consecrated
to the work whereunto he has been called." [38]

There is no juridical authority in the Churches of Christ beyond the local congregation. Only denominations are ruled by "ecclesiastical forms of government." But in so doing, say the Christians, "they have ignored the head of the church (Christ) and have assumed the right of self-government." Clearly this is against the Scriptures which tell us that, "Shortly before Christ ascended to the right hand of God, he said, 'All authority hath been given unto me in heaven and on earth.' Christ has all authority; therefore man has none." Yet "we hear much of 'synods,' 'presbyteries,' 'councils,' 'general assemblies,' and 'conferences.' In these delegations, men legislate rules" independently of the law of God.[39]

Also congregational in polity but fully organized as a denomination, the Disciples are grouped on three levels above the local church, into district and state conventions, and an International Convention which meets annually as a representative body of all the churches. There is no national body comparable to the Southern Baptist Convention or the Methodist General Conference. In fact, the Disciples' conventions have only advisory power and no final authority over the member churches. More direct supervision is exercised through a variety of boards, e.g., the Board of Church Extension, whose purpose is to assist Christian churches in the planning and financing of buildings; the Board of Higher Education, with 36 affiliated institutions like Texas Christian, Butler, and Drake Universities, "concerned with the education of youth in an atmosphere of Christian influence" and the training of the clergy; and the Christian Board of Publications, which operates a "Brotherhood-owned publishing house" with a current investment of two million, "to propagate and support an effective program of Christian education," by providing a home journal, *The Christian Evangelist,* books, audio-visual materials "and all other supplies" necessary for "Christian teaching, Christian evangelism and Christian stewardship in the local church."

While accurate figures are not available there is good reason for believing that the Christian schism of 1906 was only the high-point in a permanent trend within the Disciples of Christ towards an undistinguishable form of non-sectarianism. This is strikingly illustrated in the history of the *Christian Century,* founded in 1884 as a rival periodical to the denomination-minded *Christian Evangelist.* Remaining under the aegis of the Disciples, in 1908 the *Christian Century* was bought by Charles Clayton Morrison, and dedicated to "a new era of frank commitment to liberalism." Morrison was "far ahead of Disciple sentiment (in) advocating open membership" to all comers, regardless of their creedal prepossessions. By 1918, the paper carried the subtitle, "An Undenominational Journal of Religion." What many considered a "suicidal boldness in cutting loose from the position of the vast majority in the denomination of its origin," resulted in making the *Christian Century* acceptable to a wide circle of "liberals in all churches," until today it is the most popular interdenominational magazine in the country, with a weekly circulation upwards of 50,000.[40] After forty years as editor of the *Christian Century,* Morrison is still a member of the Disciples' ministry. Without apology, historians of the denomination speak of his lifetime opposition to Protestant sectarianism, including the Disciples, as a "distinguished career in the public and ecclesiastical field."[41] Early in 1956, he was elected president of Protestants and Other Americans United for Separation of Church and State.

STATISTICS

Disciples of Christ

Total World Membership	2,029,963
Countries where Church is established	16
United States of America	
Membership (Resident and Non-Resident)	1,897,736
Churches	7,951
Ministers having charges	5,269
Church schools	7,966
Church school enrollment	1,248,495
Affiliated institutions of higher learning	35
Student enrollment	23,211
National publications	8

Churches of Christ

Total United States Membership	1,600,000
Churches	16,500
Pastors having charges	14,000
Sunday schools	2,935
Sunday school enrollment	209,615
National publications	7

REFERENCES

1. Alonzo W. Fortune, *Origin and Development of the Disciples,* St. Louis, Christian Board of Publication, 1953, pp. 48, 51.
2. *Ibid.,* p. 52.
3. *Ibid.,* pp. 81-82.
4. *Ibid.,* p. 101.
5. *Ibid.,* p. 151.
6. *Ibid.,* p. 152.
7. Winfred E. Garrison, *Religion Follows the Frontier, A History of the Disciples of Christ,* New York, Harper, 1931, pp. 297-298.
8. Leroy Brownlow, *Why I Am A Member of the Church of Christ,* Fort Worth, Brownlow Publications, 1945, pp. 84-85.
9. B. A. Abbott, *The Disciples, An Interpretation,* St. Louis, Bethany Press, 1926, p. 71. Biblical inspiration, according to the Catholic Church, is a direct, supernatural, charismatic influence on the mind, will, and executive faculties of the human writer, by which he mentally conceives, freely wills to write and actually writes correctly all that God intends him to write and nothing else, so that God is truly the author of the sacred book produced.
10. *Ibid.,* pp. 87, 91.
11. *Ibid.,* pp. 86-87.
12. *Ibid.,* pp. 88-89.
13. G. C. Brewer, *Is the Church of Christ a Denomination?,* Nashville, Gospel Advocate Co., n.d., p. 14.

14. Brownlow, *op. cit.*, p. 71.
15. *Ibid.*, p. 72.
16. Leslie G. Thomas, *Restoration Handbook*, Nashville, Gospel Advocate Co., 1954, p. 76. Campbell and his followers equate the Catholic Church with the sects of Protestantism as "man-made" first by denying that Christ founded a visible Church—against the unanimous evidence of Christian antiquity; and then ignoring the historical continuity of this visible Society, which Christ established, as the Roman Catholic Church—as seen, for example, in the uninterrupted succession of Roman Pontiffs from Peter the Apostle to Pope Pius XII.
17. Abbott, *op. cit.*, p. 117.
18. *Ibid.*, p. 120.
19. *Ibid.*, pp. 123, 125, 127.
20. Brownlow, *op. cit.*, p. 168.
21. Abbott, *op. cit.*, p. 134.
22. *Loc. cit.*
23. *Ibid.*, p. 143.
24. Benjamin L. Smith, *Minister's Manual*, St. Louis, Christian Board of Publication, 1951, p. 7.
25. James DeForest Murch, *Christian Minister's Manual*, Cincinnati, Standard Publishing Foundation, 1937, p. 10.
26 Alexander Campbell, *The Christian System*, Cincinnati, Standard Publishing Co., n.d., p. 40.
27. Smith, *op. cit.*, p. 151.
28. Murch, *op. cit.*, p. 79.
29. *Ibid.*, p. 84. The baptismal formula, "I baptize thee *into* the name of the Father . . . ," is valid according to Catholic teaching, and, in fact, used by certain Churches in union with Rome. It follows the Greek text of Matthew 28/19. The Roman rite follows the Latin translation, which dates (originally) from the end of the first century of the Christian era.
30. *Ibid.*, p. 47.
31. Smith, *op. cit.*, p. 163.
32. Murch, *op. cit.*, p. 63.
33. *Ibid.*, p. 17.
34. Brownlow, *op. cit.*, p. 177.
35. *Ibid.*, p. 180.
36. Murch, *op. cit.*, pp. 205-206.
37. Smith, *op. cit.*, p. 179.
38. *Ibid.*, p. 181.
39. Brownlow, *op. cit.*, pp. 38-39. By their opposition to ecclesiastical authority in any form, the Campbellite Christians deny that Christ established a Church to carry on His work for the salvation of souls, since there cannot be a Church without ecclesiastical authority. Moreover when they argue from Scripture that "Christ has all authority; therefore man has none," they prove too much. If it ever became true that men had no authority, civil and domestic society would cease to exist. The fact is that God has delegated His authority, naturally, to parents and the state; and supernaturally to the Catholic Church, when Christ gave the Apostles and their successors the power to bind and loose and to teach all nations "all that I have commanded you" (Matt. 28:20).
40. Winfred E. Garrison and Alfred T. DeGroot, *The Disciples of Christ, A History*, St. Louis, Christian Board of Publication, 1954, pp. 431-432.
41. *Loc. cit.*

5. Episcopalians

IN MANY WAYS Episcopalianism has more profoundly affected the history and fortunes of the Catholic Church, and is more closely akin to its doctrine and spirit than any other Protestant denomination. The defection under Henry VIII and Queen Elizabeth was not only numerically considerable but, otherwise than in Germany or France, it involved the loss to the Church of a whole nation, and not only of one nation, but of many peoples who were later on to belong to the British Commonwealth. Our only canonized English saints in modern times, John Fisher and Thomas More, and scores of beatified, were the victims of a persecution sanctioned by the Church of England. The same persecution, under God, contributed to solidifying the faith of the Irish people and to give the United States and other countries a large Catholic immigration and Catholic leadership whose benefits are past counting. From the ranks of the Anglican communion has come a stream of converts, including some of the Church's outstanding priests and lay apostles. From the Episcopalian point of view, even though firmly attached to the doctrine, sacraments, and canonical position of their own church, many of them "hope ardently for ultimate reunion with Rome." In their opinion, "the Roman problem is the key problem of Christian unity, not only because the Roman is the most numerous Christian communion but because the papacy has within itself the potentiality of becoming many of the things which Roman Catholics now claim that it is." [1]

HISTORY

The historical origins of Episcopalianism cover a period of thirty-six years, from 1527 when Henry VIII first proposed a divorce from his wife, Catherine of Aragon, to 1563, when his daughter, Queen Elizabeth, by an act of Parliament promulgated the Thirty-nine Articles of the Anglican Church. Between these two dates, in rapid succession, the religious character of the English nation was radically changed. After seven years of vain effort to obtain papal sanction for his divorce, Henry made himself supreme head of the Church of England, Parliament declaring that, "the Roman Pontiff has no greater jurisdiction bestowed on him by God in the Holy Scriptures in this realm of England than any other foreign bishop." [2] During the minority of his son, Edward VI, the Book of Common Prayer was published in two editions (1549 and 1552), first along Lutheran and then Calvinist lines; a new Ordinal was issued (1550-1552), following a Lutheran pattern, in which every mention of a priesthood offering sacrifice was carefully omitted from the ordination ritual; and the first draft of forty-two Articles of Faith was authorized in 1553. However the complete rupture with Catholicism on a national scale did not come until 1563, when the Elizabethan Parliament made the Thirty-nine Articles of Religion obligatory on all citizens under heavy penalties.

Episcopalianism was brought to the American colonies by a group of English settlers who landed at Chesapeake Bay on May 6, 1607, and a week later founded what is now Jamestown, Virginia. For more than a hundred years, "The story of the Church of England in the thirteen colonies . . . is the story of what happens to an episcopal Church when it tries to live and thrive without a bishop." [3] England feared that allowing an indigenous colonial episcopate would produce an independent denomination in America. But in spite of these precautions, secession came as a result of the American Revolution. First a distinctive name was adopted. In 1783 the American Anglicans became known officially as the Protestant Episcopal Church: Protestant to distinguish them from Catholics, and Episcopal to mark them off from the Presbyterians and Congregationalists. In the same year ten representatives of the Church of Connecticut elected and sent Samuel Seabury to Scotland to be consecrated bishop by the Non-Jurors; in 1786 William White of Pennsylvania and Samuel Provost were sent to England for episcopal consecration. Finally in 1789 the church was united as a national body at the first General Convention in Philadelphia. Among the resolutions adopted and still in force, it was decided that the Protestant Episcopal Church should be independent of all foreign authority, civil and ecclesiastical, and have full power to regulate its own affairs; its liturgy should conform to that of the Church of England; its ministry should consist of three orders, bishops, presbyter, and deacon; the canons of church doctrine and policy should be made by representatives of both clergy and laity; no powers should be delegated, as in England, to a general ecclesiastical government, except such as could not be conveniently exercised by individual state conventions; there should be bishops in each state, and they should have seats in the General Convention.

This first Convention also revised the English Book of Common Prayer. Though some writers call the revision slight, the nature of the changes was significant. Sixty-nine feast days were dropped from the church calendar, mostly of "persons subsequent to New Testament times or events not based on New Testament evidence"; the "Ornaments Rubric" requiring vestments was omitted; the Athanasian Creed was removed; in the Catechism, the sentence, "the Body and Blood of Christ . . . are verily and indeed taken and received by the faithful in the Lord's Supper," was changed to read, ". . . spiritually taken and received." [4]

For the first generation of the nineteenth century, the Protestant Episcopal Church was notoriously lax in its home missionary efforts, and as a consequence lost most of its communicants who migrated west of the Alleghenies. State dioceses felt this was the responsibility of the National Convention; the latter insisted it was the duty of the states. In 1829 the bishops decided that their mission society was the Church itself and not just a few zealous individuals. A missionary episcopate was therefore established, and, by tacit agreement, the Evangelical segment of the Church concentrated on foreign missions, while the High Church party emphasized the domestic field. The earliest surviving mission outside the country was in Liberia.

American Episcopalianism was deeply affected by the English Oxford Movement, led by Keble, Newman, and Froude. Although the full effect was slower coming in the States, the impact was felt already in the mid-nineteen hundreds, especially among the younger clergy, who began to wince at the appellation "Protestant." They were "inclined to be apologetic about the deplorable conditions of a Church which had so nearly forgotten its Catholic heritage. For them the Reformation was a de-formation, and the ancient Church of Rome, instead of being a target for their abuse, began to exert upon them an uneasy fascination." [5] Between 1825 and 1855, thirty American Episcopalian clergymen went over to Rome; and in the decade 1830-1840, out of fourteen bishops elected, eleven were High Church advocates. This provoked a reaction, and in

1847 the Society for the Promotion of Evangelical Knowledge (S.P.E.K.) was established to combat Tractarianism. Though unhampered by schisms as other denominations, even during the Civil War, the growth of the Protestant Episcopal Church in the nineteenth century was comparatively slow, as indicated in the following table:

Year	Members	Clergy	Ratio to National Population
1800	12,000	250	1 to 441
1830	31,000	760	1 to 417
1866	160,000	2,450	1 to 209
1901	751,000	5,067	1 to 102

During the same century, the Catholic population in the country grew from 50,000 to 12,041,000 in membership; from 50 to 11,987 in the number of priests; and in population ratio from 1:1061 to 1:6.3.

Among the major changes which the Protestant Episcopal Church has undergone in the past fifty years, the most significant is in the reshaping of its liturgy. The American Book of Common Prayer was first revised in 1892 under the aegis of William Huntington, who began at Harvard as a Liberal and "as time went on became more Orthodox, more Catholic,"—in fact, too Catholic for the General Convention which adopted only a fraction of his suggested modifications. Meantime an "unofficial revision" of the liturgy went on apace. In 1891 the standard directory of ceremonial recommended interpolations from the Latin Mass, e.g., Offertory prayers and the Last Gospel. Later on *The People's Missal* boldly advocated the admission of the entire Latin Canon, and introduced a whole sequence of Introits, Secrets, Offertory prayers and Communion verses. Still later came the *English Missal* which was "nothing but a bald translation of the Roman Missal, with side glances toward the Book of Common Prayer." [6] Ceremonial books simply reflected the changed liturgical

practices. "Colored stoles, vested choirs, processional
crosses, fixed altars, choral services—all of which had at one
time been the stigmata of a very 'advanced' parish—were
by 1900 commonplaces; indeed, an Episcolapian church
which lacked them was scarcely orthodox. Eucharistic vestments, which had caused such a furor in the eighteen-
sixties, were now nothing out of the way." [7] In the experience of one clergyman, in 1892 the altar of his church was
a plain wooden structure without any ornaments, in 1903
this was replaced by a marble altar furnished with a cross,
in 1908 a vested choir and processional cross were introduced, in 1913 candles and an early communion celebration every Sunday, in 1933 Eucharistic vestments, and in
1938 the reservation of the Sacrament.[8]

The Book of Common Prayer was revised again in
1928, this time from cover to cover, so that only the title
page remained the same, and even here Bishop Guerry of
South Carolina moved to strike out the word "Protestant,"
but his motion was killed in committee. An effort to drop
the Thirty-nine Articles failed by a narrow margin, "but
they were relegated to a harmless position as a sort of appendix." [9] Most of the changes took the form of a revision
of the ultra-Protestant Prayer Book of 1552, and a return
to that of 1549. In the offertory, "the revision by-passed
Cranmer, with his pathological fear of giving any countenance to the doctrine of sacrifice in the Eucharist." [10] New
Collects, Epistles, and Gospels were added to the Eucharistic ceremony. In response to the demand for adding post-
Scriptural saints to the liturgy, a new proper was included,
corresponding to the *Proprium Sanctorum* of the Roman
Missal. The Requiem Mass for the Dead, which High
Churchmen had denounced in the 1870's, was now made
legal. Reacting against the Protestant tradition, prayers
for the dead were formally sanctioned. "After 1928, the
Church at every Eucharist was remembering all the faith-

ful departed, and beseeching God to grant them continual
growth in His love and service . . . This was change of
doctrine with a vengeance." [11] In the same way, the sacrament of extreme unction was restored, at least partially,
"as a sacrament of healing." Impetus to this innovation
came from Boston, the center of Christian Science, where
an Episcopalian rector who was also a professional psychol-
ogist "began in 1906 to make his church a center of faith
healing." [12]

DOCTRINE AND WORSHIP

While the Thirty-nine Articles are still included in the
American Book of Common Prayer, they are not considered representative of the doctrinal and ritual position
of the Protestant Episcopal Church. For years it was felt
that American Episcopalians needed a quasi-official exposition of their beliefs and practices, at once faithful to
their Anglican tradition and yet embodying the distinctive
characteristics of the Church in this country. A series of
books was therefore "written to provide adults with the
basic content teaching of the Episcopal Church." The
present analysis is based largely on these volumes, produced under the auspices of the Department of Christian
Education of the National Council, with parallel sources
used when necessary.

The Church. By definition, "Episcopalians belong to a
Church that is a member of the family known as the Anglican Churches." However, the term Anglican "does not
imply adherence to the teachings of a religious leader as
does 'Lutheran' or 'Calvinist.' " It means "that Christian
tradition which became the ethos of the Church of England and spread thence to become the distinguishing mark
of a vast world-wide Communion of Churches." [13] If we
ask what is the most striking characteristic of the Anglican
tradition, we are told it is the "combination in a single

church life of Christian elements sometimes sharply divided by the words 'Catholic' and 'Protestant.' " Or, as
affirmed by the Anglican Congress of 1954, the Anglican
Communion is "a fellowship of Churches at one and the
same time Catholic in seeking to do justice to the whole-
ness of Christian truth, in emphasizing continuity through
the Episcopate and in retaining the historic Creeds and
Sacraments of undivided Christendom; and Evangelical in
its commission to proclaim the Gospel and in its emphasis
on personal faith in Jesus Christ as Saviour." [14]

The tension between these contraries has produced
three types of Episcopalian parishes, sometimes mistaken
as separate denominations—the high, low, and broad. In
general, a high parish "emphasizes sacramental worship,
the supreme value of the 'Catholic tradition' and a rather
elaborate service of worship." At the other extreme, the
low parish minimizes the liturgy; its "services are simple
and a stronger emphasis is placed on the gospel and on
personal religion." Between the two is the broad parish,
"which may be either High or Low, (where) the importance of a rational understanding of the Christian tradition is stressed, with a concern for 'liberal' values." [15] Summarily, therefore, the High Church stresses what may be
called the Catholic viewpoint, the Low Church is Protestant and Evangelical, and the Broad Church is more
Liberal, Modernist, and Latitudinarian. Much of the conflict in present-day Episcopalianism, notably among the
clergy, arises from the attempted assimilation of these
disparate elements in a single body.

In spite of these tensions, there is a common core of
beliefs and attitudes which Episcopalians regard as their
special heritage. Their faith and worship are epitomized
in the Lambeth Quadrilateral, which the Americans accepted in 1892: sufficiency of Scripture, the Apostles' and
Nicene Creed, baptism and the Lord's Supper, and the

historic episcopate. More realistically, however, and admitted by their writers, what has kept the Anglicans together is a triple visible bond of unity: "They all use the Book of Common Prayer; they are all in communion with the Archbishop of Canterbury; they all recognize bishops as their chief pastors." [16]

Sacraments. Technically only two sacraments are accepted as "ordained of Christ Our Lord," baptism and the Lord's Supper. While baptism is universally regarded as the sacrament of initiation into the Church, the degree of membership through baptism is still a matter of dispute. In his opening address to the General Convention in 1955, the presiding bishop urged the necessity of "a different . . . approach to the whole problem of Church membership." [17] As presently worded, the canons require after baptism one year of church attendance—hence rational maturity—for full membership in the Episcopalian communion. One of the main issues, still unsolved, is "whether a newly baptized baby would have to wait till he had attended church for a year before he could be counted as a member in good standing," i.e., a full-fledged member of the Protestant Episcopal Church.[18]

The Episcopalian concept of the Lord's Supper ranges from very "Catholic" to the opposite extreme, depending on two factors: the notion of the presence in the Eucharist, and the attitude towards the Eucharistic service. As regards the real presence, "The manner in which Christ is present and communicates Himself to His people in the Holy Communion has never been precisely defined by the Anglican Churches, although the certainty and reality of His presence have been strongly affirmed." [19] So too the Communion service. Since the Prayer Book revision of 1928, countenance has been given to a sacrificial idea of the Lord's Supper, comparable to the Mass in the Roman Rite. However this must be sharply qualified by the still officially uncertain meaning of the Eucharist itself. In High Church circles, of course, there is no doubt about the Eucharist as a sacrifice, or about the sacrament as containing the Body and Blood of Christ.

Among other benefits in America, the Oxford Movement has made the Episcopal Church willing to admit, in effect, the sacramental character of the five rites which the Thirty-nine Articles proscribe as "not to be counted for Sacraments."[20] Thus confirmation is elevated to sacramental dignity, as a divinely ordained complement to baptism. Performed by the bishop, "with the outward and visible sign of the Laying on of Hands," it "calls down upon the candidates the Holy Spirit of God to strengthen them in their Christian profession."[21]

The same with penance. "Many Christians . . . have found it helpful to make a private and specific acknowledgement of their sins to God through sacramental confession in the presence of a priest of the Church. When they do this, they can receive from him both absolution from sin and assurance that they are restored by God to living membership in Christ's Body."[22] Church publications regularly list the times of confession in various churches. In many places confessions are heard at stated hours, e.g. Saturday from 12 to 1, 4 to 5, "and by appointment."

In matrimony, the ministers are said to be "the couple who are undertaking the marriage; by their promises they marry themselves . . . For Christians who are members of the Church of Christ, marriage is not merely a means of legalizing sexual relations; it is sacramental in nature, permanent in character, and must reflect the spiritual marriage and unity that exists between the Lord and His Church."[23] Consistent with the concept of marriage as a permanent contract, the canons of the Protestant Episcopal Church do not authorize the Church itself to grant divorce, in the technical sense. But they do provide ample grounds for annulment. Moreover bishops may permit divorced persons to remarry, on certain conditions, and re-admit them to Holy Communion, if they show themselves to be in good faith and trying to live a good Christian life.

Without clarifying the fundamental ambiguity on the Eucharist as a sacrifice, and therefore of the ministry as a priesthood, the Episcopal Church nevertheless declares that "the act of ordination (of the clergy) has a sacramental character." By the imposition of hands, "God the Holy Ghost sets apart and authenticates these persons as minis-ters of Christ in His Church." [24] In the rite of ordination to the priesthood, the bishop and clergy present lay their hands "severally upon the head of every one that receiveth the Order of Priesthood." Then the bishop says: "Receive the Holy Ghost for the Office and Work of a Priest in the Church of God, now committed unto thee by the Imposi-tion of our hands. Whose sins thou dost forgive, they are forgiven; and whose sins thou dost retain, they are re-tained. And be thou a faithful Dispenser of the Word of God, and of his holy Sacraments; in the name of the Father, and of the Son, and of the Holy Ghost. Amen." [25] The word "priest" was inserted into the prayer of ordina-tion in 1661, attempting to correct the century-long defect in form which was one reason why Leo XIII, in 1896, de-clared Anglican Orders invalid. When the change was made in the seventeenth century, "a number of ministers, amounting it is said to two thousand, resigned their bene-fices," in protest against this and similar "Catholic" resto-rations.[26]

Extreme unction is proved to be scriptural by an ap-peal to the familiar text in St. James. Moreover, "the sacramental nature of this action is shown in the direction that the minister may use a prayer in which he says: 'I anoint thee with oil (or I lay my hand upon thee) . . . be-

seeching the mercy of Our Lord Jesus Christ, that . . .
the blessing of health may be restored unto thee.' Coupled
with this prayer is another, in which God is asked . . .
'to release thy servant from sin.' Here an outward and visible means is being employed so that an inward and spiritual gift may be received." [27]

De Novissimis. The Episcopalian position on hell is
obscure. To the question of whether death in sin is punished by an irrevocable separation from God, the answer,
in theory, or "in principle (is), yes . . . To deny hell in
principle would be to deny man's freedom; to confine it
to anything short of eternity would be to limit that freedom." But in practice, "when we come to think of how
things will in fact work out, we must take into account our
experience with God in this life . . . In that experience
God never gives up His dealing with an individual soul."
Of course, "whether His persistence and His loving in-
genuity . . . will be enough to move all men eventually
to turn to God, we do not know. We can hope and pray
that the time will come, perhaps deep into eternity, when
there will be no rebel areas, no pockets of resistance." [28]
Thus the matter is left, admitting eternal punishment
theoretically from the nature of man's freedom, while
postulating universal salvation, not from reason or revelation but from our "experience" of God's mercy.

More clear-cut and a departure from the Protestantism
in the Thirty-nine Articles is the teaching on purgatory.
"The Romish Doctrine concerning Purgatory," says Article 22, "is a fond thing, vainly invented, and grounded
upon no warranty of Scripture, but rather repugnant to
the Word of God." [29] Yet now the Church allows belief in
"purgatory (for) those whose enjoyment of God is not
lessened by any defect in themselves, but it is not the full
consummation in which the whole creation participates." [30]

This attitude is fully sanctioned by the Prayers for the Dead in the revised (1928) American Book of Common Prayer, e.g., "O God, whose mercies cannot be numbered; Accept our prayers on behalf of the soul of thy servant, and grant him (her) an entrance into the land of light and joy, in the fellowship of thy saints." [31]

Doctrinal Liberalism. American Episcopalianism seems not to have been plagued with such eminent liberals in its ranks as the late Anglican Bishop of Birmingham, Ernest Barnes, who taught that "miracles do not happen," [32] and that St. John the Evangelist "thinks of the son of God in terms of a solar deity such as Mithra." [33] However, the liberal party in the Protestant Episcopal Church is neither small nor uninfluential. A popular manual on *The Episcopal Church,* currently in use, describes the Bible as "the literature of a great race, the literature of a great movement toward realizing the relation of God to man . . . But the Church does not ask you to make a formal statement of belief in the Bible." The writer admits that "every minister of the Church makes solemn affirmation at his ordination that he believes 'the Holy Scriptures of the Old and New Testaments contain all things necessary to Salvation.' But the Church imposes no such obligation upon its members." [34] In 1934, a group of "American priests" of the Episcopalian Church published a volume of essays called *Liberal Catholicism and the Modern World,* in which they defended the title "Liberal" as a good term. "It connotes freedom, adventure, independence, and that dignified quality of the human spirit by which it affirms its hostility to all enslavements." [35] A contributing factor in this de-Catholicization has been the practice of future Episcopalian scholars making their graduate studies at Union Theological Seminary. "There they came under the influence of Reinhold Niebuhr, Paul Tillich, and Richard

Kroner, who were bringing to bear on the general American theological scene the latest ideas of Protestant theology from the continent of Europe." [36]

GOVERNMENT, LAWS, AND ORGANIZATION

The organizational structure of the Protestant Episcopal Church is strictly hierarchical, but unlike the government of the Catholic Church the Episcopalian hierarchy does not begin on an international level; it starts more locally with a separate denomination in each country. Also unlike the Catholic Church it includes a large measure of lay participation and aims to maintain a balance of power between the executive and legislative branches.

Anglican Communion. At the highest theoretical level, Anglican Churches in various countries regard themselves as members of a world association which they describe as the Anglican Communion. There is no juridical bond, however, uniting these national churches, i.e., "there is no joint central executive or legislative body in the Anglican Communion. No archbishop or bishop is supreme, and no national Church has authority or jurisdiction over any other. A special position of honor is accorded to the Archbishop of Canterbury as head of the primatial See of the mother Church of England, and the test of membership in the Anglican Communion has traditionally been whether or not a diocese is in communion with the See of Canterbury. It is this background that gives this Church on the world scene the name Anglican, though the actual titles of the different Churches vary a great deal." [37] At the 1954 World Anglican Congress, which met in Milwaukee, the name of Geoffrey Fisher, Archbishop of Canterbury, Primate of All England and Metropolitan, headed the list of attending dignitaries, and his speech was the concluding address of the Assembly.

Protestant Episcopal Church. The largest juridical

unit, therefore, is always the national church, e.g., in England, the Church of England, in Scotland, the Scottish Episcopal Church, and in the States, the Protestant Episcopal Church. The latter comprises not only the churches in Continental United States, but also three other divisions, missionary in character, operating in eleven countries, including Hawaii, Alaska, Liberia, Mexico, and Brazil.

As a national church, the denomination is governed by two executive-legislative bodies, one permanent, called the National Council, and another which meets every three years, called the General Convention. The National Council has thirty-one members, representing the denomination both nationally and as a composite of dioceses; among the members are bishops, priests, laymen and laywomen. Heading the National Council is the Presiding Bishop. According to canon law, this central executive body "shall have charge of the unification, development and prosecution of the missionary, educational, and social work of the Church." [38] The changing status of the Presiding Bishop during the past century and a half is typical of the Church's adaptability to variable circumstances. Until 1919, he was always the senior member of the hierarchy, but this proved highly inefficient because of the man's age and often his ineptitude for the office; then a diocesan bishop was elected, who retained all the duties of his own see while managing the National Council—but this too was unworkable; finally in 1934 the Constitution was changed, providing for the election of a Presiding Bishop, to hold office until his sixty-eighth year, who is automatically relieved of diocesan responsibilities when he assumes the presidency.

Triennially the General Convention meets, usually in September, as the legislative arm of the Protestant Episcopal Church. Like the American Congress, the General Convention is bicameral, made up of a House of Bishops, composed of all the bishops of the Church, both active and retired, and a House of Deputies, consisting of eight delegates—equally clerical and lay—from each diocese. Meetings of the two Houses are held separately; and all acts of the Convention must pass both Houses. Perhaps the greatest difficulty in running the Convention arises from the large number of delegates, over 100 bishops and upwards of 700 deputies. Plans are being made for reducing the required number of delegates, while still preserving adequate representation.

Provinces. Immediately below the national Church are the Provinces, composed of a number of dioceses, presently eight in number for the entire Protestant Episcopal Church. Territorially the largest are the western Provinces; the smallest are in the east, where the Church's concentration is greatest. Organized after the pattern of the national body, the Provinces have their own representative governing organ, called the Provincial Synod, divided into a House of Bishops and a House of Clerical and Lay Deputies. However the legislative power of the Synods is very restricted. They are "little more than official conferences by which the work of the Church in any given area may be increased in effectiveness and co-ordination." [39]

Dioceses. The fundamental ecclesiastical unit is the diocese, governed by the bishop in conjunction with the Diocesan Convention. Depending on its size, a diocese is named either after the principal city or the state. On the east coast, the State of New York has six dioceses; in the mid-west, Iowa and Minnesota are separate diocesan territories. Although supreme in his diocese in many ways, the bishop is helped—and controlled—in the administration by a Diocesan Convention, sometimes called the Council, Synod or Convocation, which consists of all the clergy and a number of lay representatives from each parish and mission. On certain major issues, the Convention must divide and vote as two Houses, clerical and lay, as on the national and provincial level. One of its chief functions is to adopt an annual budget, besides promoting the mission work of the diocese and its cooperation with the national Church. It also has the right to elect a bishop in case of vacancy, choose delegates to the General Convention and Provincial Synods, give financial aid to churches and missions, amend the diocesan Constitution, pass or repeal local canons, and receive the annual report of the bishop and intra-diocesan organizations.

A large part of the national Church, especially in the west, is still too sparsely populated to be divided into dioceses. Missionary districts are temporarily set up, along state territorial lines, e.g., Nevada, Utah, and Arizona, which function analogously to a fully erected diocese, but with missionary bishops, and less rigidly, according to the amount and complexity of the work in the district.

Local Parish. At the lowest grade in the Church are the local parishes, which are not geographically distinct but draw their membership from all those who regularly attend the parish church (or mission) and contribute to its support. As a legal corporation, often called, "The Rector, Wardens and Vestrymen of ————— Church," the parish is canonically united to the diocese and headed by the rector who must be an ordained priest. Temporal administration is in the hands of vestrymen, men or women, from whose number are chosen wardens, who are vice-presidents of the vestry and *ex officio* delegates to the Diocesan Convention. Where a parish is still missionary, the bishop appoints the minister; but independent parishes have the right to call their own rector. According to canon law, a vestry may not elect a new rector until the bishop has been notified of the proposed candidate in sufficient time to discuss the matter with the vestry. Normally the bishop recommends certain candidates, on whom the ves-

try then votes and resubmits the name chosen for episcopal approval. Once appointed, a rector cannot resign
without the consent of the vestry, "nor may he be removed
except the bishop give his godly judgment thereto after a
long canonical process." [40] A regular feature in the classified section of Episcopalian church magazines is the request for a priest to take charge of some parish or mission
and giving the advantages of the position offered, or a
priest advertizing his services for parochial work and describing his special qualifications.

RELIGIOUS ORDERS

After three centuries of suppression in the Established
Church, religious life was finally restored, "against tremendous obstacles, active opposition, not infrequently
breaking out in persecution (and) general apathy." [41] In
1930, the Lambeth Conference expressed its appreciation
of the work of those "who have given their lives in complete sacrifice as a supreme act of worship of God and for
His immediate service." [42] Episcopalian canon law governing the ministry now recognizes the vocation of men and
women who dedicate themselves by vow to the religious
life, and provides for the regulation of their communities.
Since 1842, when the Nashotah Community was first organized in Wisconsin, fifty-three different religious congregations have been established in the United States,
twenty of men and thirty-three of women. Twenty-three
of these (17 of women and 6 of men) have since become
extinct, and four (3 of men and 1 of women) have been received into the Catholic Church, among them the well-
known Society of the Atonement (men and women) at
Garrison, N. Y., which became Catholic in 1899. At present (1956), there are twenty-six religious orders or congregations (11 of men and 15 of women) in the United States
belonging to the Protestant Episcopal Church.[43]

Perhaps the best known among the communities for men is the Society of St. John the Evangelist or, more popularly, the Cowley Fathers, founded in 1865 at Cowley-St. John, a suburb of Oxford, England. Associated with the founder, the Rev. Richard Benson, were an Englishman, Simeon O'Neill, and an American, Charles Grafton, later Bishop of Fond du Lac, Wisconsin. After living together for a year to test their vocation, these three men, in one another's presence, pronounced the vows of poverty, chastity, and obedience, on the Feast of St. John the Evangelist, 1866. This was the first successful effort in the Church of England to re-establish religious life for men. The rule of the society is described as modern, but based on a careful study of the rules of ancient and modern orders, with special affinity to those of the Society of Jesus and the Congregation of the Mission (Lazarists). There is a novitiate of at least two years, and no life profession under the age of thirty. Personal sanctification is fostered by sacramental confession, daily recitation of the Divine Office in choir, and daily meditation, an hour for priests and a half hour for lay brothers. Work in the apostolate includes parish ministry, retreats, missions, directing hostels, hearing confessions, spiritual direction of religious women, and the foreign missions. Cowley Fathers have been in the States since 1870; in 1914 they organized a separate American Province, and since 1921 are an autonomous congregation.

The Order of St. Augustine is a purely contemplative society of ordained clerics and lay brothers, who follow the "Holy Rule written in A.D. 423." Their daily order is divided between prayer, study, and manual labor. Community Mass and the eight breviary Offices are the center of devotional life. Referred to as "monks," all the members assist with the manual labor, in the monastery and on the farm, besides taking care of a guest house for retreatants.

After six months of postulancy and two years of novitiate, perpetual vows may be taken. Their one foundation in this country is at Orange City, Florida.

Among women religious, the Community of St. Mary was the first Anglican sisterhood established in America. Founded in 1865 by Harriet Starr Cannon with only five sisters, the Society now has two American Provinces and a mission school in the Philippines. The Constitutions are based on the Rule of St. Benedict, with the twofold object of "advancing the glory of God and performing the spiritual and corporal works of mercy." Mass is offered each morning, and the Divine Office, "to which nothing is preferred," is recited daily from the *Monastic Diurnal,* an English translation of the Benedictine Office. Six months of postulancy and two years of novitiate are followed by perpetual vows. Heading the Community is the Mother Superior General, residing in New York City, who has the power of visitation and presides at meetings of the General Chapter, which is the basic source of authority in the organization. In 1935 the Community bought Racine College, Wisconsin, and renamed it the De Koven Foundation for Church Work. As a center for retreats and conferences, it has become a "stronghold of the Catholic movement in the Episcopal Church." [44]

Comparable to the Augustinian monks, the Poor Clares of Reparation and Adoration are a contemplative order, dedicated to prayer and penance, under the spiritual direction of the Order of St. Francis. Founded in 1922, they represent the Second Order of the American Congregation of the Franciscans, and follow "the primitive Rule of St. Clare," adapted to modern conditions. In the spirit of Franciscan poverty, they have no fixed source of revenue but are supported entirely by alms. Several hours a day are spent in the chapel, assisting at daily Mass, reciting the Divine Office, making meditation, "offering the community intercessions," and watching before the sacrament reserved and exposed on the altar. Regarded as austere, the Rule of St. Clare is not considered "beyond the strength of normal human beings." Among the requirements for admission are: age limit between 18 and 40, freedom from obligation of debt or marriage, good health of mind and body, emotional stability, and a love of prayer sufficient to enable the candidate to live a cloistered life. A six months' postulancy is followed by at least a year's novitiate, three years under annual vows, and then perpetual profession. One of their forms of apostolate is the Fellowship of Prayer, by which they pledge themselves to pray daily, by name, for all who are duly enrolled. The Motherhouse is at Mt. Sinai, Long Island.

In recent years, the Episcopal Church has been actively promoting vocations to the religious life. "Many Churchpeople," it is said, "are asking why monks and nuns do not take over or open parochial schools—why they do not administer more homes for the aged and more hospitals. The answer is simple: there are not enough monks and nuns. Already many religious communities find themselves 'spread too thin,' their members over-worked, and the duties they have already undertaken suffering from lack of thoroughness. What is the answer to this problem? The solution is to be found in more vocations to the religious life." Contrary to the prevalent notion that only pious people are called to the religious life, the fact is that "those in the cloister are striving toward sanctity, but are a long way from the goal; for the monk or nun is after all just a sinner trying to live close to God in a very special way. The religious life is a school for sanctity, not a museum of saints." [45]

APPROACHES TO CHURCH UNITY

Church unity efforts in the Protestant Episcopal Church on a major scale began in 1867, when nineteen American bishops joined in the first Lambeth (London)

Conference to strengthen the solidarity of Anglican bodies throughout the world. Twenty years later in 1888, the American delegation successfully promoted the adoption of what has since become the doctrinal cohesive of world Anglicanism. Originally conceived by William Huntington, of Worcester, Massachusetts, the Lambeth Quadrilateral reduced to four statements the basic principles to which the Anglican Church subscribes, namely:

I. The Holy Scriptures of the Old and New Testaments, as "containing all things necessary to salvation," and as being the rule and ultimate standard of faith.

II. The Apostles' Creed, as the Baptismal Symbol; and the Nicene Creed, as the sufficient statement of the Christian faith.

III. The two sacraments, Baptism and the Supper of the Lord, ministered with unfailing use of Christ's words of institution, and of the elements ordained by Him.

IV. The Historic Episcopate, locally adapted in the methods of its administration to the varying needs of the nations and peoples called of God into the unity of His Church.

Since 1888, the Lambeth Quadrilateral has been reinterpreted, but never revised. "It still expresses the official position of the Church in relation to projects for union with Protestant bodies." [47]

Before the end of the century, invitations for union on the basis of the Quadrilateral were sent to eighteen Protestant denominations. But only one, with the Presbyterians, reached anything like a negotiable stage, though even this was finally called off by the Episcopalians. Union efforts broke down over the crucial question of orders. Advocates of the Episcopalian-Presbyterian merger suggested holding formal services of "extension of authority to minister in the united Church," at which time the clergy of each denomination were to be told: "The Ministry of the Word and Sacraments which thou hast already received is hereby recognized; and the grace and authority of Holy Orders as conferred by this Church is now added." [48] In 1946 the "Catholic" minority in the Protestant Episcopal Church successfully vetoed the Proposed Basis of Union, mainly on the grounds that the recommended formula for extension of orders was in no sense a supplementary ordination, and that, consequently, if adopted, "the united Church would have no priesthood in the Catholic and Prayer Book sense of the term." [49]

Equally unsuccessful were attempts at union with the Eastern Orthodox churches. "The chief obstacle on the other side was that the Orthodox Church was not prepared to affirm the validity of Anglican orders. The chief obstacle on this side was the watchful suspicion of the Evangelicals, who regarded these Eastern Churches as little better than the Church of Rome." [50]

However, a close degree of union was established with the Polish National Church, founded in 1900 and directed for fifty years by Francis Hodur, schismatic Catholic priest who was consecrated bishop at Utrecht by the Old Catholic Church. In October, 1946, the House of Bishops of the Episcopal Church accepted the overtures of the Polish Nationals and received them into full intercommunion on the basis of the so-called Bonn agreement, which stated: [51]

I. Each Communion agrees to admit members of the other Communion to participation in the Sacraments.

II. Each Communion recognizes the catholicity and independence of the other, and maintains its own.

III. Intercommunion does not require from either Communion the acceptance of all doctrinal opinion, sacramental devotion, or liturgical practice character-

istic of the other, but implies that each believes the
other to hold the essentials of the Christian Faith.

On a global scale, the World Council of Churches directly owes its existence to the reunion efforts of the
American Episcopalians. In 1910 Bishop Brent, Philippine
missionary and later Bishop of New York, asked the House
of Bishops of the Protestant Episcopal Church to appoint
a committee inviting "all Churches which accept Jesus
Christ as God and Saviour to join in conferences following the general method of the World's Missionary Conference, for the consideration of all questions pertaining to
the Faith and Order of the Church of Christ." [52] Out of
this grew the World Conference on Faith and Order, which
in 1938 developed into the World Council of Churches.

Paradoxically, though, it was not till 1940 that the
Episcopal Church joined the Federal Council of Churches
of Christ in America, since become the National Council
of Churches. While cooperating with the Council in many
ways, the Catholic party in the Episcopalian Church opposed formal entrance into the Federation on doctrinal
grounds. When the opposition was finally overcome and
the Episcopalians became constituent members, "the
Council signalized its joy over this by promptly electing
(their) Bishop Tucker as its head." [53]

STATISTICS

Anglican Churches
    World Membership (1954 estimate)   40,000,000
    England and Wales (Members of Church of
        England)   2,989,702
    Canada (Members of Church of England)   2,060,720
Protestant Episcopal Church, U.S.A.
    World Membership (1956)   3,013,570
    Continental United States (1956)
        Membership (baptized persons)   2,757,944
        Parishes and Missions   7,262

Clergy	7,193
Living American Bishops (Active, Retired, Missions)	538
Dioceses and Missionary Districts	87
Lay Readers	9,060
Communicants	1,781,262
Sunday schools (1951)	5,619
Number of pupils (1956)	655,818
Day schools (elementary and high schools)	100
Church colleges and universities	6
Theological seminaries	12
Hospitals and convalescent homes	62
Church periodicals	121

REFERENCES

1. "The Problem of Rome," *The Living Church*, Aug. 30, 1953, p. 10.
2. Henry O. Wakeman, *The History of the Church of England*, London, Rivingtons, 1904, p. 222.
3. James T. Addison, *The Episcopal Church in the United States*, New York, Scribner, 1951, p. 27.
4. *Ibid.*, pp. 70-71.
5. *Ibid.*, p. 158.
6. George E. DeMille, *The Episcopal Church Since 1900*, New York, Morehouse-Gorham, 1955, p. 74.
7. *Ibid.*, p. 75.
8. *Loc. cit.*
9. *Ibid.*, p. 83.
10. *Loc. cit.*
11. *Ibid.*, p. 85.
12. *Ibid.*, p. 86.
13. Powel M. Dawley, *The Episcopal Church and Its Work*, Greenwich, Conn., Seabury Press, 1955, p. 5.
14. *Anglican Congress, 1954: Report of Proceedings*, Greenwich, Conn., Seabury Press, 1954, p. 195.
15. W. Norman Pittenger, "What Is an Episcopalian?", *A Guide to the Religions of America* (Leo Rosten, ed.), New York, Simon and Schuster, 1955, p. 54.
16. *Ibid.*, p. 48.
17. "Handle With Care," *The Living Church*, Nov. 6, 1955, p. 14.
18. *Loc. cit.*
19. James A. Pike and W. Norman Pittenger, *The Faith of the Church*, Greenwich, Conn., Seabury Press, 1951, p. 153.
20. "Articles of Religion," No. 25, *The Book of Common Prayer*, New York, Oxford Univ. Press, 1944, p. 607.
21. Pike-Pittenger, *op. cit.*, p. 156.
22. *Ibid.*, p. 158.
23. *Ibid.*, p. 159.
24. *Ibid.*, p. 160.
25. *Book of Common Prayer*, p. 546.
26. Wakeman, *op. cit.*, p. 385.
27. Pike-Pittenger, *op. cit.*, p. 161.
28. *Ibid.*, pp. 177-178. Anglican hesitancy about the eternity of hell is in contradiction to the clear testimony of Scripture. The wicked, says Christ, "will go into everlasting (aiōnios)

punishment, but the just into everlasting (aiōnios) life" (Matt. 25:46). Christian tradition from the earliest centuries confirms the teaching of Scripture. When the Origenists (fourth century) began to teach that "the punishment of devils and wicked men is temporary and will eventually cease," they were condemned as heretics.

29. "Articles of Religion," No. 22, *The Book of Common Prayer*, p. 607.

30. Pike-Pittenger, *op. cit.*, p. 173.

31. *Book of Common Prayer*, p. 334.

32. Ernest W. Barnes, *The Rise of Christianity*, London, Longmans-Green, 1948, p. 66.

33. *Ibid.*, p. 93. The extent to which liberalism has penetrated the ranks of Anglicanism is revealed in a current Anglican study of the relation of Freemasonry to Christianity. Sixteen members of the Anglican Hierarchy, including the Archbishop of Canterbury, and 525 clergymen are listed, by name, as Freemasons in Higher Degrees in 1954. "A complete list of all the (Anglican) clergy in the Craft would be many times larger." Walton Hannah, *Christian By Degrees*, London, Augustine Press, 1954, pp. 207-216.

34. George P. Atwater, *The Episcopal Church: Its Message for Men of Today*, New York, Morehouse-Gorham, 1952, p. 74.

35. F. S. B. Gavin (Ed.), *Liberal Catholicism and the Modern World*, Vol. I, Milwaukee, Morehouse, 1934, p. vii.

36. DeMille, *op. cit.*, p. 118.

37. *Anglican Congress*, pp. 1-2.

38. Powel M. Dawley, *The Episcopal Church and Its Work*, Greenwich, Conn., Seabury Press, 1955, p. 103.

39. *Ibid.*, p. 141.

40. *Ibid.*, p. 125.

41. "The Religious Life," *The Living Church*, Apr. 29, 1951, p. 14.

42. *Report of the Lambeth Conference, 1930*, London, Society for Promoting of Christian Knowledge, pp. 62, 184.

43. Peter F. Anson, *The Call of the Cloister: Religious Communities and Kindred Bodies in the Anglican Communion* London, Society for Promoting of Christian Knowledge, 1955, pp. 594-596. The revival of religious life in the Church of England (and American Episcopalianism) began "with the dawn of the Oxford Movement and the publication of the first of the *Tracts for the Times* in 1833, (when) the 'dry bones' of Anglicanism began to stir." *Ibid.*, p. xiii.

44. *Ibid.*, p. 559.

45. *Living Church*, Apr. 29, 1951, pp. 14-15.

46. Addison, *op. cit.*, pp. 274-275.

47. *Ibid.*, p. 275.

48. DeMille, *op. cit.*, p. 152.

49. *Ibid.*, p. 155.

50. Addison, *op. cit.*, p. 278.

51. Theodore Andrews, *The Polish National Catholic Church*, London, Society for Promoting of Christian Knowledge, 1953, p. 89.

52. William A. Brown, *Toward A United Church*, New York, Scribner, 1946, p. 58.

53. DeMille, *op. cit.*, p. 67.

6. Evangelical United Brethren

IN THE Church of the Evangelical United Brethren we see a confluence of practically all the major streams of classic Protestantism. Among its founders were a Dutch Calvinist, a Mennonite perfectionist, a Methodist exhorter, and a converted Lutheran. Its organizational structure is fundamentally Methodist, and the sect might have been incorporated into John Wesley's society except for the language obstacle. The Methodist Bishop, Asbury, was reluctant to allow preaching in German. Its doctrinal position is modeled on the Thirty-nine Articles of the Anglican Church.

While professedly non-liturgical, Evangelical United Brethren are becoming unusually interested in the liturgy, which points to the influence of pre-Reformation Christianity at work in the denomination. They are finding that ritual worship can be "a vital factor in the faith and life of Christian people." One recommendation is that church buildings be "remodeled for the purpose of making the sanctuary more suggestive of worship." Recently the General Council of the church ordered the publication of *Christian Worship in Symbol and Ritual,* which leaves nothing to be desired in careful direction to ministers on how to prevent the liturgy from becoming "an empty form or passing fad." They are instructed in the historical background and development of the liturgy from early Christian times, and in the meaning of liturgical symbols and practices. And though "public worship in non-liturgical Protestant churches has no fixed pattern," the clergy are even advised to follow uniform directives so that services "be performed in a manner fitting to their purpose." [1]

HISTORY

As a distinct denomination, the Evangelical United Brethren Church is only ten years old. It was born of a merger at Johnstown, Pennsylvania, in 1946, between the Church of the United Brethren in Christ and the Evangelical Church, each with a history that goes back to the early nineteenth century.

The Church of the United Brethren was founded in Frederick County, Maryland, in 1800, by two itinerant preachers, Philip Otterbein (1726-1813) and Martin Boehm (1725-1812). Otterbein was a missionary of the Reformed Church, having migrated to Pennsylvania in 1752 from the German duchy of Nassau. His religious training at home and in school was an "emphatic though moderate" Calvinism. Later he was influenced by the prevalent German pietism, in which "the core of religion was held to be life committed to God, not baptism nor assent to creed. Bible reading, confession, free prayer, hymn singing—these were the avenues to achieve an active, biblical faith." [2]

Martin Boehm was of Swiss ancestry, born in Lancaster County, Pennsylvania. At the age of 31 he was chosen by lot to be pastor of the local Mennonite Church. But his use of English instead of German and his promotion of revivals aroused opposition. The Mennonites denounced him for "associating with men that allow themselves to walk on the broad way, preaching warfare and the swearing of oaths," and finally expelled him from the denomination.[3] Meantime Boehm had met Otterbein, and together they formed a fellowship of seven evangelist preachers. By 1800 this voluntary association was formalized into a group called The United Brotherhood in Christ Jesus. Otterbein and Boehm were elected superintendents or bishops. Depending on the locality, the organization was known by different names: The Freedom People, The New Reformed, The New Mennonites. At the foundation conference in 1800, they considered themselves "unsectarian." By 1821, however, the name was permanently changed to The United Brethren in Christ. As early as 1817, a *Discipline* of doctrines, ritual, and organizational rules was published, in order to raise the United Brethren above the "free and easy fellowship of unsectarian revivalism." An elaborate Constitution was formulated in 1841, with special emphasis on prohibition of membership in secret societies and opposition to slavery.

Parallel with the steady growth of the Brethren and before their merger with the Evangelicals, there arose a domestic conflict over lay participation and secret societies, with a proposed change of the Constitution. A minority group seceded in 1889 to form the Church of the United Brethren in Christ (Old Constitution), with a current membership of 20,000, permitting the ordination of men and women and forbidding participation in war and membership in secret societies like the Freemasons.

Independently of the Brethren, the Evangelical Church was started as a revivalist movement by Jacob Albright (1759-1808), a Lutheran by baptism but a Methodist preacher by profession. Alternating between preaching and farming, Albright was finally "certified" in 1803, when "evangelical and Christian friends" from five mission centers drafted a statement declaring "Jacob Albright . . . a truly evangelical minister in every sense of the word and deed."[4] This was the only ordination Albright received. Before his premature death of overwork in the ministry, Albright had converted a Lutheran youth, George Miller (1774-1816), who in 1809 organized his master's followers into The So-Called Albright People. In 1816 they held their first General Conference as The Evangelical Association. A schism was averted in 1831 when John Hamilton was deposed for his anti-denominationalism. Finally in 1839 John Seybert was elected the first bishop of the Association, and through twenty-one years of tireless preaching and administration did more than any one else "in molding the expansion and character of the Evangelical Church" in America.

As the denomination spread, the German language was replaced by English in preaching and the religious press. Missionary work was organized in a separate society in 1839, and gradually expanded to Germany, Switzerland and Russia, Africa, China and Japan. Like the United Brethren, the Evangelicals were divided by a schism, but on a larger scale. In 1894, delegates of the opposition met in Naperville, Illinois, to organize The United Evangelical Church, thus splitting the parent denomination in a 60-40 ratio. "A chain of untoward events, a number of incompatible leaders, coupled with varying opinions regarding the character of episcopal power," formed the background of the secession. After thirty years of separation and bitter recrimination on both sides, the two segments were re-united in 1922 to form The Evangelical Church.[5]

When the United Brethren and The Evangelical Church merged in 1946, the union came as a result of more than a century of ecumenical efforts by both parties. In the early 1800's, the United Brethren were negotiating a union with the Methodists, planning the formation of a Wesleyan Methodist—United Brethren Church, which never materialized. In the mid-century, the Evangelical

Conference actually approved by a majority of one to unite with the Methodists, but failed to carry out the resolution. At the turn of the present century, a fusion of Presbyterians, Christians, Methodists, Congregationalists and United Brethren was discussed but unrealized after the Christians and Congregationalists dropped out. In 1933 the United Brethren and Evangelicals entered into active negotiations, "which resulted in the happy union of the two" on November 16, 1946. Historians of the new denomination trace its creation to almost fifty years of collaboration of Brethren and Evangelicals in the world ecumenical movement, working together as delegates to the Foreign Mission Conference at New York in 1900, at Edinburgh in 1910, at Madras in 1939. When the World Council of Churches was formed, Evangelicals and Brethren joined. Inevitably a union took place, on the assumption that "the creedal statements of these two Churches grew out of common and profound religious experience of the fathers, and were formulated in accord with their discerning interpretation of the Holy Scriptures and by careful study of other ecclesiastical confessions." Consequently, states the Plan of Union, "it is not strange that these creedal statements are found to be in agreement. In all basic and enduring verities of the Christian faith, their respective positions are in the most intimate and beautiful accord." [6] At the time of the merger, the United Brethren had a membership of approximately 450,000; the Evangelical Church, 250,000.

DOCTRINE AND WORSHIP

The "Confession of Faith" is prominently placed at the head of the *Discipline of the Evangelical United Brethren Church,* and summarized in 32 Articles, comparable to the 25 Articles of Faith of the Methodist

Church, and largely derived from Methodist and Anglican sources. But whatever merger took place in 1946, it did not produce a common statement of belief. The 32 Articles of Faith are really two sets of doctrinal statements, 13 for the Brethren and 19 for the Evangelicals, not combined but juxtaposed, and in more than one instance hard to reconcile dogmatically.

Along with an express belief in the Trinity, the Incarnation and the inspiration of Scripture, there is considerable deviation from the teaching of many Protestants, notably in the acceptance of certain doctrines that have been either glossed over or abandoned by the more liberal communions.

The Church. In keeping with the Calvinist tradition, the "holy Christian Church" is said to be "composed of true believers in which the Word of God is preached by men divinely called, and ordinances are duly administered." [7] To avoid misunderstanding of the word, "Catholic," in the Apostles' Creed, the term is explained to mean, "the holy general church," divinely instituted for the three-fold purpose of "maintenance of worship . . . the edification of believers, and the conversion of the world to Christ." [8]

Depravity and Justification. There is no compromise with Reformation theology on the state of man since the fall. "Apart from the grace of our Lord Jesus Christ," man is considered "not only entirely destitute of holiness, but is inclined to evil, and only evil, and that continually." [9] Originally the United Brethren used the expression, "depravity," with reference to man's condition, and only after years of controversy was the offensive word omitted from the examination of candidates for the ministry. But the concept remains unchanged. Reminiscent of John Wesley, the Evangelical United Brethren conceive justification of the sinner as a personal experience of the divine presence.

Accordingly, "the witness of the Spirit is an inward impression on the soul, whereby the Spirit of God, the heavenly Comforter, immediately convinces the regenerate believer that he has passed from death unto life, that his sins are all forgiven, and that he is a child of God." [10]

Sacraments. In spite of protestations to the contrary, the doctrine on the sacraments is an instance of the incompatibility that still exists between the Evangelical and United Brethren in spite of the merger. The Brethren part of the Confession of Faith admits two sacraments, baptism and the Lord's Supper, and then liberally adds that "the mode of baptism and the manner of observing the Lord's Supper are always to be left to the judgment and understanding of each individual." [11] A few pages later, the Evangelist statement leaves practically nothing to free choice. Baptism is described at length as "not merely a token of the Christian profession . . . but it is also a sign of internal ablution or the new birth." [12] Likewise the Lord's Supper is "not merely a token of love and union . . . but is rather a mystery or a representation of our redemption by the sufferings and death of Christ." [13] Without denouncing transubstantiation as does the Methodist *Discipline*, the real presence is simply denied, declaring that "the changing of the bread and wine into the body and blood of Christ cannot be supported by the Holy Writ." [14]

Baptism is administered by pouring, sprinkling, or immersion, according to the preference of a child's parents or the adult convert. The Trinitarian formula is used.

More than anywhere else, in the administration of the Lord's Supper there is evidence of a liturgical rebirth among the Evangelical United Brethren. Ten years have elapsed since the publication of the first *Discipline* (1947) of the united denomination. In the latest (1955) edition of the *Discipline* issued by order of the General Conference,

the changes in the service of Holy Communion can only
be described as radical. Self-consciously the new directive
tells the people that this Eucharistic service "is thoroughly
evangelical in theology;" but actually it is notoriously not
evangelical and betrays the rising dominance of the "High
Church" party. Ten years ago, the *Discipline* prescribed
that "unfermented wine shall be used." [15] Now there is
no prescription and "fermented wine" is freely allowed.
Formerly the clergy were told that "this order is . . . in
accordance with the usage of non-liturgical Churches." [16]
Now the "form and order for celebration of the Holy
Communion is an adaptation of the traditional order
which can be traced back to early history of the Church." [17]
In the previous directives, "The Prayer of Consecration"
avoided all mention of Christ's body and blood and referred only to "this memorial of his death" and "this bread
and wine in remembrance of his passion." [18] All this is
changed. There is now an explicit "Consecration of the
Elements," during which the minister prays, "that we . . .
may be partakers of his most blessed body and blood."
Following this, he separately takes up the bread, breaks
it, and says, "This is my body," and the chalice, saying,
"This cup is the new covenant in my blood." [19] Then to
remove any lingering doubt about the new attitude
towards the Eucharist, after the words of Institution are
pronounced, the bread and wine are said to be "Consecrated Elements," and after giving Communion to the
people, the minister is charged to "return the sacred ves-
sels to the Lord's Table and reverently cover them." [20]
The "end result" of this reformed Eucharistic rite "is to
give us the consciousness that we are part of the church
catholic in all ages and in all places." [21]

Moral Standards. Correlative to the idea of Christian
perfection, the Evangelical United Brethren Church
makes considerable demands on its members for the prac-

tice of the moral virtues. Against the human tendency to idleness and sloth, "The Church believes in the proper use of time. The waste and misuse of idle hours . . . obligate every church to provide wholesome activities . . . through worship, music, reading, study, fellowship, recreation and service" facilities. Accordingly, "the Church views with alarm the widespread circulation and reading of salacious literature . . . Strict censorship of motion pictures in order to protect society from evident evils is advocated." [22] Alcoholic beverages, gambling, narcotics and tobacco are forbidden, but in descending order of emphasis. "The manufacture, sale and use of intoxicating liquors as beverage . . . are strictly prohibited." [23] Less absolute but still forbidden is gambling, which is "a menace to society," so that "all members of the Church are expected to abstain from gambling in any form." [24] In like manner "the Church is unalterably opposed to the use of and the traffic in habit-forming drugs . . . and calls upon its members to abstain from the use of narcotics." [25] Lastly "the Church believes that the use of tobacco in any form is injurious and a needless waste of time . . . All members of the church are urged to abstain from its use." [26] Along with these restrictions is a leniency in the matter of divorce which loses none of its compromise by an appeal to the Scriptures. After stating that "the Church shall consistently regard as valid only such divorces as are granted on the ground of adultery," and ministers are told not to solemnize "marriages in cases where there is a divorced husband or wife living," a concession is granted which practically negates the prohibition, since "this does not apply to the innocent party to a divorce caused by adultery." [27]

Occasional Services. A notable feature of Evangelical United Brethren worship is the variety of services for special occasions. There is a service for the Dedication of an

Organ, for the Dedication of a Parsonage, for the Charge
of the Trustees of a Parsonage, for Commissioning of Missionaries, and even for the Burning of a Mortgage. The
ritual is quite impressive. For example, the solemn Dedication of a Home begins with the singing of an "instrumental prelude," and a declaration by the minister that,
"Before the state, the school, or the church were established, the home had come into being . . . We have come
to invoke the divine blessing upon this home." [28] After
prayer, said by the minister, and Scripture reading, the
husband, wife and family alternate in a "Responsive Service" which includes the lighting of a candle and reciting
a series of invocations:

> *Husband*—To thee, O God, who dwellest with the
> humble . . . and maintainest their lot;
> *Family*—We dedicate this home and light the can-
> dle of devotion.
> *Wife*—As a house of friendship, where others may
> come for fellowship . . . and be enabled to go forth
> strengthened, in body, mind and spirit;
> *Family*—We dedicate this home and light the can-
> dle of friendship.
> *Husband*—To beauty in art and literature, where
> pictures and books shall be friends, and music and
> song the language of comfort and inspiration;
> *Family*—We dedicate this home and light the can-
> dle of beauty.
> *Wife*—To the Great Guest, Jesus Christ, our Lord
> . . . who brought the light of heaven and the peace of
> God to people like ourselves;
> *Family*—We dedicate this home and light the can-
> dle of service and hospitality.[29]

The dedication closes with a triple blessing by the minister, asking that, "Jehovah lift up his countenance upon
thee and give thee peace. Amen." [30]

GOVERNMENT AND ORGANIZATION

The organization of the Evangelical United Brethren follows the general plan of the Methodist Church, with thirty-three Annual Conferences or jurisdictional areas which roughly correspond to the territory of one or more States. In addition there are eleven Missionary and Overseas Conferences which cover such areas as Florida, Kentucky and Puerto Rico. Subordinate to these are the Quarterly Conferences, supervised by district or conference superintendents. The major Conferences are grouped into Episcopal Areas, currently eight in number, presided over by a bishop.

Bishops are simply elders who have been chosen by the General Conference for a term of four years to supervise and administer the territory committed to their care. "They are agents of supervision, not a separate order. Their distinctiveness is administrative, not priestly, and they lack the special 'grace' which pertains to bishops in genuinely episcopal churches. Such prerogatives as they hold are entrusted to them for a specific term of office." [31] Behind this severe limitation of episcopal power lies a theory of ecclesiastical structure which the Evangelical United Brethren believe was inspired by John Calvin. They proudly regard it as "the golden mean" between congregationalism and episcopalianism, affirming that "the people through their chosen representatives should administer the Church, thus providing a church government that was democratic without being subject to chaos (as among Baptists and Congregationalists), and authoritative without the peril of tyranny (as among Episcopalians and Roman Catholics)." [32]

In contrast with the purely administrative function of bishops, Evangelical United Brethren ordain their elders in order to give them definite spiritual powers. As the bishop lays hands on the head of the candidate, he asks that, "The Lord pour upon thee the Holy Spirit for the office and work of an Elder," and bids him receive "authority to preach the Word of God, and to administer the holy sacraments in the Church." [33] Inconsistently, however, even before ordination a man may be "licensed to preach in accordance with the Order and Discipline of The Evangelical United Brethren Church," and also administer the sacraments.[34] The latter privilege is granted to "probationers" who are looking forward to eventual ordination, "by special annual grant from (their) Annual Conferences." [35] Since 1946, the question arose whether this concession of administering the sacraments without ordination refers also to ministers from other churches who are serving as licensed, though unordained, preachers in the E.U.B. The General Conference answered that while "it is not the policy of the denomination to provide such rights for unordained Ministers of other denominations serving in our pulpits, however, where the emergency exists, the Annual Conference itself must determine" and may grant the privilege.[36]

Great care is taken to provide maximum lay participation in the church government. Laymen have equal representation with the clergy in the Annual and General Conferences. To forestall clerical intrusion beyond set limits, the meaning of what constitutes a lay person is clearly defined. Not only elders, but "no Minister (who may be a layman), Minister's wife, nor anyone recommended to the Annual Conference for licence to preach, should be eligible for election as a Lay Member or Alternate for an Annual Conference." [37] In governing the church, therefore, "laymen and ministers sit side by side during the conference session, enjoying equal rights and privileges," with two exceptions: only the clergy may vote on granting a licence to preach and in advancing a lay candidate to eldership.[38]

The federated character of its organization enables the church to operate numerous boards and agencies on a national scale that would be impossible in a less closely knit society. The Board of Missions, for example, directs the church's evangelism on all levels, from the local town and county to the foreign missions in West Africa. Besides other duties, the Board of Christian Education has general supervision of the two denominational seminaries with authority to "make such recommendations as will be of assistance in increasing the effectiveness of these institutions." [39] Typical of the ecumenical changes taking place in the church is the constitution of the new United Theological Seminary, formed since 1947 by the merger of the Bonebrake and Evangelical Schools of Theology. The statutes of Bonebrake had required each professor on the day of his inauguration publicly to declare that he would not teach or insinuate anything contrary to the Constitution, the Confession of Faith and the rules of the Evangelical United Brethren Church.[40] United Theological Seminary no longer requires such a declaration.

One feature of the denomination which is rather singular among American Protestants is its attention to the status of women and an organized effort to solicit their cooperation in the church's activities. There is a Women's Society of World Service, operating on a national and local level, whose purpose is "to unite all the women of the church in Christian fellowship to make Christ known throughout the world, to deepen the spiritual life of each of its members and to develop a sense of personal responsibility for the whole task of the Church, through a program of education, service, prayer and giving for the maintenance and advancement of the missionary work of the Evangelical United Brethren Church." [41] A Girls' Missionary Guild has the same general purpose on a minor scale. Growing out of these women's societies is a denomination-wide program of Missionary Education for Children, whose aim is to develop in boys and girls "a spirit of friendship for all children, to create in them a desire to help all children to know and love Jesus Christ, to lead to a desire to share with others the good things of life which Christianity has brought to the world." [42] One result of this enlistment of women and interest in the children is an unusually high enrollment in Sunday School classes: 700,000 children for a church membership of 750,000. By comparison, the Episcopalians have only the same number of children in their Sunday Schools for a total church membership of almost three million.

STATISTICS

Total Church Membership	746,206
Churches	4,498
Ordained Clergy	3,621
Clergy Having Charges	3,071
Sunday Schools	4,391
Enrollment	687,719
Church Periodicals of National Circulation	4
Colleges and Seminaries	10
Orphanages and Homes for the Aged	9

REFERENCES

1. Paul W. Milhouse, *Christian Worship in Symbol and Ritual*, Harrisburg, Evangelical Press, 1953, p. 5.
2. Paul H. Eller, *These Evangelical United Brethren*, Dayton, Otterbein Press, 1950, p. 23.
3. *Ibid.*, p. 27.
4. *Ibid.*, p. 45. Quotation from R. Yeakel, *Geschichte der Evangelische Gemeinschaft*, vol. I, Cleveland, 1890, p. 56.
5. Eller, *op. cit.*, p. 75.
6. *The Discipline of the Evangeli-*
   cal United Brethren: 1947, Dayton, Otterbein Press, 1947, p. 14.
7. *The Discipline of the Evangelical United Brethren: 1955*, Dayton, Otterbein Press, and Harrisburg, Evangelical Press, 1955, p. 19.
8. *Loc. cit.*
9. *Loc. cit.*
10. *Ibid.*, pp. 27-28.
11. *Ibid.*, p. 19.
12. *Ibid.*, p. 25.
13. *Loc. cit.*
14. *Ibid.*, p. 26.

15. *Discipline: 1947*, p. 439.
16. *Loc. cit.*
17. *Discipline: 1955*, p. 403.
18. *Discipline: 1947*, p. 443.
19. *Discipline: 1955*, pp. 412-413.
20. *Ibid.*, pp. 404, 414.
21. *Ibid.*, p. 403.
22. *Ibid.*, pp. 364-365.
23. *Ibid.*, p. 366.
24. *Ibid.*, p. 365.
25. *Ibid.*, p. 366.
26. *Loc. cit.*
27. *Ibid.*, p. 368.
28. *Ibid.*, p. 482.
29. *Ibid.*, pp. 483-484.
30. *Ibid.*, p. 484.
31. Eller, *op. cit.*, p. 121.
32. *Ibid.*, pp. 121-122.

33. *Discipline: 1955*, p. 451.
34. *Ibid.*, p. 88.
35. *Ibid.*, p. 100.
36. *Ibid.*, p. 604.
37. *Ibid.*, p. 46.
38. Eller, *op. cit.*, p. 122.
39. *Discipline: 1955*, p. 236.
40. *Discipline: 1947*, p. 567.
41. *Discipline: 1955*, p. 210.
42. *Discipline: 1947*, p. 239. Recent legislation has created a new agency, the Boys and Girls Fellowship, "to provide a total program of Christian education and evangelism for the children of the Church . . . from birth through eleven years of age." *Discipline: 1955*, p. 259.

7. Lutherans

WHERE OTHER Protestant churches are satisfied to describe their religious similarities and differences without analysis, Lutheran writers are concerned with telling their people and others what they consider the essence of Lutheranism. A recent symposium allowed Lutheran theologians of varying degrees of orthodoxy to express their opinion on, "What is Lutheranism's *raison d'être* as a distinct communion in the twentieth century." [1] While there was no agreement on the answer, there was revealed a basic divergency of attitude. On one side are the conservatives, who distinguish Lutheranism as essentially an adherence to the principles enunciated in a half dozen "symbolic documents," beginning with the Confession of Augsburg (1530) and ending with the Formula of Concord (1577). Without this adherence, it would be quite impossible "correctly to acknowledge God and call upon Him to preserve harmony in the Church and to bridle the audacity of such as invent new doctrines." [2]

At the other extreme are unionists who are looking for a fusion of Lutheran and other denominations, and liberals who do not hesitate to dismiss the Lutheran Confessions as dated, outmoded, and no more binding than any other statement of religious sentiment. Arguing against rigid conservatists, they insist that, "Symbolism is

no part of original Lutheranism . . . The full symbolic
system contended for . . . was not adopted until 1580,
after the Lutheran Church had existed more than half a
century." [3] Moreover the Formula of Concord itself declares that the Scriptures alone are the norm by which "all
doctrines are to be examined." Since "the official declaration of historic Lutheranism plainly declares that with new
light and more adequate interpretation of the biblical
writings, changes in doctrine are not only anticipated but
necessary." There is scarcely need, say the modernists, to
point out that the Lutheran Confessions "contain many
views no longer tenable. We would, for instance, hesitate
to call the Pope the Antichrist . . . We might well question . . . the Christological doctrine on the ubiquity of
Christ's body . . . Even the position which Luther himself took on the interpretation of the Eucharist may fairly
be challenged." [4]

Between these extremes is a variety of opinion that
defies classification, while retaining enough historical continuity to permit a descriptive analysis of the melange
called American Lutheranism.

HISTORY

Lutheranism dates from October 31, 1517, when Martin Luther affixed his 95 theses to the church door of the
castle of Wittenberg. Three years later, June 15, 1520, he
was formally excommunicated by Pope Leo X, who also
condemned 41 propositions from Luther's writings, notably the denial of free will and the Roman Primacy; and
the claim that no matter how ostensibly good, every human act is a sin.

The religious chaos which Luther and his followers
provoked in Germany occasioned a series of conferences
or diets which became landmarks in the history of the
Reformation. Summoned by Charles V to the Diet of

Worms (1521), Luther refused to recant and was condemned as an outlaw, but the Elector of Saxony took him into protective custody. Eight years later, at the Diet of Speyer (1529), five Lutheran princes rejected the compromise of King Frederick that would allow their estates to practice the new religion while demanding the same rights for Catholics. Their statement of protestation has become historic since it gave the name Protestant to the whole opposition movement to the Catholic Church.[5] When the Diet of Speyer proved inoperative, the Emperor summoned the Diet of Augsburg (1530) to effect a reconciliation between the Catholics and Reformers. A profession of the Protestant faith was drafted with Luther's assistance and approval and submitted to the Diet. After the Confession of Augsburg was refuted by the Catholic delegation, Melancthon was commissioned to write an "Apology for the Confession of Augsburg." Both documents are now doctrinal standards in the Lutheran Church.

A year after Augsburg, the Lutherans organized an offensive and defensive alliance, the Schmalkaldic League, for which Luther wrote a set of Articles in 1537, thus marking "the final establishment of the Lutheran *Landeskirche* as a distinct outward body completely separated from the Roman Church." [6] Before his death in 1546, besides voluminous other writings now mostly of historical interest,[7] Luther published (1529) two catechisms, a larger and smaller, originally intended "for the improperly indoctrinated Roman clergy who had joined the evangelicals and to the teachers of the parochial schools," which have since become recognized as "probably the most useful and the most unique of his original publications." [8]

Already during Luther's lifetime, conflicts over doctrine arose among the leaders of the Reformation. With characteristic passion, Luther stigmatized his rival, Zwingli, as a pagan, Oecolampadius as having a corrupt heart

and lying mouth, and Calvin and his followers as possessed
of "in-devilled, over-devilled and through-devilled hearts."[9]
After the reformer's death, the area of conflict was widened
where different groups favored Calvinism or Zwinglianism
in opposition to the orthodox Lutheranism of their
founder. Questions of sin and grace, justification by faith,
the use of good works, the Person and work of Christ, and
especially the Lord's Supper were the ground of violent
dissension. A partial solution was effected, at least among
Lutheran churches, by the Formula of Concord, the last
of the Lutheran symbols, which was drawn up in 1577.

By the middle of the seventeenth century Lutheranism
had been propagated not only in Germany and Central
Europe but in Denmark, where the Lutheran Church was
organized (1536) with the king as supreme bishop; in
Sweden, where the Reformation was formally established
in 1529; in East Prussia in 1525; in Iceland by 1550; and
temporarily or among scattered regions in Poland (1573),
Transylvania (1545), Hungary (1606), and Silesia (1524).

Although a Lutheran Christmas service was held at
Hudson Bay as early as 1619, the first European Lutherans
to make a permanent settlement in America came from
Holland to the Dutch New Netherlands (Manhattan Island) in 1623. Under Governor Stuyvesant they had to
conform to the Reformed (Calvinist) ritual, but freedom
of worship came when New Amsterdam (New York) was
captured by the English in 1664. A second distinct body
of Lutherans came from Sweden in 1637. Two years later
they had a minister and organized the first independent
Lutheran congregation in the New World at Fort Christina (Wilmington, Delaware). After 1771, the Swedes of
Delaware and Pennsylvania dissolved their union with
the Mother Church in Sweden and, not having English-
speaking pastors of their own, chose ministers from the
Episcopalian Church. Since 1846 these congregations have

entered into full communion with the Episcopalians. The first colony of German Lutherans came from the Palatinate, arriving in 1693 and settling in Germantown, now a part of Philadelphia. Before the mid-1800's about 30,000 German Lutherans found a permanent residence in Eastern Pennsylvania, besides scattered groups along the Atlantic Coast, in New Jersey, Virginia, Georgia, and South Carolina.

The first systematic organization of Lutheran churches in the colonies was undertaken in 1742 by Henry Muhlenberg (1711-1787), a Hanoverian, who is regarded as the patriarch of American Lutheranism. The basis of unity was the synod, territorial in extension and compassing all the churches in a given area. Thus in 1748 Muhlenberg founded the Synod of Pennsylvania, and in 1773 his son, Frederick, organized the Ministerium of New York, the second synod in America. The elder Muhlenberg was a pietist, his successors were tainted rationalists—with the result that indifferentism and schism crept into the churches. In 1792 the Pennsylvania Synod eliminated all confessional tests in its constitution, and the New York Ministerium substituted more liberal books for the older Lutheran catechisms and hymnals. Transition from German to English, and sympathy in the German party for the German-speaking Reformed Churches caused divisions in many congregations. Added to these disrupting elements were the growing immigration from Europe and the westward movement, so that in 1820 a General Synod for all the Lutherans in America was formed at Hagerstown, Pennsylvania, to prevent a complete disintegration. Yet even at the beginning, some district ministeria remained aloof, and as time went on rival synods developed. In spite of opposition from confessional Lutherans, the General Synod rapidly absorbed new state organizations as they arose, until by 1860 it had 26 member synods, 864 minis-

ters and a reported 164,000 communicants. As a federation
comprising more than half the Lutherans in America, the
General Synod was directed by men who were "avowed
enemies of the Lutheran Confessions. They denounced the
Lutheran doctrines of baptism, the Lord's Supper, absolution, and the personal union of the two natures of Christ.
They loved the doctrines of the Reformed Church, cham-
pioned the revival, and advocated a union with the sects." [10]

At the time of the Civil War, when hopes ran high that
the General Synod would form a solid national body, a
schism occurred that was not healed for half a century.
The slavery question and doctrinal differences occasioned
the break. In 1863 five southern synods withdrew to form
the General Synod of the Confederate States, reorganized
in 1886 as the United Synod of the South. Three years
later, the Pennsylvania Synod, "contending for theological
conservatism," sent out invitations to all American and
Canadian synods to join in forming a new body. In answer to the invitation, thirteen synods consolidated into
the General Council. Separated for fifty years, these three
units were reunited in 1918 to form the United Lutheran
Church in America, currently the largest Lutheran body
in the States. It has 14 colleges and 9 theological seminaries, three of the largest being in Chicago, Philadelphia,
and Gettysburg, Pennsylvania. Over 600 missionaries are
maintained in the States, and about 2,200 mission congregations in Liberia, Argentina, British Guiana, India, and
Japan. There are 23 family service agencies, 41 hospitals
and adult welfare institutions, and 37 agencies and institutions for children. Catering to a wide variety of nation-
alities, the United Lutheran Church uses 16 languages in
its various rituals and publications, including Spanish,
Hungarian, and Yiddish.

Meantime the conservatives were busy organizing their
own synods, on the triple basis of doctrinal fidelity to the

Lutheran symbols, territorial limitation, and usually a common European background. In 1847 a group of Saxon immigrants, led by Carl Walther, organized the Missouri Synod. They had come to America "because of their religious convictions," to escape the Prussian government's imposition of union of the Lutheran and Reformed churches. A like group of German immigrants founded the Wisconsin Synod in 1850; "from a mild and conciliatory attitude, the Lutheranism of this synod developed into one of uncompromising fidelity to the Lutheran confessions." [11]

In 1869 the Missouri and Wisconsin Synods, while remaining autonomous, "joined fellowship" in a cooperative society, which has since aggregated three other groups (Norwegian, Slovak, and Negro) to form the Lutheran Synodical Conference of North America. Out of a total membership of 2,300,000 in the Conference, 1,900,000 belong to the Missouri division and 300,000 to the Synod of Wisconsin. Mission work is limited to the Indians and Negroes in the Wisconsin segment; but the Missouri Synod, besides maintaining over 1,000 congregations in home mission fields, has about 400 foreign mission congregations in India, Japan, New Guinea, and the Philippines. In 1955, the Synodical Conference conducted 1,427 day schools, enrolling about 140,000 pupils, 18 colleges and academies, 20 hospitals and sanatoria, 36 homes for children and the aged, and through the Missouri Synod served a total of 750 colleges and universities by its Student Service Commission. Three seminaries are operated: two Concordia Seminaries in St. Louis and Springfield, Illinois, and the Evangelical Lutheran Seminary at Thiensville, Wisconsin.

The present-day American Lutheran Church grew out of three German branches: the Ohio, Buffalo, and Iowa Synods, individually organized between 1818 and 1854, but not merged into a single body until 1930. Although the Iowa Synod originated as a secessionist party from the Missouri organization (1854), which it regarded as too congregational and doctrinally rigid, it is now cooperating with the parent organ in an attempted union of the American Lutheran Church and the Missouri Synod. The American Lutheran Church owns and operates 4 colleges and 2 seminaries (Wartburg Seminary in Dubuque, and Evangelical Lutheran Seminary of Capital University in Columbus, Ohio), besides 38 day schools. Remarkably well organized, the Church concentrates on home mission work among the Mexicans and Negroes, and foreign missions in India and New Guinea.

Swedish Lutherans formed the independent Scandinavian Augustana Synod in 1860, in company with sympathetic Danes and Norwegians, and in protest against the Illinois Synod which was accepting "new Lutherans (who) recognized no standards of doctrine and who did all in their power to tear down every barrier which might hinder the instream of free thought." [12] The word "Scandinavian" was dropped in 1894. Besides 300 home mission stations, foreign missionaries are supported in Africa and India. Contributions to the missions in 1955 totalled over 10 million dollars. Membership in 1956 was 510,000; with 850 ministers taking care of 1,200 parishes. Six colleges, a seminary (at Rock Island, Illinois), 24 hospitals and children's homes, and 18 homes for the aged are maintained by the Synod.

Like the Swedes, Norwegian Lutherans felt the need for a separate denomination, but doctrinal differences kept them apart for years. By 1887 there were six competing Norwegian synods. Finally in 1917, three of the largest united to form the Norwegian Lutheran Church, which was renamed the Evangelical Lutheran Church in 1947. Localized in the North Central States, especially in Minne-

sota, the Evangelical Lutheran Church has a current enrollment of 900,000 in 2,460 churches, served by 1,340
ministers. In 1955 there were 13 day schools operated by
the denomination, and the Sunday School enrollment was
about 300,000. It operates 33 hospitals and welfare homes,
8 colleges, and supports over 100 missionaries in South
Africa, Latin America and Madagascar. In addition to a
theological seminary in St. Paul, Minnesota, the Church
conducts a Bible Institute in Saskatchewan.

DOCTRINE

While Lutherans as a class have the reputation for
being the most orthodox among Protestant denominations,
this needs to be severely qualified. If by orthodoxy is
meant fidelity to the principles of the Reformation, then,
it is true, a sizable portion of American Lutherans is still
orthodox, and on this basis we may find a substantial
agreement among the various divisions. But there are wide
deviations, not unlike the situation among Baptists in
their adherence to Calvinism, or among the Methodists
in their fidelity to John Wesley.

Our analysis will cover two aspects: the common doctrinal elements, and the differences in matters of faith.
The creedal bases for whatever agreement there is among
American Lutherans are the Ecumenical Creeds: Apostles',
Nicene, and Athanasian; and the Lutheran Confessions
composed during the first fifty years of the Reformation
and comprehended in the Book of Concord, namely, the
Augsburg Confession and its Apology, the two catechisms
of Luther, his Smalcald Articles and the Formula of Concord. The evidence of disagreement is the various doctrinal statements made by the Lutheran churches, either
officially or as found in their representative theologians.

The Church. Claiming to base its position on the teaching of the Fathers, the Augsburg Confession defines the

Church as "the Congregation of saints, in which the Gospel is rightly taught [purely preached] and the Sacraments rightly administered [according to the Gospel]." [13] In the revised edition of 1540, the ambiguous "congregation of saints" was specified, in parentheses, as "the assembly of all believers." [14] This concept of the Church is equivocal, apparently defining it as invisible, since it is composed of all believers, and yet visible, because it exists wherever the Gospel is rightly preached and the sacraments are rightly administered. As a result, two antithetical theories have arisen among the Lutherans. Liberals admit the Church's invisible character, but emphasize that, "There could never be a Church which is merely invisible . . . Wherever the Word of God is preached and the sacraments are administered, there is the true Church of Jesus Christ." [15] Evangelicals teach the opposite, holding that, "The Church is *invisible* because the constitutive factor of the Church, faith in the heart, is invisible for men and known only to God." Consequently, "all who declare the Church to be wholly visible—Romanists—or at least semi-visible—recent Lutherans—are perverting the nature of the Christian Church." [16] It should be added that this reference to the "Romanists" is a misrepresentation of Catholic doctrine, which holds that the Church is not only visible but also, and especially, a spiritual entity—the Mystical Body of Christ—animated by the invisible Spirit of God.

Justification. Again appealing to the Fathers, the Augsburg Confession teaches that, "Men can not be justified [obtain forgiveness of sins and righteousness] before God by their own powers, merits or works; but are justified freely [of grace] for Christ's sake through faith, when they believe that they are received into favor . . . God imputes this faith for righteousness before Him (Christ)." [17] Moreover, "ours teach that . . . by faith alone is apprehended remission of sins and grace." [18] As explained by confessional Lutherans, salvific faith is a blind trust in God's mercy, to the exclusion of any good work on the part of man, so that "faith is said to be the beginning, middle and end of justification . . . Man cannot prepare himself for God's activity by a deep sorrow, an earnest longing . . . Man is justified solely by faith." [19]

It is a matter of history that Luther mutilated a famous passage in the Epistle to the Romans when translating the Bible into German, to make it square with his theory of justification. He inserted the adverb *allein* in St. Paul's statement that, "A man is justified by faith *alone* (Rom. 3:28)." When a correspondent brought his attention to Catholic criticism of the interpolation, he told him, "Your papist is tormented by this word *alone* which I have added. Tell him Dr. Martin Luther wants it so . . . I am not the papists' pupil, but their judge." [20] Modern Lutheran commentators either ignore the mutilation or defend it on the grounds that it "is demanded by the whole context of the Epistles to the Galatians and to the Romans,"—interpreted in Luther's sense.[21]

Free Will and Total Depravity. More devastating in the light of future developments was the denial of free will to do any spiritual good, expressed by the Augsburg Confession. Consequent on Adam's sin, "Man's will has no power to work the righteousness of God, or a spiritual righteousness, without the Spirit of God." [22] Man is utterly corrupt, according to Luther; and this opinion is echoed by his literalist disciples who teach that, "Original sin . . . has so totally corrupted human nature that man is incapable of any spiritual good and inclined to all evil." Whatever good he may do is attributable solely to God. The truth of this teaching, it is said, "has been, is now, and will ever be confirmed by every Christian who has made a practical experience of the Law and the Gospel." [23] Liberal-minded Lutherans properly reject this doctrine.

They feel that "Luther's insistence . . . upon man's total
depravity is hardly tenable either on Christian, moral, or
reasonably considered grounds . . . To propound the
utter worthlessness of man implies the curious paradox in
which salvation is conceived to be effected upon a worthless object . . . We must, therefore, on Christian, moral
and reasonable grounds regard such extreme doctrine as
nonessential in character." [24]

The Sacraments in General. Unexpectedly, Lutheran
symbolical books are not clear on the exact number of the
sacraments, which are defined as "rites which have the
command of God and to which the promise of grace has
been added;" [25] or as "signs of the New Testament, i.e.,
signs of the remission of sins." [26] First, in general, it is said
the number of sacraments is unimportant. According to
the Apology for the Augsburg Confession, "We do not
believe it to be of any consequence if, in teaching, different persons count (the number of sacraments) differently." [27]
However, in Luther's large catechism baptism and the
Lord's Supper are considered essential, since they were
"instituted by Christ," and therefore "without them there
cannot be a Christian." [28] Melancthon's Apology inclines
to fix the number at three, popularly so-called, saying that
"Baptism, the Lord's Supper, and Absolution, which is the
Sacrament of Repentance, are truly Sacraments." [29] In the
same way, the term "Sacrament" is conceded to "Holy Ordination," by the Apology and the Smalcald Articles.
While denying that priests in the New Law are "called to
offer any sacrifice," the Apology admits that "if Order is
understood thus, neither will we refuse to call the imposition of hands a Sacrament." [30] With reservation, even matrimony is described as sacramental in the Apology. Older
than the New Testament, marriage and its promises "per-
tain to the life of the body. Wherefore, if anyone wants to
call it a Sacrament, he ought still to differentiate it from

the preceding ones."[31] The objection to this use, that, "calling Holy Matrimony a Sacrament opens the way to calling other vocations which have God's command, e.g., the magistracy, Sacraments,"[32] indicates how vague the term "Sacrament" is in the Lutheran Confessions. Finally confirmation and extreme unction are denied any sacramental quality, being only "rites received from the Fathers which even the Church does not require as necessary to salvation because they do not have God's command."[33] Most Lutherans, however, would allow them to be called sacraments, but "only in an improper sense."[34]

Baptism. There is an inconsistency between the wording of the symbolical books and the teaching of the Lutheran Churches, even the most orthodox, on the necessity of baptism. The Augsburg Confession, for example, without qualification states that baptism "is necessary to salvation," and condemns "the Anabaptists who allow not the Baptism of children, and affirm that children are saved without Baptism."[35] But the churches found this doctrine too difficult and, in fact, went to Luther himself to mitigate the absolute necessity of the first sacrament. "It may happen," wrote Luther, "that one has faith without having been baptized . . . If a person dies a believer but lacks Baptism, he would not be condemned."[36] To speak of faith without baptism in children would be unintelligible except that Luther held the theory of "infant faith" before the age of reason. Consequently, while modern writers admit that "Baptism is not a matter of choice, but a divine ordinance," they explain that "still one may not assert an absolute necessity of Baptism."[37] The "Papist" doctrine on Limbo for unbaptized children is dismissed as an effort "to soften somewhat the cruel nature of their error," which teaches that "infants dying without Baptism are deprived of the beatific vision of God, but subject to no torment."[38]

In the administration of the sacrament, although "the Matthew 28:19 (Trinitarian) formula of Baptism is" said to be "the most fitting, the simplest and the safest," still even otherwise rigid Lutherans "acknowledge as valid a Baptism performed 'in the name of Jesus Christ,' if the baptizers are known as Trinitarians and confess their faith in the Holy Trinity." [39]

The Lord's Supper. In his small catechism, Luther asks: "You believe, then, that the true body and blood of Christ are in the Sacrament?" and answers, "Yes, I believe it." [40] Also, according to the Augsburg Confession, "The true body and blood of Christ are truly present in the Supper under the form of the bread and wine and are there distributed and received;" [41] and still more clearly in the Apology, which says that, "The body and blood of Christ are truly and substantially present in the Supper." [42]

What is the nature of the "Real Presence" in the Lord's Supper? The symbolical books define it mostly in negative terms. First against the Catholic doctrine, they reject "papistic transubstantiation, when it is taught that in the Holy Supper the bread and wine lose their substance and natural essence . . . that they are changed into the body of Christ and the outward form alone remains." [43] Then against the Calvinist position, "We unanimously reject and condemn . . . the doctrine that the bread and wine are only figures, similitudes and representations of the far absent body and blood of Christ." [44] More positively, however, "the expressions 'under the bread,' 'with the bread,' 'in the bread,' are used . . . to indicate the sacramental union of the intransubstantiated essence of the bread and of the body of Christ." [45] Again, "we do not hold that the body and blood of Christ are confined in the bread *localiter,* i.e., locally, or are otherwise permanently united therewith apart from the use of the Sacrament." There-

fore, "apart from use," when the Supper ritual is actually
taking place, "we do not hold that the body of Christ is
present." [46]

American Lutherans understand the "Real Presence"
in different ways, depending on their adherence to the
basic Confessions. At the orthodox level is the Missouri
Synod, which teaches that, "as far as the 'what' of the Real
Presence is concerned, we occupy the same ground as the
Roman—that is, the Western—and Greek—that is, the Eastern Churches." [47] More liberal positions identify the body
of Christ with His person, explaining that, "The Greek
term 'soma' means person." Consequently, in the Lord's
Supper, "we get fellowship with the entire person of
Christ," much as "in the right preaching of the Word, too,
we get fellowship with God." [48]

Sacrament of Penance. Without calling it a sacrament,
Lutheran symbolical books speak favorably of "Absolution, or the Power of the Keys," calling it "an aid and consolation against sin and a bad conscience." Furthermore,
the "Keys truly remit sins before God, because God quick-
ens through the word." [49] Beyond this, however, the rest
is a departure from Catholic doctrine. Luther's catechism
denies that penance is a distinct sacrament. "Repentance,"
he says, "is simply a return and approach to Baptism," although normally requested for Communion, since "it is
not usual to give the body of the Lord except to them that
have previously been examined and absolved." [50] Lutheran
sources also distinguish between absolution and confession: the former is admittedly scriptural, the latter only
human. Accordingly, "since private absolution originates
in the Office of the Keys, it should not be despised, but
greatly and highly esteemed." [51] As regards the confession
of one's sins to a minister, though only "instituted by the
Church," yet "on account of the great benefit of absolu-

tion, which is the chief and pre-eminent part (of confession), for the consolation of straitened consciences, and for a number of other reasons, we retain confession." [52]

Lutheran Churches in America practice auricular confession, depending on how closely they follow the symbolic formulae. While maintaining "there is no essential difference between what is known as *Privatbeichte* (private confession) and *Allgemeine Beichte* (general confession)," pastors are told that "private confession offers a certain advantage." For example, "A Christian may be troubled because of a certain sin or certain sins which he has committed; he may fear he has committed a sin which cannot be forgiven; he may need spiritual advice; and he must needs positively know that God absolves him from his sins." For these reasons, "his pastor, whom God has given him for that purpose, shall hear his confession privately, advise him from the Scriptures, and, if he be penitent, absolve him." [53] One formula of absolution reads: "Be it unto thee according to thy faith. And I, by the command of Our Lord Jesus Christ, upon this thy confession, forgive thee all thy sins, in the name of the Father, and of the Son and of the Holy Ghost. Amen." [54]

Marriage and Divorce. While Luther did not go as far as Calvin in secularizing marriage, and still spoke of it as "Holy Matrimony," like Calvin he permitted divorce with remarriage. Although the basic Confession of Augsburg is silent on the subject, Lutheran tradition holds there are two legitimate grounds for divorce: infidelity and wilful desertion. Manuals of pastoral theology explain that, in case of infidelity, the pastor should first try to persuade the offended party to condone the injustice. But he must leave the final decision "to the option of the innocent party, and if the latter has applied for, and obtained a legal divorce, the pastor, sufficient proof thereof having been submitted, cannot, after the expiration of a proper period, refuse the solemnization of another marriage." [55] The same in cases of "malicious desertion," with a distinction. Desertion is regarded, "in itself divorce," whereas infidelity "is not itself divorce, but cause of divorce." [56] Arbitrarily referring the Pauline privilege to all cases of desertion, ministers are instructed that, "after having secured a legal divorce," the deserted party is "no longer bound to the former spouse, and must not be denied remarriage at the proper time." [57] Significantly, pastors have to be cautioned against too great severity, lest they fail in charity by refusing to marry divorced persons.

Universal Priesthood. One of the most radical errors of Reformation theology was Luther's denial of a distinct sacerdotal office or power, and the corresponding claim that all believers are equally priests before God. Ignoring the context which refers to offering "spiritual sacrifices," he rested his case on the words of St. Peter, saying, "You are a chosen race, a royal priesthood" (I Pet. 2:9). "By this text," he said, "I have proved that all Christians are priests, for Peter addresses all Christians, as the words themselves clearly prove." [58] This notion was later incorporated into the Smalcald Articles, and thus made confessional doctrine, after Luther had taken up the Catholic challenge and repudiated the very idea of a visible priesthood to be consistent with his theory of a purely invisible Church.

A great part of modern Lutheranism finds its basis and justification in the hypothesis of a universal priesthood. As a logical consequence, it rejects as unscriptural the doctrine, "that only such are true ministers of the Church as have been ordained by bishops . . . that the different offices and ranks of the clergy are not of human but of divine origin . . . that only priests can forgive sins . . . that the power of excommunication does not belong to the whole congregation, but to the spiritual rulers of the Church." [59] But along with the denial of a

distinct sacerdotal office, Lutherans inherited a problem
which they have not yet resolved, namely, the exact status
of the ministry, whether it is a divine or merely human
institution. If there is no sacerdotal office instituted by
Christ and all believers are equally priests, where does the
Lutheran ministry derive its authority to teach, celebrate
the Eucharist, absolve from sin, demand obedience, and
punish the unworthy? In trying to answer this question,
two schools of thought have arisen. The evangelical party
"grants that the ministry is divinely ordained, but only in
the sense as everything wise, appropriate, morally necessary can be said to have divine sanction, not in the sense
that an express divine command for the establishment of
the public ministry can be shown." [60] Against this position
is the "strongly Roman doctrine of the ministry, namely,
that the office of the public ministry is not conferred by
the call of the congregation as the original possessor of all
spiritual power, but is a divine institution in the sense
that it was transmitted immediately from the Apostles to
their pupils, considered as a separate 'ministerial order'
or caste, and that this order perpetuates itself by means of
the ordination." [61]

To date no solution has been found for the dilemma,
and no compromise seems possible, as evidenced by the
number of schisms in American Lutheranism that have
centered around one or another of these conceptions of
the ministry, which if not divinely ordained has no title
to authority, and if divinely ordained is the negation of a
cardinal principle of Lutheran theology.

RITUAL AND WORSHIP

As much as they differ in ritual emphases, Lutheran
churches at least have in common the evangelical principle
bequeathed by their founder, who made preaching of the
Gospel instead of the Mass the center of the Christian

liturgy. Around this nucleus, however, even the most confessional bodies have developed a liturgical system that is
in striking contrast with the cold formality of churches in
the strict Calvinist tradition. A representative example is
the liturgy of the Synodical Conference of North America.

Hymns. Luther's love of music is proverbial. Faithful
to this memory, the number and variety of hymns in regular use can only be described as bewildering. The current
Lutheran Hymnal lists 668 full-length hymns, giving the
words and music, author, composer, and date of composi-
tion, and frequently extending to eight and ten stanzas.
There is an alphabetical index of all the songs, an index
of first lines, a metrical index of tunes, a classification of
general doxologies, arrangement according to season and
doctrinal content, and separate lists of authors, composers,
and translators, giving their dates of birth and death.
Among the authors are Sts. Ambrose, Bede, and Bernard
of Clairvaux, the Dominican Savonarola, non-Lutheran
reformers like Hus and John Wesley, and more recent
writers like John Keble and William Cullen Bryant. Although most of the composers (161) are Protestant, they
include several names familiar to Catholics, like Pales-
trina, Prätorius, Gounod, and Tallis. Out of 700 hymns,
not one is directed to the Blessed Virgin; one, the *Magnificat,* quotes her song of praise, and another makes reference
to her virginity. This silence is consistent with Lutheran
opposition to having "Mary, the Mother of Mercy . . .
called upon for help." [62]

Holy Communion Service. The most elaborate liturgical service in the Lutheran Church is the "Order of Holy
Communion," which is celebrated with varying frequency
and closely approximates the sequence and even the words
of the Roman missal.

1. The ritual opens with a public sign of the cross, followed by the *Confession of Sins,* in the form of a prayer

recited by the congregation. The minister then pro-
nounces the *Absolution,* saying: "Upon this your confession, I, by virtue of my office, as a called and ordained
servant of the Word, announce the grace of God unto all
of you, and in the stead and by the command of my Lord
Jesus Christ, I forgive you all your sins, in the name of
the Father and of the Son and of the Holy Ghost." [63]

2. An *Introit* is either chanted by the choir or recited
by the minister. Different introits are provided for the
changing seasons of the year. In form and content they are
translations or paraphrases from the Catholic Mass.

3. *Kyrie Eleison,* in the vernacular, is said or chanted
by the minister and the congregation; followed by the
Gloria in Excelsis Deo, similarly recited or sung—somewhat abbreviated from the Latin Mass.

4. *Salutation,* "The Lord be with you," with the response, "And with thy spirit;" *Collect* for the day, taken
verbatim or adapted from the Missal; the *Epistle,* an-
nounced and read to the people; one of a number of
Graduals, chanted or recited, and concluded with a *Halle-
luyah,* which also differs for different seasons; the reading
of the *Gospel,* facing the people, after which the congregation answers, "Praise be to Thee, O Christ."

5. The *Nicene Creed* is then recited by the people, followed by a hymn and the *Sermon.*

6. The *Offertory Prayer,* which may be sung or recited,
is always the same: "Create in me a clean heart, O God,
and renew a right spirit within me. Cast me not away from
Thy presence; and take not Thy Holy Spirit from me. Restore unto me the joy of Thy salvation; and uphold me
with Thy free spirit. Amen." [64] Then follows a series of
General Prayers: for the Church, civil rulers, enemies,
those in "trouble, want, sickness, anguish of labor, peril
of death, or any other adversity."

7. The *Preface* is preceded by three versicles and responses: "The Lord be with you . . . Lift up your hearts . . . Let us give thanks to the Lord our God." Nine proper Prefaces are provided, for Advent, Christmas, Epiphany, Lent, Easter, Ascension, Pentecost, Trinity, and "Days of Apostles and Evangelists." The wording is practically the same as in the Catholic Mass, e.g., the Trinity Preface:

> It is truly meet, right and salutary, that we should at all times and in all places give thanks unto Thee, O Lord, holy Father, almighty everlasting God, through Jesus Christ Our Lord, Who with Thine only-begotten Son and the Holy Ghost art one God, one Lord. And in the confession of the only true God we worship the Trinity in Person and the Unity in Substance, of Majesty co-equal. Therefore with angels and archangels and with all the company of heaven we laud and magnify Thy glorious name, evermore praising Thee and saying: Holy, Holy, Holy, Lord God of Sabaoth.[65]

After the *Sanctus*, the *Lord's Prayer* is recited, with the people adding, in song, "For Thine is the kingdom and the power and the glory for ever and ever. Amen." [66]

8. The *Words of Institution* of the Eucharist are recited or chanted by the minister. They are a literal translation of the words of Consecration from the Mass.

9. Immediately after are the *Pax Domini*: "The peace of the Lord be with you always . . . Amen," and the *Agnus Dei*, saying three times the invocation: "O Christ, Thou Lamb of God, that takest away the sin of the world, have mercy on us." [67]

10. *Communion* is distributed while the congregation sings one or more hymns. In the act of distribution, "when the Minister giveth the bread," he says, "Take, eat; this is

the true body of Our Lord and Savior Jesus Christ, given
into death for your sins." And "when he giveth the cup,"
he says, "Take, drink; this is the true blood of Our Lord
and Savior Jesus Christ, shed for the remission of your
sins." [68] After each distribution, he adds: "May this
strengthen and preserve you in the true faith unto life
everlasting." [69]

11. After distributing the elements, the minister recites a *Prayer of Thanksgiving,* following the chant of
Nunc Dimittis by the congregation and preceding an optional *Post Communion Hymn.* The service is closed with
the *Benedicamus Domino* and the *Benediction* said by the
minister over the congregation, and answered by the
people with a chanted, "Amen."

Rite of Confirmation. The confirmation ceremony is
the solemn conclusion to a long period of instruction in
the Lutheran religion. Since the ritual itself is denied to
be sacramental, the emphasis is on the human element,
technically called "indoctrination," which is "the necessary prerequisite of confirmation." Children must be at
least twelve years old when confirmed; the usual age is
fourteen, and "a year or two older is always better."

In the "Order of Confirmation," the two essentials are
profession of faith and promises, and the imposition of
hands by the presiding minister. Among the promises
asked of the candidate is: "Do you . . . as a member of
the Evangelical Lutheran Church, intend to continue
steadfast in the confession of this Church, and suffer all,
even death, rather than fall away from it?", to which the
person answers, "I do so intend, with the help of God." [70]
During the imposition of hands, a choice of five formulas
may be used by the minister, e.g., "N., May God, who hath
begun the good work in thee, perform it until the day of
our Lord Jesus Christ." [71] Adults who are baptized do not
have to receive Confirmation.

ORGANIZATION AND GOVERNMENT

In the United States, the congregation is the basic unit of Lutheran church government. Normally the parish is administered by a church council, headed by the pastor, and composed of laymen elected to the office and variously called elders, deacons or trustees. Pastors are elected and called by the congregation, but not deposed from the ministry.

Beyond the local level, the organization assumes two different forms. It may be a synod, like the Missouri or Norwegian Synods, composed of pastors and elected lay delegates from the congregations; or, more commonly, though organized on synodical lines, it is simply called a Church, like the American Lutheran or the Danish Evangelical Lutheran Churches. In either case, this constitutive body is the denomination in a full juridical sense. Meetings are held at least triennially; between sessions the corporate work of the body is directed by a president, his officers and a number of boards, commissions, and auxiliaries.

Some Lutheran sects are not organized beyond the level of a synod. Generally, however, a group of synods bands together to form a conference (also called a "Church"), in which the member bodies relinquish a certain amount of autonomy for the privilege of mutual benefits in the larger organization. For example, the late American Lutheran Conference (2,331,451 members), which collaborated with the National and World Councils of Churches, included the American Lutheran, Augustana, Evangelical Lutheran, Lutheran Free, and United Evangelical Lutheran Churches. Organized in 1930, it was dissolved in 1954. The Lutheran Synodical Conference of North America (membership 2,331,451) is an ultra-conservative society, committed to a strict adherence to the

six fundamental Lutheran Confessions, including the
Apology, Luther's large catechism, the Smalcald Articles,
and the Formula of Concord, which are optional in other
Lutheran churches, especially those of Scandinavian origin. According to its constitution, the United Lutheran
Church (2,113,779), in spite of its name, is also a conference, which was proximately formed in 1918 by a union
of the General Synod, the General Council, and the
United Synod of the South, but ultimately is composed of
all the sub-synods within the three larger constituents.

Recent events in American Lutheranism have high-
lighted the tenuous character of its church government,
which is more constantly changing through schism and
merger than that of any other Protestant body. On a wide
doctrinal level, the Synodical Conference is facing a crisis
which threatens to disrupt the organization. Its Norwegian section accuses the Missouri Synod of unionist activities, i.e., of compromising in matters of doctrine by cooperating with Lutheran churches of questionable dogmatic
character. Similarly, the Wisconsin group is dissatisfied
with the "Common Confession" to which the members of
the Conference subscribe, calling it "inadequate." In a
statement from the President of the Missouri Synod, he
admits, "We are saddened beyond words. Of course if the
Norwegian and the Wisconsin Synods decide to suspend
or terminate relations of fellowship with our Synod . . .
we cannot prevent it. However . . . we do not admit the
charges . . . It is one thing to make charges; it is another
thing to furnish convincing evidence from the Word of
God." [72]

Originally on a smaller scale, the Wisconsin heresy
trials (1955) of three ministers have since developed into
another major problem which cuts across several Lutheran denominations. Pastors George Crist, John Gerberding, and Victor Wrigley had been tried by their

Northwest Synod on charges of denying the Virgin Birth, the Resurrection of Christ, and the value of intercessory prayer. Crist and Wrigley were found guilty, Gerberding was acquitted but resigned his pastorate. The synod then suspended Crist from the ministry, but Wrigley was defended by his congregation, which stood by him, with the result that the congregation withdrew from the Northwest Synod. All the while, liberal-minded Lutherans felt that an injury had been done not only to the three pastors but to the reputation of American Lutheranism. They tried to have the cases re-examined by the supposedly higher authority of the United Lutheran Church to which the Northwest Synod belongs, but without success. The reason was a fear of schism. Any attempted exercise of jurisdiction over the Northwest Synod would have been against the constitution of the U.L.C. which is ostensibly a Church, and yet so loosely federated that "it has no authority in constituent synods or their congregations or seminaries, and no official way to enter an affair like this one." [73]

Negotiations are under way for a reunion of four parties to the recently defunct American Lutheran Conference, to form a new merger as the American Lutheran Church. Expected to mature in five years, the new denomination will join the American, Evangelical, United Evangelical, and Free Lutheran Churches, but excluding the Augustana Synod. On its part, the Augustana Synod is planning a union of its own with the United Lutheran Church in America. One of the major differences still to be ironed out illustrates the compromise nature of Lutheran ecclesiastical structure. Some U.L.C.A. synods openly tolerate their pastors' membership in Masonic Lodges; the Augustana Synod to date forbids the practice. Confessional Lutherans look upon the Lodges as, "antichristian societies . . . destructive of the best interests of the Church and the individual soul." [74] But the President

of the Augustana Synod did not consider this a serious obstacle to mutual recognition, declaring that opponents of
the merger were using the Lodge question to "cover up
certain provincial reasons" for their hostility.[75]

On a country-wide scale, the National Lutheran Council was organized in 1918 to act as a liaison between the
churches and the Federal Government for the spiritual
welfare of the members of the Armed Forces, and to carry
on relief work among the war victims. Current membership in the Council includes most of the Lutheran
Churches with the exception of the Synodical Conference.
As a national agency, its function has since been extended,
"to witness for the Lutheran Church on matters which require an expression of common faith, ideals and program
. . . to represent Lutheran interests in America in matters which require common action, before national and
state government (and) before organized bodies and movements outside the Lutheran Church." [76] The success of the
Martin Luther film is an example of the Council's cooperative effort in the field of propaganda.

On the international level, in 1923 the Lutheran
World Convention first met at Eisenach, Germany, and
was attended by 147 delegates, representing 22 nations.
After two other meetings in Copenhagen (1929) and Paris
(1935), the Convention was reorganized in 1947, at Lund,
as the Lutheran World Federation. Its doctrinal basis is,
"the Holy Scriptures of the Old and New Testaments as
the only source and the infallible norm of all church doctrine and practice," and its main purpose is, "to cultivate
unity of faith and confession among the Lutheran Churches
of the world," yet in such a way as "to foster Lutheran
participation in ecumenical movements." [77] It was in the
spirit of this ecumenism that Lutheran Bishop Eivind
Berggrav, one of the Presidents of the World Council of
Churches, would not attend the Lutheran communion

service at Evanston in 1954 because he disapproved its closed character. The service was open only to those "who believe in His actual presence."

STATISTICS

Estimated Lutheran World Population (1951)	71,000,000
Membership, World Lutheran Federation (1952)	51,000,000
Evangelical (Lutheran-Reformed) Churches	
West Germany (1954) (51% of population)	25,000,000
East Germany (1954) (80% of population)	14,000,000
Lutheran Churches	
Sweden (1951)	7,000,000
Norway (1952)	3,400,000
Denmark (1954)	4,300,000
Finland (1953)	4,000,000
United States, 19 bodies (1955)	6,818,283
Churches (1955)	16,265
Day-Schools (1955)	2,470
Enrollment (1955)	240,000
Clergy (1955)	15,429

REFERENCES

1. *What Is Lutheranism?* (Vergilius Ferm, ed.), New York, Macmillan, 1930, p. x.
2. William H. T. Dau, *Ibid.*, p. 218.
3. Vergilius Ferm, *Ibid.*, p. 278.
4. *Ibid.*, p. 280.
5. According to a modern non-Catholic historian, the extension of the term "Protestant" after the Diet of Speyer "is justified in that the official protest has become the only thing that all the multifarious institutions and cultural manifestations known as Protestant have in common. This is the opposition to the Catholic Church and all Catholic thought as expressed in literature, art, science, and culture in general: an opposition in the name of individual responsibility before God." Gerhard Ritter, "Protestantism," *Twentieth Century Encyclopedia of Religious Knowledge*, Grand Rapids, Baker Book House, 1955, vol. II, p. 914.
6. E. G. Schwiebert, *Luther and His Times*, St. Louis, Concordia, 1950, p. 741.
7. There are four Weimar editions of Luther's writings, amounting to a total of 83 volumes.
8. Schwiebert, *op. cit.*, pp. 637-638.

9. *D. Martin Luthers Saemtliche Schriften* (Johann Walch, ed.), Halle, 1740 sqq., vol. XX, p. 223.

10. Walter A. Baepler, *A Century of Grace*, St. Louis, Concordia, 1947, pp. 5-6.

11. J. L. Neve and Willard D. Allbeck, *History of the Lutheran Church in America*, MS (third edition), n.d., p. 124.

12. *Ibid.*, p. 50.

13. Philip Schaff, *The Creeds of the Evangelical Protestant Churches*, "The Augsburg Confession," London, Hodder and Stoughton, 1877, pp. 11-12.

14. *Ibid.*, p. 11.

15. Eric H. Wahlstrom, "Lutheran Church," *The Nature of the Church: Papers Presented to the Theologiacal Commission of the World Conference on Faith and Order* (R. Newton Flew, ed.), London, S.C.M. Press, 1952, p. 266.

16. Francis Pieper, *Christian Dogmatics*, St. Louis, Concordia, 1953, vol. III, p. 408.

17. Schaff, *op. cit.*, p. 10.

18. *Ibid.*, p. 24.

19. F. E. Mayer, *The Religious Bodies of America*, "Lutheranism," St. Louis, Concordia, 1954, p. 154. The Council of Trent condemned Luther's notion of saving faith as a blind trust that one's sins are covered over by the merits of Christ. Salvific faith, the Council defined, is an assent of the mind to the truths of revelation which, coupled with supernatural hope and charity, places a man on the road to heaven.

20. The letter was written to Wenceslaus Link (1530), and includes the now famous expression of Luther's arbitrariness: "Sic volo, sic jubeo, sit pro ratione voluntas (I want it so, I command it so, the will must take the place of reason.)" *Luthers Saemtliche Schriften* (Walch edition), vol. XXI, p. 314.

21. Pieper, *op. cit.*, vol. II, p. 533. In context, St. Paul refers to the saving power of faith in Christ independently of the detailed prescriptions of the Mosaic Law. Luther twisted Paul's words by inserting "alone," so as to mean that faith, independently of good works, is sufficient for salvation.

22. Schaff, *op. cit.*, p. 18.

23. Dau, *op. cit.*, p. 215.

24. Ferm, *op. cit.*, pp. 294-295.

25. Arthur C. Piepkorn, *What the Symbolical Books of the Lutheran Church Have to Say about Worship and the Sacraments*, "Apology of the Augsburg Confession," St. Louis, Concordia, 1952, p. 16.

26. *Loc. cit.*

27. *Ibid.* The Catholic doctrine on the sacraments was vindicated by the Council of Trent (A.D. 1547) in a series of propositions directed against the innovations of Luther and his followers. Summarily, the Council defined that there are seven sacraments in the New Law, instituted by Christ; these sacraments are essentially and not only externally different than the ritual ceremonies in the Old Testament; they are necessary for salvation and cannot be replaced by mere faith in God's promises, nor were they instituted simply to nourish the faith; they contain the grace which they signify and confer grace on anyone who places no obstacle in the way; and, with the exception of baptism and matrimony, they

cannot be administered by anyone, but only by those who are duly ordained to the priesthood or the episcopate.

28. *Ibid.*, "Luther's Large Catechism," p. 17.
29. *Ibid.*, "Apology," p. 17.
30. *Loc. cit.*
31. *Ibid.*, p. 18.
32. *Loc. cit.*
33. *Loc. cit.*
34. *Loc. cit.* (Editor's comment).
35. Schaff, *op. cit.*, p. 13.
36. Pieper, *op. cit.*, vol. III, p. 281.
37. *Ibid.*, p. 280.
38. *Ibid.*, p. 281.
39. *Ibid.*, p. 261.
40. *Dr. Martin Luther's Small Catechism*, St. Louis, Concordia, 1943, p. 33.
41. Schaff, *op. cit.*, p. 13.
42. Piepkorn, *op. cit.*, p. 29.
43. *Ibid.*, "Formula of Concord," p. 31.
44. *Loc. cit.*
45. *Loc. cit.*
46. *Loc. cit.* Among the original Reformers, Luther was quite singular in admitting the real presence; but inconsistently he denied that a change of substance takes place at the Consecration. To explain this apparent contradiction, he invented the thory of "Christ's Ubiquity." Then he argued that since Christ, as God and Man, is everywhere independently of the Mass, there is no need of transubstantiation to account for His presence in the Sacrament. Catholic teaching from apostolic times held that the whole Christ, God and Man, is really and truly present in the Eucharist, *and* that this presence is effected uniquely by the words of the Consecration in the Mass.
47. *Ibid.*, "Apology," p. 30. Besides the difference already noted,

Catholic theology further denies (what many Lutherans hold) that the substance of the bread remains in the Eucharist, along with the Body of Christ.

48. Luther A. Weigle, *What Is Lutheransim?*, p. 33.
49. Piepkorn, *op. cit.*, "Smalcald Articles," and "Apology," p. 40. When Lutherans say that the "keys remit sin," they refer to the declaration by the minister that God has forgiven a sinner; they do not mean (as Catholics do) that any words of absolution effect this forgiveness.
50. *Ibid.*, "Augsburg Confession," p. 40.
51. *Ibid.*, "Smalcald Articles," p. 41.
52. *Ibid.*, "Augusburg Confession," p. 41.
53. John H. C. Fritz, *Pastoral Theology*, St. Louis, Concordia, 1945, p. 119.
54. *The Lutheran Agenda*, St. Louis, Concordia, n.d., p. 64.
55. Fritz, *op. cit.*, p. 167.
56. *Loc. cit.*
57. *Loc. cit.*
58. *Works of Martin Luther*, Philadelphia, Castle Press-Holman Co., 1930, vol. III, p. 319.
59. John T. Mueller, *My Church and Others*, St. Louis, Rudolph Volkening, 1945, p. 47.
60. Pieper, *op. cit.*, vol. III, p. 445.
61. *Ibid.*, p. 447.
62. Mueller, *op. cit.*, p. 31.
63. *The Lutheran Hymnal* (Authorized by the Synods Constituting the Evangelical Lutheran Synodical Conference of North America), St. Louis, Concordia, 1941, p. 16.
64. *Ibid.*, p. 23. While keeping the name, "Offertory," modern Lutherans are faithful to Luther's hatred of the sacrificial terminology in this part of the Mass.

"That complete abomination (the) *Offertorium,*" he wrote, "on account of which nearly everything sounds and reeks of oblation." *Works of Martin Luther,* Philadelphia, Muhlenberg Press, 1932, vol. VI, p. 88.

65. *Lutheran Hymnal,* pp. 25-26.
66. *Ibid.,* p. 27.
67. *Ibid.,* p. 28.
68. *Ibid.,* p. 29.
69. *Loc. cit.*
70. *Lutheran Agenda,* p. 24.
71. *Ibid.,* p. 25.
72. *The Lutheran Witness,* August 2, 1955, LXXIV, p. 6.
73. *Christian Century,* February 8, 1956, p. 167.
74. *Doctrinal Declarations* (Collection of Official Statements on the Doctrinal Position of Various Lutheran Synods in America), "Minneapolis Theses of The American Lutheran Conference," St. Louis, Concordia, n.d., p. 21. One of the pastoral problems for the minister is how to deal with members of his congregation who are also affiliated with the Lodge. Each case is to be judged individually, pastors are told, above all trying to "show the individual the sinfulness of his lodge affiliation." However, "it is impossible to say how long one must continue to deal with such a person before excommunicating him." Fritz, *op. cit.,* pp. 373-374.
75. *Christian Century,* July 6, 1955, LXXII, p. 796.
76. Mayer, *op. cit.,* p. 186.
77. *Ibid.,* 187.

8. *Methodists*

IF EVER A Protestant society was built around a dynamic personality and its continued existence was due to the infusion of his spirit, that society is Methodism. John Wesley not only founded the Methodist Church but left his followers with a reverence for himself which is unique among the Reformers. "The flame of John Wesley's early devotion," they say, "still burns in the hearts of his children, and the evangelical gospel which he preached to the common people of England in the eighteenth century continues to bear spiritual fruitage in the minds and hearts of this present generation." [1]

This is not a study of Methodist theology. If it were, we should have to examine in detail Wesley's character and doctrine to see how his insistence on "salvation for all" diverted the course of Protestantism in the English speaking world and brought it closer to the Catholic teaching on freedom and good works. Although our present concern is more practical and limited to a review of Methodism as an ecclesiastical institution, even here the organizing genius of John Wesley, his personal asceticism and inflexible pursuit of an ideal believed to be from God are still discernible. Where Methodists have compromised in matters of faith or allowed material interests to obscure the spiritual, they have, on their own admission, departed from the principles of their founder.

HISTORY

The founder of Methodism was born in Epworth, England, June 17, 1703. He died in London, March 2, 1791. Graduated from Oxford with an M.A., he was ordained a priest in the Church of England in 1728. Returning to Oxford as a lecturer, he joined a group of Bible-reading students, nicknamed Methodists by a cynical wit because of their methodical application to Scripture study and prayer. Wesley came to the American colony of Georgia late in 1735, but returned to England two years later, after an unfortunate court trial involving the "excommunication" of a woman in his parish. He had hoped to marry the lady, but could not reach a decision; meantime she married someone else, and then her being repelled from the Lord's Supper looked like revenge. Disillusioned, Wesley remarked on what he had learned from his American stay, "that I, who went to America to convert others, was never myself converted to God." [2]

The turning point in Wesley's life and the birthday of Methodism came on May 24, 1738, at a prayer meeting in London, during the reading of Luther's preface to the Epistle to the Romans. He felt his heart "strangely warmed" as Luther's teaching on justification by faith penetrated his soul. Immediately he set on a career of evangelization that for zeal and magnitude has no counterpart in the history of Protestantism. He preached three times a day for over fifty years, traveled over 200,000 miles on horseback throughout the British Isles, including forty-two visits to Ireland, published four hundred books and pamphlets, and with his brother, Charles, composed 6,500 hymns. His labors and exertions, described by admirers as "wholly dedicated to God and the service of his fellow-men," have earned for him the title of "Methodism's saint."[3]

Moral laxity among the clergy and people of the Church of England was the background of Wesley's evangelism, although it was never intended by him to mean a complete severance with the Anglican Communion. A year before his death, Wesley still proclaimed his loyalty to the Established Church, declaring that, "I live and die a member of the Church of England, and none who regard my judgment will ever separate from it."[4] When his doctrine on the internal witness of the Spirit and free grace barred him from the pulpits, he answered, "The world is my parish," and began field-preaching. Societies of the "saved" were formed throughout England with Wesley as the final authority in all matters of doctrine and discipline. He drew up a list of rules for his followers as early as 1739, but the Methodists were not legally recognized in England until 1784.

American Methodism had three independent beginnings. In 1760, the Irish Robert Strawbridge from Ulster organized a group of Methodist preachers in Maryland; the following year another group of Irish immigrants from County Limerick founded the first Methodist meeting house in New York; and finally, between 1769 and 1772, Wesley personally appointed and sent chosen missionaries from England to the colonies.

The Methodist Church in America grew in numbers during the Revolutionary War, but also weakened to the point of near disintegration for lack of Anglican-ordained clergy to care for its needs. When the Bishop of London refused to ordain ministers for Methodist societies in the colonies, Wesley on his own authority first ordained Thomas Coke, Richard Whatcoat, and Thomas Vasey, and then consecrated Coke to the episcopacy. "I can scarcely believe it," wrote his brother Charles, "that in his eighty-second year my brother, my old, intimate friend and companion, should have assumed the episcopal character, ordained elders, consecrated a bishop, and sent him to ordain our elder preachers in America." [5] On his part, Wesley believed he had been divinely inspired to this action. "Know all men," he stated in a formal manifesto, "that I, John Wesley, think myself to be providentially called, at this time, to set apart some persons for the work of the ministry in America." [6] Besides the inspiration, he argued that "he had been convinced of his scriptural authority as a presbyter to ordain, since it had been the practice of the ancient church in Alexandria for presbyters to ordain bishops, never suffering the interference of a foreign bishop." [7] This assumption of episcopal powers is still the main barrier of separation between the Episcopal and Methodist Churches.

During Christmas week of 1784, within two months of the landing of Coke, Whatcoat, and Vasey in New York, the Methodist Episcopal Church in America was juridically constituted and established as a religious body independent of the Church of England. The immediate fruit of this founding Conference, held in Baltimore, was the publication in 1785 of the first Methodist *Discipline*. As a carefully planned and detailed code of doctrine, ritual and policy, drawn up according to directives received from John Wesley, the Discipline became an instrument of ecclesiastical unity for American Methodism, much as the Book of Common Prayer is in Anglicanism.

The greatest name in American Methodist history is Francis Asbury, who was ordained elder and consecrated bishop during the Christmas Conference of 1784. As an evangelist, he outrode Wesley in distance covered (275,000 miles) and revivals held (4,000), during his thirty years of missionary travel. His genius in organizing lay preachers

(1,000 by 1816) placed laymen into governing power in the church, and thus completely severed Methodism in the United States, both legally and doctrinally, from the Church of England.

Three years after the church's American establishment occurred the first secession from the parent body. In 1787 a group of Negro Methodists met in Philadelphia to organize the African Methodist Episcopal Church. Their grievance was the discrimination practiced against their brethren by the white members of the denomination. A few years later, in 1796, the African Methodist Episcopal Zion Church was similarly started because of racial discrimination in New York. The present (1956) combined membership of these two Methodist segments is about two million.

Within a dozen years of Asbury's death, lay representation in church policy contributed to the third major schism in American Methodism. In 1828 the Methodist Protestant Church seceded over the juridical question of appeal for restoration of expelled ministers, and the more basic issue of equal participation of laymen and clergy in church government.

In 1845 another division occurred over the slavery question, bisecting the Methodist Episcopal Church into the Methodist Episcopal Church, North, and the Methodist Episcopal Church, South. The proximate occasion for the split was the mandate of the 1844 General Conference, ordering Bishop Andrew of Georgia to desist exercising his office so long as he remained a slaveholder. This enraged the southern delegates, who went home to begin their own denomination the following year.

Shortly after the Emancipation Declaration, the Methodist Episcopal Church, South, was faced with the problem of retaining in its body the thousands of liberated negro slaves. On the negroes' own initiative, the Colored Meth-

odist Episcopal Church was founded in 1870. Its current
(1956) membership is 400,000 in 2,500 churches.

The last two decades of the nineteenth century witnessed an "ominous change" in American Methodism. "No
longer were Methodists drawn from the lower and hum-
bler economic and social groups, but rather represented
the great middle class, and, as Mr. (Theodore) Roosevelt
asserted, constituted 'the most representative church in
America.' " [8] Moreover, "to an increasing degree the business of the church fell more and more into the hands of
laymen." [9] Illustrative of this new spirit was the celebrated
Vanderbilt University case, tried in the courts, which resulted in the university's withdrawal (1914) from Methodist auspices in order to obtain the funds under control of
the Peabody Foundation.

As a balance to this secularizing tendency, Methodist
organizations like the Church Extension Society upheld
traditional Wesleyan principles of evangelization. The
Church Extension Society was founded "to secure suitable
houses of public worship and such other church property"
as might assist the propagation of the faith. Within the
first ten years, the Society collected $3,000,000 for its proj-
ects, and at present is promoting missionary enterprises in
Hawaii, Alaska, Central America, and among the Negroes
and Indians in the States.

Comparable to the evangelical balance to the inroads
of secularism was the tendency towards reunion among
Methodist bodies to offset the century and a half of schismatic fragmentation. After years of negotiation, on May
10, 1939, a Plan of Union was adopted at Kansas City,
which united the Methodist Episcopal Church, the Methodist Episcopal Church, South, and the reformed Methodist Protestant Church into one organic body. The Methodist Church. The historical basis for the fusion, as stated
in the Plan of Union, was that all three denominations

"had their common origin in the organization of the Methodist Episcopal Church in America in 1784, A.D., and have ever held, adhered to and preserved a common belief, spirit and purpose, as expressed in their common Articles of Religion." [10]

DOCTRINE OF FAITH AND MORALS

The Methodist Church accounts for eighty per cent of the membership of all Methodist bodies in the country and substantially expresses their common principles and policy. Its codification, therefore, of belief and worship in the *Doctrines and Discipline of The Methodist Church* may be taken as fairly representative of the nature and function of American Methodism at the present day. Going back to the first days of the church's establishment in Colonial America, the *Discipline* has become an authoritative source book which the clergy urge the people to have "found in every Methodist home." It is revised every four years by the delegates to the General Conference, and currently runs to 800 pages in duodecimo.

The heart of the Methodist profession of faith is the *Articles of Religion* which John Wesley sent to America in 1784, and which now hold the place of honor in the *Discipline*. Although based on the Thirty-nine Articles of the Anglican Church, they have been modified and supplemented to meet the needs of a growing democratic society.

Explicit faith is declared in "one living and true God, everlasting, without body or parts, of infinite power, wisdom and goodness." In the "unity of this Godhead are three persons, of one substance, power and eternity—the Father, the Son and the Holy Ghost." [11] Having stated that the Son of God "took man's nature in the womb of the blessed Virgin," the *Discipline* explains that He "truly

suffered, was crucified, dead and buried, to reconcile His
Father to us." After His passion and death, He is said to
have risen from the dead, ascended into heaven, until He
"return to judge all men at the last day." [12] Then follows
a series of propositions, briefly worded in the *Articles of
Religion* and expanded elsewhere in the *Discipline,* more
than half of which the Methodists admit, "are a protest
against the errors of Roman Catholicism," since "our
Methodist Articles are protestant articles." [13]

Scripture and Revelation. Without using the term, tradition is eliminated as a source of revelation, because "the
Holy Scriptures contain all things necessary to salvation;
so that whatsoever is not read therein nor may be proved
thereby, is not to be required of any man that it should be
believed as an article of faith, or be thought requisite or
necessary to salvation." [14] In listing the canon of Scripture,
those books are accepted "of whose authority (there) was
never any doubt in the Church." [15] Accordingly seven
books of the Old Testament are dropped, notably the
Book of Wisdom and the two Books of Machabees.

Sin, Faith, and Justification. Original sin is first declared against the Pelagians not to consist in the mere
"following of Adam," and then erroneously identified,
with Luther and Calvin, as "a corruption of the nature of
every man," which is so deep that "of his nature" man is
"inclined to evil, and that continually." [16] As a result of
this condition, "we have no power to do good works, pleasant and acceptable to God, without the grace of God pre-
venting us." [17] Luther's doctrine of justification by faith
alone is restated almost in the words of the Tridentine
condemnation, that "We are accounted righteous before
God only for the merit of our Lord and Saviour Jesus
Christ, by faith, and not for our own works or deservings.
Wherefore, that we are justified by faith only is a most
wholesome doctrine, and very full of comfort." [18]

For an adequate concept of the Methodist idea of faith
and conversion, the statements in the *Discipline* must be
seen in the context of Wesley's own writings on the subject. As regards salvific faith, by which a sinner feels that
he is converted to God, Wesley conceived it as something
deeply personal, involving a direct quasi-sensible experience of the divine presence, a consciousness of "the imma-
nent activity of the Holy Spirit." [19] In Wesley's own words,
"Faith is the divine evidence whereby the spiritual man
discerneth God, and the things of God. It is with regard
to the spiritual world, what sense is with regard to the
natural. It is the spiritual sensation of every soul that is
born of God." [20] His attitude toward man's cooperation
in the work of salvation is ambiguous. Faced with parallel
passages from Wesley, in which he first seems to favor and
then to oppose the Catholic notion of good works, some
Methodists confess that, "if . . . Wesley is here falling
back upon human causality in salvation, then we must be
content with a final unresolved contradiction in Wesley's
thought. Wesley has rendered man powerless and, in spite
of that, requires him to respond freely to grace." [21] Whatever may be said in theory, Wesley's constant exhortation
to the practice of Christian virtue meant an implicit repudiation of the denial of man's freedom and an admission that liberty must be rightly used as a condition for
salvation.

Definition of the Church. The Methodist concept of
the Church includes three aspects, the universal, the visible, and the local, clearly defined by the *Discipline*:

> The Church Universal is composed of all who ac-
> cept Jesus Christ as Lord and Saviour, and which in
> the Apostles' Creed we declare to be the holy catholic
> Church.[22]

> The visible Church of Christ is a congregation of

faithful men in which the pure word of God is preached, and the Sacraments duly administered.[23]

The local church is a connectional society of persons who have professed their faith in Christ, have been baptized, have assumed the vows of membership in The Methodist Church, and are associated in fellowship as a local Methodist Church.

According to Methodism, therefore, the Church is not essentially a visible society founded by Christ. It was not He but His followers who may be said to have established a church by their common acceptance of Him as their Savior. Not even a common faith in a definite body of doctrine, but only a trustful hope in the mercy of God is required to belong to the invisible society called the Church Universal. However, if they wish, Christians may further express their solidarity by forming a visible church with not only a mutual trust in their Redeemer, but a common preaching discipline and sacramental ritual, like the Lutherans or Episcopalians. Finally on the local level, the members are united by a voluntary submission to the Methodist form of Christianity, which makes no claim to exclusiveness as the true Church of Christ, but only has the title to individuality, to distinguish it from other equally orthodox bodies.

Rites and Ceremonies. Since the Church is essentially invisible, it has no need of visible symbols to express and preserve its unity. Negatively, then, "It is not necessary that rites and ceremonies should in all places be the same, or exactly alike; for they have always been different, and may be changed according to the diversity of countries, times and men's manners." And positively, "every particular church may ordain, change or abolish ceremonies and rites, so that all things may be done to edification."[25] It is interesting to note that in drafting this last regulation, Wesley substantially altered Article 34 of the Thirty-nine Articles of the Anglican Church, which allowed the churches to modify rites and ceremonies that have been "ordained by man's authority." [26] Wesley deleted the restrictive clause.

The Sacraments. Only two sacraments, baptism and the Supper of the Lord, are said to be found in the Gospel. The other five, commonly called sacraments, "are not to be counted for Sacraments of the Gospel; being such as have partly grown out of the corrupt following of the apostles, and partly are states of life allowed in the Scriptures." [27] Directly aimed at the Catholic doctrine of the reserved presence in the Eucharist, the *Discipline* states that "the Sacraments were not ordained of Christ to be gazed upon, or to be carried about; but that we should duly use them." [28] This is substantially Article 25 of the Thirty-nine Articles. Although baptism is not explicitly said to effect the remission of sins, yet implicitly this function is suggested in the two synonyms given in its definition. It is "not only a sign of profession and mark of difference whereby Christians are distinguished from others that are not baptized; but it is also a sign of regeneration or the new birth." [29] Still there is strong evidence that Wesley, and the Methodists after him, would not regard baptism as remissive of moral guilt. Article 16 of the Anglican Articles begins: "Not every deadly sin willingly committed after Baptism is sin against the Holy Ghost." [30] The corresponding Article 12 of the Methodist Creed begins: "Not every sin willingly committed after justification is the sin against the Holy Ghost." [31] A reasonable conclusion is that Wesley substituted "justification" for "Baptism" to fit more logically into his system of justification by faith alone, since infants are presumably incapable

of making an act of justifying faith; consequently whatever else happens to them at baptism, it is not the remission of sin.

The Supper of the Lord. The term "Eucharist" is nowhere used to describe the Sacrament of the Altar. Instead
it is called the Lord's Supper or Holy Communion. Like
the Episcopalians, the Methodists deny the real presence
of the Body and Blood of Christ. Thus "transubstantiation, or the change of the substance of bread and wine
in the Supper of the Lord" is said to be contrary to the
plain words of Scripture, following the Protestant tradition in the Church of England. However, there is a sense
in which Christ may be considered present in the Lord's
Supper, "after a heavenly and spiritual manner. And the
means whereby the body of Christ is received and eaten
in the Supper is faith." [32] Unlike the Anglicans, from
whom the wording of this doctrine is drawn, there is no
evidence of a sacramental or "Catholic" interpretation of
the real presence among the Methodists.

Marriage and Divorce. Although the marriage ceremony is taken almost verbally from the Roman Ritual, the
contract itself is denied to be a sacrament instituted by
Christ. Correspondingly it is not a permanent union, but
may be dissolved in a variety of ways. The full text from
the Discipline reads:

> No minister shall solemnize the marriage of a di-
> vorced person whose wife or husband is living and un-
> married; but this rule shall not apply (1) to the inno-
> cent person when it is clearly established by competent
> testimony that the true cause for divorce was adultery
> or other vicious conditions which through mental or
> physical cruelty or physical peril invalidated the mar-
> riage vow, nor (2) to the divorced persons seeking to

be re-united in marriage. The violation of this rule concerning divorce shall be considered an act of malad-ministration.[33]

Hence the Methodist Church does not claim the right to grant a divorce on its own authority, but it concedes this right to the state and the married persons under several conditions:

1. The subsequent marital union of one party automatically gives his (or her) partner the right to a valid re-marriage before a Methodist minister.

2. The innocent party in case of adultery, physical, or mental cruelty may be validly remarried.

3. The victim of vicious conditions, or one exposed to physical danger may be validly remarried.

Religious Education. Since Methodist churchmen like G. Bromley Oxnam, Secretary of the Council of Bishops, have been outspoken in their opposition to government aid for Catholic schools, it is instructive to see the official mind of their church on the subject of religious education. In the words of the *Discipline*:

> The Methodist Church is committed to the public schools as the most effective means of providing common education for all our children. We hold that it is an institution essential to the preservation and development of our true democracy.
>
> We are unalterably opposed to the diversion of tax funds to the support of private and sectarian schools. In a short time this scattering process can destroy our American public school system and weaken the foundations of national unity.
>
> We believe that religion has a rightful place in the public school program, and that it is possible for public school teachers, without violating the traditional

American principle of separation of church and state, to teach moral principles and spiritual values.[34]

While admitting that "opponents of the public schools call the schools 'godless,'" the first impression is that the Methodist Church is against sectarian education in general as a remedy for this godlessness, on the grounds that it may "weaken the foundations of national unity." However statistics show that there are at present in the United States, 118 educational institutions professedly affiliated with the Methodist Church, including 98 universities and colleges. Moreover a large section of the *Discipline*, under "Administrative Agencies," sets down the policy for the erection and management of "educational institutions related to the Methodist Church," which suggests that this body is not opposed on principle to sectarian education.

Temperance. The traditional Methodist reform attitude towards alcoholic beverages goes back to John Wesley, who wrote in his sermon on "The Use of Money," that "Neither may we gain by hurting our neighbor in his body. Therefore, we may not sell anything which tends to impair health; such is evidently all that liquid fire, commonly called drams or spirituous liquors." [35]

In accordance with this principle, the *Discipline* declares in forthright language what is the official Methodist stand on the sale and use of intoxicating drinks:

> Our Church reasserts its long-established conviction that intoxicating liquor cannot be legalized without sin. The Church of Jesus Christ from its very nature stands at variance with the liquor traffic. For it to be silent in its opposition would be to be disloyal in its function. Therefore, to be true to itself the Church must be militant in opposition to the liquor traffic . . . Adequate relief can come only through total ab-

stinence for the individual, and effective prohibition for the state.[36]

These norms are given positive expression in the Board of Temperance, with headquarters in Washington, D. C., whose duty it is "to promote by an intensive educational program . . . voluntary total abstinence . . . to promote observance and enforcement of constitutional provisions and statutory enactments which suppress the traffic in alcoholic liquors and in narcotic drugs; and to aid and promote such legislation." [37] Since the General Conference of 1872, American Methodists have steadily promoted the necessity of "total legal prohibition." They were the most influential group in securing the passage of the 18th Amendment, and in 1932, just before the Amendment was repealed, the General Conference stated that, "As a church we can follow no course except the one that will reduce the consumption of beverage alcohol to the minimum. We are convinced that national prohibition is that method." [38]

WORSHIP AND RITUAL

The contrast between Methodist doctrine and worship is striking. Where the Articles of Religion describe the church as fundamentally invisible, whose only bond of unity is a common trust in the Redeemer, the Methodist Ritual emphasizes the need for a corporate and visible worship that goes into minute details of posture, gesture, and order of procedure.

Methodist Orders of Worship. To avoid imposing complete uniformity on the ministers, the *Discipline* allows four types of religious service called "Orders of Worship," suitable for Sunday or week-day celebration. "But while liberty is given in the use of these orders of worship, it is urged that all ministers and congregations make use of

some one of these orders." [39] Order III, which is the simplest, will illustrate the general procedure: [40]

ORDER OF WORSHIP III

Let the service of worship begin at the time appointed.
Let the people kneel or bow in silent prayer upon entering the sanctuary.

PRELUDE. The people in devout meditation.

CALL TO WORSHIP. Which may be said or sung.

HYMN. If a processional, the hymn shall precede the call
  to worship, and the people shall then rise at the second
  stanza and join in singing.

PRAYER OF CONFESSION. To be said by all, the people seated
  and bowed, or kneeling.

SILENT MEDITATION

THE LORD'S PRAYER

ANTHEM

LESSON FROM HOLY SCRIPTURES

PASTORAL PRAYER

PRESENTATION OF OFFERINGS

HYMN. People standing.

THE SERMON

INVITATION TO CHRISTIAN DISCIPLESHIP

HYMN OR DOXOLOGY. People standing.

SILENT PRAYER

BENEDICTION

POSTLUDE

The Lord's Supper. Two different services for the administration of the Lord's Supper are allowed by the
Methodist *Discipline,* substantially alike, and both "intended to replace the regular order of morning worship
when the Sacrament of the Lord's Supper is administered." [41] A preliminary rubric directs that "The Lord's
Table should have upon it a fair linen cloth. Let the pure,

unfermented juice of the grape be used." [42] The Communion ritual is long and elaborate. Alternating prayers are said by the minister and congregation, texts from the Old and New Testaments, e.g., the Decalogue and Isaias 53:1-10, portions from the Sermon on the Mount, and finally the Prayer of Consecration, which is practically verbatim from various parts of the *Missale Romanum*:

> O merciful Father, we most humbly beseech thee, and grant that we, receiving this bread and wine, according to thy Son our Saviour Jesus Christ's holy institution, in remembrance of his death and passion may also be partakers of the divine nature through him, who in the same night that he was betrayed took bread (Here may the minister take the plate in his hands); and when he had given thanks, he broke it, and gave it to his disciples, saying, Take, eat; this is my body, which is given for you; do this in remembrance of me. Likewise after supper he took the cup (Here may the minister take the cup in his hands); and when he had given thanks, he gave it to them, saying, Drink ye all of this; for this is my blood of the new covenant which is shed for you, and for many, for the remission of sins; do this, as oft as ye shall drink it, in remembrance of me. Amen. [43]

After another short prayer, the minister communicates himself and then distributes the elements to the people. The substitution of "bread and wine" for "body and blood" in the Prayer of Consecration, and the reference to "faith" in the Communion Prayer reveal the Methodist idea of the Eucharist as mainly subjective; there is no physical reality independently of the mind of the communicant. In giving the bread, the minister says: "Jesus said, 'This is my body, which is given for you.' Take and eat this in remembrance that Christ died for you, and feed

on him in your heart by faith, with thanksgiving." And
in giving the grape juice, he concludes, "Drink this in remembrance that Christ died for you, and be thankful." [44]

The closing prayers are an orthodox paraphrase of the
Hanc Igitur and *Agnus Dei* of the Latin Mass, and a short
doxology taken verbally from the *Gloria* of the Roman
Missal. Most of these prayers, which last about ten minutes, are recited aloud by the congregation, led by the presiding minister.

The Administration of Baptism. The only other sacrament admitted by the Methodists is baptism, in which
"every adult person, and the parents of every child to be
baptized, have the choice of sprinkling, pouring or immersion." [45] Three rituals are provided for the administration
of the sacrament, one each for infants, youths, and mature
adults. The sequence in each is an explanation of the
meaning of the rite, a prayer to God, an exhortation and
questions addressed to the sponsors or candidates for baptism, a passage from the Gospels and the actual conferring
of the sacrament. The words of administration are the
same in all three cases, namely: "N., I baptize thee in the
name of the Father, and of the Son, and of the Holy Spirit.
Amen." [46]

There is a significant difference in the questions asked
of sponsors presenting an infant and a youth or adult presenting himself to be baptized. In the infant ritual, there
is no reference to sin infecting the soul. Only one question
is put to the sponsors, whether they solemnly promise to
see that the child is brought up a Christian. Whereas in
adult baptism, there is explicit reference to sin and sorrow, when the candidate is asked: "Will you faithfully put
away from you every known sin, of thought, word or deed,
and accept and confess Jesus Christ as your Saviour and
Lord?" The answer is: "God helping me, I will." [47] Nevertheless even in the baptismal rite for youths and adults,
the context shows that the sin factor pertains only to actu-

ally committed faults, since there is no suggestion of inherited sin being deleted in the sacrament.

Minister of the Sacraments. The Methodist *Discipline*
distinguishes four grades in the ministry of the church,
one lay and three clerical. To the lay ministry belong the
preachers, who may be either local (stable) or traveling
(itinerant). To the clerical belong deacons, elders, and
bishops, who are specially ordained to their office.

All the above classes of persons, even lay preachers
with a permanent pastorate who have never been ordained,
are permitted to administer the sacraments of baptism
and Holy Communion. Here is a flagrant conflict between
ritual and practice. On the one hand, the ritual of the
Lord's Supper uses the words of institution and prescribes
the "Prayer of Consecration." What before the prayer was
referred to as bread and unfermented grape juice, after it
is called "Holy Communion," which is to be received by
the people "while they are devoutly kneeling." Also in the
rite of ordination of elders, when the bishop imposes
hands on the ordinand, he says, "Be thou a faithful dispenser of the Word of God and of his holy Sacraments,"
whereas in ordaining deacons he explains that, "It apper-
tains to the office of a deacon . . . to assist the elder when
he ministereth the Holy Communion." [48] Thus a clear
distinction is set up between the order of elder and deacon,
the latter being ordained only to help in the ministration
of Communion, while the former is ordained specifically
to dispense the Sacred Mysteries. But in practice no distinction is made between deacon or elder, cleric or layman, in conducting the full ritual of the Lord's Supper,
which requires a formal "consecration" of the elements.

LIBERTY OF DOCTRINE AND PRACTICE

To the casual reader of the *Doctrines and Discipline
of the Methodist Church* it would seem that Methodism
represents a body of stable principles to which the mem-

bers of Wesley's society are expected to conform. Actually
this is not the case.

Some indication of the freedom permitted Methodists
is already found in the *Discipline* itself, for example,
where no distinction is made in the invitation to receive
the Lord's Supper. The elder says:

> Ye that do truly and earnestly repent of your sins,
> and are in love and charity with your neighbors, and
> intend to lead a new life, following the commandments
> of God, and walking henceforth in his holy ways; draw
> near with faith, and take this holy Sacrament to your
> comfort.[49]

Commenting on this invitation, one of their bishops
explains that, "Any follower of Christ is invited to commune with us." And "the Methodist Church admits to the
Sacrament of the Lord's Supper all followers of Christ who
desire to partake with us of the symbols of the body and
blood of our Lord and Saviour Jesus Christ." [50] No doubt
this "open Communion" is practiced because the Methodist sacrament does not pretend to contain the reality
but only the symbol of Christ's body and blood.

Another bishop thus summarizes the tolerance of the
Methodist Church, whose "doctrines are broad and are
based on Scripture," covering every kind of religious faith
and practice:

> Methodism teaches that ordination by any estab-
> lished evangelical Church is valid. A letter from any
> Christian Church may be accepted as the only condi-
> tion of membership. Moreover it has been our historic
> custom with other Churches in evangelism, missions,
> education . . . and the promotion of various move-
> ments for the extension of the Kingdom. Any follower
> of Christ is invited to commune with us. Any minister

in good standing may be invited to our pulpits. We lay no claim to exclusiveness in doctrines, rites or authority. We request only a place of fellowship and service in the ranks of those who love our Lord Jesus Christ in sincerity.[51]

The apology for this absence of principle in the Methodist creed is an appeal to the words of John Wesley that, "The distinguishing marks of a Methodist are not his opinions of any sort. His assenting to this or that scheme of religion, his embracing any particular set of notions . . . are all quite wide of the mark. Whosoever imagines that a Methodist is a man of such or such an opinion is grossly ignorant of the whole affair." [52] The proud boast of his church, therefore, is that it "recognizes the Christians of other Churches and the Churches of other Christians" without discrimination.[53]

ORGANIZATION AND GOVERNMENT

The government of the Methodist Church is highly organized. Centering around the Conference, the duties and functions of Methodist officials form an integrated unit which is an elaboration of the norms set down by John Wesley and which historians of Protestantism regard as "unsurpassed for the accomplishment of the spiritual mission of the Church." [54] The same organizational structure is duplicated, on a minor scale, by the smaller Methodist sects.

Conferences. There are six types of Methodist Conferences, hierarchically stratified from the General Conference on a global level to the Church Conference in the local congregation.

The General Conference, which meets every four years, is "the legislative body for the entire church . . . having full legislative powers over all connectional matters." [55]

It has authority to enact laws which define the powers, duties and privileges of the bishops; to decide on the content and form of the Hymnal and Ritual; to initiate and direct church publications, evangelization and the missions, social and charitable enterprises; to direct and decide the Church's judicial administration.[56] Lesser Conferences are ultimately responsible to the General Conference for all matters of common interest to the whole denomination. Delegates to the General Conference are elected by the Annual Conferences. One half the delegates are ordained ministers and one half lay members, the total not to exceed 800 or be less than 600. The Judicial Council, elected by the General Conference, is the final court of appeal in the Methodist Church. Indicative of its detailed operation, a decision handed down in 1953 declared that when a candidate for the traveling ministry is asked about his abstinence from tobacco, he must answer "in the affirmative and without qualification." [57]

The Jurisdictional Conference is "the representative body in the United States, established by the Plan of Union (1939), composed of ministerial and lay delegates (50-50) from the several Annual Conferences of a jurisdiction and meeting every four years." [58] There are six jurisdictions in the country; all are geographically distinct, with the exception of the Central, or Negro Conference, which overlaps the others. Election of bishops is the Jurisdictional Conference's most important function.

The Annual Conference is "the basic administrative body in the Methodist Church, having supervision over the affairs of the Church in a specific territory." [59] Technically the territories so administered are also called Annual Conferences, most of which correspond to the individual States. Three fundamental items referred to the Annual Conference are: Constitutional Amendments, Election of Delegates to the General and Jurisdictional Conferences, and matters relating to the Character and Function of the

Clergy. Reading of official appointments at the close of the Annual Conference is one of the most spectacular events in Methodist procedure.

The District Conference is "an assembly held annually in each district where authorized by the Annual Conference." [60] Its duties include inquiry into the spiritual state of the church, promotion of mission work in the district, support of churches and colleges, hospitals and publications, and examination of candidates for the Methodist ministry.

The Quarterly Conference is "the governing body of the pastoral charge." [61] It unites the parish with the larger sphere of Methodist activity, and is composed of the preachers, lay leaders, and other representatives of the local churches. Although the Conference may convene four times a year, only two annual meetings are obligatory. Among the duties it may handle, the most important is to act as a "sounding-board" for the people, to determine whether a given pastor is satisfactory to his congregation. If not, the Conference is authorized to inform the minister, call for adaptation to the people's wants and, if necessary, urge the pastor's removal.

The Church Conference is "an assembly of the members of a charge or church for review and planning of the church's work and, when so authorized by the Quarterly Conference, for election of church officers." [62] Its immediate purpose is to cooperate with the pastor in carrying out the duties of his office and to extend the influence of the local church into the whole community.

Church Ministers and Officials. Highest in rank is the bishop, who is a general superintendent within his territory. He is an elder, specially ordained, and generally holding office for life. Although nominally an executive, his duties are severely limited by the democratic structure of the Methodist Church, in which the Conferences play the major role. One large power he enjoys, however, is to ap-

point pastors and other ministers of the gospel, after consultation with the district superintendents. To him also
belongs the consecration of bishops and the ordination of
elders, deacons and deaconesses. Since 1939, when the nonepiscopal Methodist Protestant Church was absorbed into
membership, the episcopacy in the Methodist Church has
become more than ever unessential. Except for the right
of appointment, which also may be challenged, "the
bishop's power and real influence . . . is largely a matter
of his personality and abilities. These lie in the direction
of his presidencies over conferences, directing business,
and maintaining accord among the members. He serves
on many boards of the church, sometimes as the presiding
officer, mostly as just a member. Often he is of much value
as Exhibit A in dedications and conventions." [63]

Next in ministerial rank is the elder who has been
"duly ordained by the laying on of the hands of a bishop
and other elders." Below the elder is the deacon, who is
also ordained by the bishop. A deaconess is "a woman who
has been led by the Holy Spirit to devote herself to Christlike service under the direction of the Church, and who,
having met the requirements prescribed by the Joint Committee on Missionary Personnel, including a period of not
less than one year of probation, has been duly licensed,
consecrated, and commissioned by a bishop." [64] As provided by the *Discipline,* deaconesses may engage in any of
the social, educational, and missionary activities proper to
the Methodist Church, in America or overseas. They receive a fixed salary, are given periodical leave of absence
or sabbatical leave, and provision is made for their financial security after retirement from active service. Of the
1,500 deaconesses in the United States in 1950, the largest
number, 800, was listed as belonging to the Methodist
Church.

Peculiar to the Methodist Church is the importance of
the laity in the religious ministry. A person may be li-

censed to serve as pastor of a charge (church) even though he is not ordained as elder or deacon. If he is properly licensed, he is technically a minister or preacher, and entitled to the full exercise of the Methodist ministry. Lay trustees manage the property interests of the local congregation; while lay stewards handle the finances and generally guide the spiritual work of the parish under the pastor's direction. The 1956 General Conference legislated the admission of women to the full exercise of the ministry, not only locally, as before, but even to serve as "itinerant preachers" and to participate in the General Conference of the Methodist Church.

STATISTICS

Methodist World Membership (1952)	13,391,034
Methodists in the United States (22 Bodies)	11,688,002
The Methodist Church (U.S.A.)	
Inclusive Membership	9,202,728
Churches	39,801
Ordained Clergy (1955)	26,165
Pastors having Churches (1955)	23,286
Bishops, Active in the U.S. (1955)	37
Universities and Colleges (1953)	98
Hospitals (1953)	71
Homes for Aged (1953)	64
Homes for Children (1953)	41
Countries where Missions Established (1953)	36
Missionaries Serving Overseas (1953)	1,500
Periodicals Published	32

REFERENCES

1. William K. Anderson, editor, *Methodism,* Nashville, The Methodist Publishing House, 1947, p. 5.
2. William W. Sweet, *Methodism in American History,* New York-Nashville, Abingdon-Cokesbury, 1933, p. 34.
3. William W. Sweet, "Methodism's Debt to the Church of England," *Methodism,* p. 50.
4. *Loc. cit.*
5. Sweet, *Methodism in American History,* p. 107.
6. *Ibid.,* p. 105.
7. *Ibid.,* p. 103.

178]

8. *Ibid.*, p. 337.
9. *Ibid.*, p. 338.
10. *Doctrine and Discipline of the Methodist Church*, Nashville, The Methodist Publishing House, 1952, p. 8.
11. *Ibid.*, pp. 25-26.
12. *Ibid.*, p. 26.
13. Charles C. Selecman, *The Methodist Primer*, Nashville, Tidings, 1953, p. 31.
14. *Discipline*, p. 26.
15. *Loc. cit.*
16. *Ibid.*, p. 27.
17. *Loc. cit.*
18. *Ibid.*, p. 28.
19. Nels F. S. Ferre, "God Can Be Experienced," *Methodism*, pp. 123-124.
20. *Ibid.*, p. 124.
21. Robert E. Cushman, "Salvation for All," *Methodism*, p. 112.
22. *Discipline*, p. 37.
23. *Ibid.*, p. 28.
24. *Ibid.*, p. 37.
25. *Ibid.*, p. 31.
26. *The Book of Common Prayer*, New York, Oxford University Press, 1935, p. 610.
27. *Discipline*, p. 29.
28. *Loc. cit.*
29. *Ibid.*, p. 30.
30. *The Book of Common Prayer*, p. 605.
31. *Discipline*, p. 28.
32. *Ibid.*, p. 30.
33. *Ibid.*, p. 120.
34. *Ibid.*, pp. 652-653.
35. Walter G. Muelder, "Methodism's Contribution to Social Reform," *Methodism*, p. 194.
36. *Discipline*, p. 639.
37. *Ibid.*, p. 385.
38. *Methodism in American History*, p. 389.
39. *Discipline*, p. 494.
40. *Ibid.*, pp. 497-498.
41. *Ibid.*, p. 502.
42. *Loc. cit.*
43. *Ibid.*, pp. 511-512.
44. *Ibid.*, p. 512.
45. *Ibid.*, p. 519.
46. *Ibid.*, pp. 521, 523, 526.
47. *Ibid.*, p. 523.
48. *Ibid.*, pp. 560, 553.
49. *Ibid.*, p. 515.
50. Selecman, *op. cit.*, pp. 36, 38.
51. *Ibid.*, p. 36.
52. Umphrey Lee, "Freedom from Rigid Creed," *Methodism*, p. 128.
53. Selecman, *op. cit.*, p. 5.
54. *Ibid.*, p. 41.
55. *Discipline*, p. 666.
56. In its most recent session (1956), the General Conference officially sanctioned artificial contraception as conformable to the Sacred Scriptures.
57. *General Minutes of the Annual Conferences of the Methodist Church, 1954*, Chicago, Council on World Service and Finance, 1954, p. 652.
58. *Discipline*, pp. 666-667.
59. *Ibid.*, p. 666.
60. *Loc. cit.*
61. *Ibid.*, p. 667.
62. *Ibid.*, p. 666.
63. James H. Straughn, "The Episcopacy," *Methodism*, p. 255.
64. *Discipline*, p. 667.

9. Mormons

MORMONS DENY they are Protestants because their founder belonged to no other sect and admitted no succession from another church society. The fact is that Mormonism is derived from the Reformation principle of religious freedom carried to the extreme of not only appealing to the inner voice of God for private interpretation of the Bible, but elucubrating a whole body of new revelation alien to the Scriptures of traditional Christianity.

As popularly conceived, Mormonism is identified with a peculiar group which at one time practiced polygamy, and still exists as a small sectarian body, but otherwise has no particular significance among the non-Catholic churches in America. This conception needs to be revised. The Church of the Latter-Day Saints, for which "Mormons" is only a nickname, is one of the largest and certainly the most closely-knit of ecclesiastical bodies in the United States. Its origin and history offer a modern study in religious psychology for which there is no counterpart in the western world; its insistence on plural marriage as divinely ordained and the conflicts this provoked, play an important role in the constitutional development of the country, especially in the currently active question of church and state authority; its phenomenal growth from one hundred thousand in 1890 to over a million in 1950, and above all its missionary zeal in every part of the world suggest the importance of the Mormon Church, even when its doctrinal system is so singular it seems well-nigh incomprehensible.[1]

HISTORY

The founder of Mormonism was Joseph Smith, a farmer's son, born at Sharon, Vermont, December 23, 1805. His family moved to Lebanon, New Hampshire, in 1811, to Palmyra, New York, in 1815, and four years later to the small town of Manchester, Ontario County, New York. Since it has a direct bearing on the origins of Mormonism, the following judgment on the Smith family should be quoted from a public statement by 62 contemporary residents of Palmyra. "We, the undersigned," they stated, "have been acquainted with the Smith family for a number of years. . . . They were particularly famous for visionary projects; spent much of their time digging for money which they pretended was hid in the earth. . . . Joseph Smith, Sr., and his son, Joseph, were, in particular, considered entirely destitute of moral character, and addicted to vicious habits."[2] Before Smith, Jr., was favored with the "revelations" for which he later became famous, he developed the habit of crystal-gazing, using an opaque stone to discover, for a fee, the location of stolen property and of buried treasure.

The first of a series of divine communications to Joseph Smith is supposed to have occurred at Manchester (near Palmyra) in 1820. He was praying for light to recognize the true church: Baptist, Methodist or Presbyterian. "I saw two personages," he later wrote, "whose brightness and glory defy all description, standing above me in the air. One of them spake unto me, calling me by name, and said, pointing to the other—This is my beloved Son, hear

Him." Then "I asked the personages who stood above me in the light, which of all the sects was right—and which I should join. I was answered that I must join none of them, for they were all wrong." [3]

Three years later occurred another revelation, regarded as the "celestial beginnings" of the Mormon faith. While in prayer on the night of September 21, 1823, a person clothed in white appeared to Smith, said he was sent from God and identified himself as Moroni. The messenger told Smith that his name "should be for good and evil among all nations," and explained how he must go about establishing a new religion. In Smith's words:

> He said there was a book deposited, written upon gold plates, giving an account of the former inhabitants of this continent, and the source from whence they sprang. He also said that the fulness of the everlasting Gospel was contained in it, as delivered by the Savior to the ancient inhabitants; also that there were two stones in silver bows—and these stones, fastened to a breastplate, constituted what is called the Urim and Thummim—deposited with the plates; and the possession and use of these stones were what constituted seers in ancient or former times; and that God had prepared them for the purpose of translating the book. [4]

After three more revelations, Smith finally went to the place designated by Moroni (Hill Cumorah), found the plates, the Urim and Thummim, and the breastplate. The plates were engraved in an unknown language, but with the help of the "spectacles," *i.e.*, the Urim and Thummim, he was able to translate the inscriptions into English. Smith later claimed that a linguistic scholar, Anthon, had certified that the characters of the unknown language were Egyptian, Chaldaic, Assyriac and Arabic. On hearing this, Anthon issued a statement denying any such certification and branded the supposed hieroglyphs as "a hoax (and) a singular scrawl." [5]

It is commonly agreed that Smith himself was incapable of producing what is now the Mormon Bible, which grew out of the Moroni revelations. In this he was assisted by a Baptist revivalist, Sidney Rigdon, who was well educated, intelligent, and bent on starting a new religion in opposition to Alexander Campbell, whose success in founding the Disciples of Christ he envied. There is ample evidence that the idea was not even original with Rigdon, but was borrowed in its historical portion from a manuscript by Solomon Spaulding, minister-archeologist of Conneaut, Ohio.[6] While disclaiming assistance from Rigdon or Spaulding, Smith admitted that at least "people besides himself had seen the golden plates" containing the heavenly message. Eventually three of the main witnesses defected from Mormonism and disclaimed their former testimony; the character of the other witnesses neutralized their veracity. In a sworn affidavit, the metal plates were identified as "gotten up" by a blacksmith and some friends, being "cut out of some pieces of copper," properly etched with nitric acid, and covered with a rusting mixture to give the appearance of antiquity.[7]

The subsequent history of the sect is a sequence of new revelations vouchsafed to Smith. He was directed to relate these revelations to the people, and his disciples following him in a strange odyssey that ended in tragedy for the prophet. On April 6, 1830, at Fayette, New York, the sect was formally organized as the Church of Jesus Christ of the Latter-Day Saints. Hostility to Mormon doctrines occasioned a revelation (1831) which told Smith that Kirtland, Ohio, was to be Zion, or the New Jerusalem, where Christ would reign after His return to the world. When trouble arose over worthless notes that Smith issued in a bank he had established, he had another revelation bidding him and Rigdon flee from Kirtland (1837) and found the new Zion in Jackson County, Missouri. Within two years, the Missourians declared war on the Latter-Day Saints, which induced a revelation telling Smith to lead his people into Illinois, where, on the banks of the Mississippi, they founded the city of Nauvoo, said to be the Hebrew for "beautiful place." The practice of polygamy, however, first led to a schism in the ranks, and then provoked an armed uprising by non-Mormons, who determined to seize "the prophet and his miscreant adherents . . . and if not surrendered, a war of extermination should be waged." [8] The result was that Smith and his brother, Hyrum, were arrested and kept in jail at Cairo, awaiting trial. But the mob wanted no trial, broke into prison, and on June 27, 1844, shot and killed the two brothers.

After the death of Smith, the Mormons split into several factions which have not been re-united to the present day. The largest segment, known as the Church of Jesus Christ of Latter-Day Saints, was led by Brigham Young to Utah, where they founded Salt Lake City in 1847. Through thirty years of uncompromising despotism, Young developed the Mormons of Utah and Idaho into a well-organized, self-sustaining religious body which grew to over one million members in 1955. At their centennial celebration in 1947, it was reported that 51,622 missionaries had been sent into the field, at their personal expense, most of them serving a full two years. About 9,000 missionaries are currently maintained in the States and at mission stations in thirty countries. The Church conducts four senior and three junior colleges in Utah, which has the highest percentage of college students of any State. A very low death rate is attributed to the practice of "Mormon abstinence" combined with an elaborate system of public welfare. Over 100 storehouses for community food and clothing are maintained by the Church.

A smaller group of Mormons protested Brigham Young's assumption of authority, claiming that Joseph Smith's son had sole title to leadership. Young was also charged, inaccurately, with having been the first to sanction polygamy. Led by Joseph Smith III, the Reorganized Church of Jesus Christ of Latter-Day Saints settled at Independence, Missouri, where the "gathering of Zion" is expected to take place before the second coming of Christ. Present membership is about 150,000, with mission stations in Australia, New Zealand and Hawaii.

Four other splinter groups, with a current total membership of less than 5,000, were organized in protest against either Brigham Young or Joseph Smith's son. Their significance in Mormon history is negligible.

DOCTRINE AND RITUAL

There are three principal sources from which Mormons derive their teachings and practices: the *Book of Mormon,* discovered by Joseph Smith; the *Pearl of Great Price,* which contains Smith's translations from the Bible, the Book of Moses and the Book of Abraham; and the *Doctrine and Covenants,* which covers the private revelations of Joseph Smith.

According to Article 8 of the Mormon Creed, "We believe the Bible to be the word of God, as far as it has been translated correctly; we also believe the Book of Mormon to be the word of God." [9] Like the Scriptures, the Mormon Bible is divided into books, chapters and verses. There are four books of Nephi, two of Mormon, and one each of Jacob, Enos, Jarom, Omni, Mosiah, Alma, Helaman, Ether and Moroni. In a modern edition, the total runs to 522 pages in duodecimo, covering perhaps 200 chapters, divided into verses, and cited like the Bible, *e.g.,* II Nephi 31:17. The Book of Mormon purports to be a record of events that took place from 600 B.C. to 421 A.D., telling the history of two nations: the Jaredites, who came to America after the confusion of tongues at Babel, and the Nephites, who migrated to America from Jerusalem about 600 B.C. The Nephites, in turn, died out at the beginning of the fifth century of the Christian era, but not before their best historian, Moroni (son of Mormon), wrote the annals of his people and hid them, along with a record of the Jaredites, "to be brought forth in the latter days, as predicted by the voice of God through his ancient prophets." It was this double record which Joseph Smith discovered in 1827, and translated from the golden plates, delivered to him by the "same Moroni, then a resurrected personage." [10]

Perhaps the most important doctrinal content of the Book of Mormon is the claim that after His Ascension Christ personally established a nascent Church among the Nephites in America; that after the passing of the Nephites a race of believers would arise as the Latter-Day Saints, blessed with the gift of revelation and prophecy and inaugurating an age of unparalleled prosperity among all nations. Underlying this mission of the Saints is the conviction that God did not intend fully to establish the true Church in Palestine at the time of Christ, but in America at the present day. All preceding events, *e.g.,* the revival of learning, the Protestant Reformation, the discovery of a new world, the landing of the Pilgrims, American independence, were a prologue to the destiny set in store for the American nation, of which the Mormons are divinely chosen prophets.

In the *Pearl of Great Price,* the Book of Moses is an interpolation between Genesis 5:21 and 23, and contains some alleged visions of Moses. Among these are revela-

tions that the devil organized the Freemasons to mislead
the human race. Later on the Mormons changed in their
opposition to Masonry, so that now some writers consider
their cultus and ritual to be modeled after that of the
Masonic Order. The Book of Abraham openly supports
the practice of plural marriage.

The private revelations of Joseph Smith, called *Doctrine and Covenants,* are the principal source of faith and
practice in present-day Mormonism. They also provide a
theoretical basis for the Church's absolute authority by
means of continued divine communications to its spiritual leaders. Believers are told that, "In view of the demonstrated facts that revelation between God and man has
ever been and is a characteristic of the Church of Jesus
Christ, it is reasonable to await with confident expectation
the coming of other messages from heaven, even until the
end of man's probation on earth." [11]

Although faith is professed in the Trinity, the Mormon concept of God is grossly materialistic. "We affirm,"
they say, "that to deny the materiality of God's person is
to deny God; for a thing without parts has no whole, and
an immaterial body cannot exist. The Church of Jesus
Christ of Latter-Day Saints proclaims against the incomprehensible God, devoid of 'body, parts, or passions.' " [12]

Mormons believe in universal salvation, allowing for
three kinds of resurrection from the dead: celestial glory,
resplendent like the sun, for those who lived perfect lives;
terrestrial, like the moon, for those who were somewhat
unfaithful; and telestial glory, comparable to the stars, for
all who did not receive Christ but were faithful to the
Holy Ghost. The wicked will be punished, but not forever. Hell is said to be eternal only in the sense that it
will last as long as there is sin to punish.

Man is defined as a union of pre-existent spirit and an
earthly body. "This union of spirit and body makes prog-

ress from the unembodied to the embodied condition, and is an inestimable advancement in the soul's onward course." [13] In line with this pre-eminence of body over spirit, "marriage is a requirement to all who are not prevented by physical or other disability from assuming the sacred responsibilities of the wedded state." [14] Through marriage, pre-existent souls are given a chance to enter the advanced state of "embodiment" that might otherwise be denied them. Mormons further distinguish between temporal and celestial marriages; the former open to everyone, the latter "permitted to those members of the Church only who are adjudged worthy." [15] Celestial marriages are performed with special, secret functions, and the offspring "are natural heirs to the Priesthood." [16]

While claiming that baptism is necessary for salvation, Mormons oppose infant baptism on the grounds of a special revelation from Moroni. "Little children," Smith was told, "are alive in Christ, even from the foundation of the world; if not so, God is a partial God, and also a changeable God, and a respecter of persons; for how many little children have died without Baptism." [17]

In a reported vision of 1830, the mode of baptism was revealed as including immersion in water and the Trinitarian formula, in which the minister says, "Having been commissioned of Jesus Christ, I baptize you in the name of the Father, and of the Son, and of the Holy Ghost, Amen." [18] As a correlative to the necessity of baptism for salvation, Mormons teach that if a person died without this rite, he may and should be baptized by proxy after death, since, "Nowhere in scripture is a distinction made in this regard between the living and the dead." [19] A living relative or friend goes through the immersion ritual in place of the deceased, with no difference in baptismal effect.

The most important ritual function of the Mormons

is the administration of the Lord's Supper, whose purpose is "to commemorate the atonement of the Lord Jesus." Participation in the communion worship is "a means of renewing our avowals before the Lord, of acknowledgment of mutual fellowship among the members, and of solemnly witnessing our claim and profession of membership in the Church of Jesus Christ." [20] A revelation to Joseph Smith commanded him, "You shall not purchase wine nor strong drink." In obedience to this authority, "the Latter-Day Saints administer water in their sacramental service, in preference to wine." [21]

For administration of the Lord's Supper, the Aaronic priesthood is required, and as a matter of policy anyone "in a higher degree" has the right to officiate at the service. The ritual words are practically the same for "consecrating the emblems" of bread and water separately. While kneeling, the elder or priest calls upon God the Father and says:

> O God, the Eternal Father, we ask thee in the name of thy Son, Jesus Christ, to bless and sanctify this bread (water) to the souls of all those who partake (drink) of it, that they may eat (do it) in remembrance of the body (blood) of thy Son, and witness unto thee, O God, the Eternal Father, that they are willing to take upon them the name of thy Son, and always remember him and keep his commandments which he has given them; that they may always have his Spirit to be with them. Amen.[22]

The real presence is denied explicitly, being called "the Great Apostasy," or the teaching that "the sacramental emblems by the ceremony of consecration lost their natural character of simply bread and wine, and became in reality flesh and blood—actually parts of the crucified body of Christ." No evidence to support the Mormon position is offered, since "argument against such dogmas is unnecessary." [23]

POLYGAMY

Plural marriage was advocated by Joseph Smith on the strength of a special revelation, in which the Lord is made to say:

> If any man espouse a virgin, and desire to espouse another, and the first give her consent; and if he espouse the second, and they are virgins, and have vowed to no other man, then is he justified; he cannot commit adultery, for they are given unto him; for he cannot commit adultery with that which belongeth unto him and to no one else.
>
> And if he have ten virgins given unto him by this law, he cannot commit adultery, for they belong to him, and they are given unto him, therefore is he justified.
>
> But if one or either of the ten virgins, after she is espoused, shall be with another man; she has committed adultery, and shall be destroyed; for they are given unto him to multiply and replenish the earth, according to my commandment.[24]

Accepted as an article of faith, polygamy became the main source of trouble for the Mormons, not only during Smith's lifetime but after the settlement in Utah. As early as 1860, a bill was introduced in the House of Representatives in Washington "to punish and prevent the practice of polygamy in the Territories of the United States." [25] Though finally passed by the House and Senate and signed by President Lincoln in 1862, the legislation was inoperative. A stronger bill failed to pass the Senate in 1869 because is was assumed impossible to convict polygamists with any juries drawn up in Utah.

In 1878 a mass meeting of women of Salt Lake City sent a petition to Congress to suppress polygamous marriages which the Mormons were contracting in so-called Endowment Houses, where people were "sealed (married) and bound by oaths so strong that even apostates will not

reveal them." [26] The next year, in his inaugural address,
President Garfield declared that, "The Mormon Church
not only offends the moral sense of mankind by sanction-
ing polygamy, but prevents the administration of justice
through ordinary instrumentalities of law." [27] President
Arthur, in his message in 1881, spoke of "this odious crime,
so revolting to the moral and religious sense of Christendom," and recommended legislation to secure convictions
in the Utah territory. [28] Inspired by these recommendations, the Edmunds Law was passed in 1882—"the first real
serious blow struck by Congress against polygamy." [29] Essentially it disfranchised any person who practiced plural
marriage. In 1890, when the U. S. Supreme Court upheld
the constitutionality of the anti-polygamy legislation, the
Mormons finally yielded to circumstances and amended
the doctrine of their Church.

This important step was not taken in the form of a new
revelation, but simply as a proclamation. There was first a
statement from the Mormon President, Wilford Woodruff:

> Inasmuch as laws have been enacted by Congress,
> which laws have been pronounced constitutional by
> the court of last resort, I hereby declare my intention
> to submit to these laws, and to use my influence with
> the members of the church over which I preside to
> have them do likewise.
>
> And now I publicly declare that my advice to the
> Latter-Day Saints is to refrain from contracting any
> marriage forbidden by the law of the land. [30]

Shortly after, the General Council of the Latter-Day
Saints unanimously voted to accept President Woodruff's
recommendation, declaring, "as a church in general conference assembled we accept his declaration concerning
plural marriages as authoritative and binding." [31] The
date of acceptance was October 6, 1890. Six years later the

State of Utah was admitted to the Union, but not before Congress had passed an act allowing Utah's admittance, "provided that polygamous or plural marriages are forever prohibited" within its territory." [32]

As regards Mormon polygamy at the present time, two distinctions should be made. The Church, in its largest segment, juridically disavowed the practice only under pressure from political forces. So far from denying, it reaffirms the claim that polygamy is divinely revealed, but its practice must be held in abeyance. Under "submission to secular authority," an official Mormon publication gives as "an illustration of . . . suspension of divine law . . . the action of the Church regarding the matter of plural marriage. This practice was established as a result of direct revelation." But when "Federal statutes were framed declaring the practice unlawful . . . the Church, through its President thereupon discontinued the practice . . . solemnly placing the responsibility for the change upon the nation by whose laws the renunciation had been forced." [33] Moreover, fundamentalists among the Mormons even now practice polygamy and defend their right to plural marriage against civil authority. As late as 1953, state officials in Arizona "raided" a polygamous Mormon colony of some 400 persons, separating the men and their wives and instituting court proceedings against the offenders.[34]

PRIESTHOOD AND GOVERNMENT

Priesthood and jurisdiction are intimately connected in Mormonism. Two types of priesthood are recognized, the lesser, called Aaronic, bestowed on Smith by John the Baptist, and the greater, known as the Melchizedek Order, given to Smith at the bidding of Peter, James and John.

The special functions of the priesthood of Melchizedek "lie in the administration of spiritual things, comprising the keys of all spiritual blessings of the Church, the right

'to have the heavens opened unto them . . . to commune
with the general assembly and Church of the Firstborn,
and to enjoy the communion and presence of God the
Father, and Jesus the mediator of the new covenant." [35] Its
officers include twelve apostles, a number of patriarchs or
evangelists, high priests "ordained with power to officiate"
but primarily administrative, seventies who are traveling
preachers "ordained to promulgate the Gospel among the
nations of the earth," and elders ordained to perform the
lower callings of the priesthood, including the power to
ordain other elders, to baptize, confirm and conduct meetings, "as they are led by the Holy Ghost."

To the Aaronic priesthood are committed the temporal
duties of the Church, operating through ministers who are
"appointed to preach, to teach, expound the scriptures, to
administer the sacrament, to visit the homes of the members." [36] They may ordain deacons, teachers and other
priests. Next in dignity are teachers, or local officers,
"whose function it is to mingle with the saints . . . They
are to see that there is no iniquity in the Church," and are
allowed to preach when directed to do so, but may not
officiate at baptism, the Lord's Supper or the laying on of
hands. Finally, to the deacons, as the lowest office in the
Aaronic priesthood, pertains the duty of caring for "the
houses of worship, the comfort of the worshipers, and
ministration to the members of the Church as the bishop
may direct." [37]

Mormon ecclesiastical structure is rigidly hierarchical.
At the head stands the First Presidency, made up of three
high priests, a president and two counselors. Its authority
is absolute and universal, binding in matters spiritual as
well as temporal. Below the Presidency is the Council of
Twelve Apostles, which supervises the lesser patriarchs.
Parallel with the Apostles is the Presiding Quorum of
Seventy, whose unanimous decisions have the same author-

ity as the Council of the Apostles. On the territorial level, working within the framework of the Church, are all the other officials. Their jurisdiction is based on geographical divisions, called stakes and wards. Heading each ward is a bishop, along with two high priests as his counselors. Being of the lower priesthood, the ward bishop has no direct authority over members of the Order of Melchizedek who are working within his territory. But subject to him are the priests, teachers, deacons and auxiliary church organizations like relief societies and mutual improvement associations.

Mormons make a great deal of what they call "practical religion," which involves the church's dictation in the lives of its members down to the smallest details. In compliance with the law of tithing, "a man should make out and lay before the Bishop a schedule of all his property and pay him one-tenth of it. . . . The next year he must pay one-tenth of the increase, and one-tenth of his time, of his cattle, money, goods and trade." [38] In matters of food, the believer is forbidden to drink "wine or strong drink"; also "tobacco is not good for men," and "hot drinks (tea and coffee) are not good for the body." While permitted to eat "the flesh of beasts and of the fouls of the air," they are to be used sparingly, and "only in time of winter, or of cold, or famine." [39] Yet with all these restrictions, the faithful Mormon professes to cherish nothing more than freedom, believing that "the right of choice is essential to salvation, and that anyone who seeks to enslave men in any sense is essentially in league with Satan himself." [40]

Current figures for the total number of ordained persons are not available and not listed in the *Yearbook of American Churches*. But in 1945, the Church of the Latter-Day Saints reported there were 149 stakes of Zion and 1,150 wards. These were ministered by 89,106 men and boys (from the age of 12) ordained to the Aaronic priesthood, besides 15,547 working in the missions. The higher priesthood of Melchizedek had 112,850 ordained men, with another 9,370 out in the mission field. Through these messengers, "the proclamation of the Gospel had been made in nearly all parts of the earth," predicting the three remaining stages in the history of the world: "the great Millenium" of prosperity, when "Satan shall be bound," followed by an interval when the devil "shall reign for a little season," and finally "cometh the end of the earth." [41]

STATISTICS

Church of the Latter-Day Saints, U.S.A.
        (Six Sects) (1956 data)

Total Membership	1,319,155
Churches	3,451
Periodicals	12
Sunday School Enrollment	1,104,387

REFERENCES

1. F. E. Mayer, *The Religious Bodies of America* (St. Louis: Concordia, 1954), p. 447.
2. William A. Linn, *The Story of the Mormons* (New York: Macmillan, 1923), p. 13.
3. Joseph F. Smith, *Essentials in Church History* (Salt Lake City: Deseret News Press, 1950), pp. 42-44.
4. *Ibid.*, pp. 51-52.
5. Linn, *op. cit.*, p. 39.
6. Two of the best witnesses for the influence of the Spaulding MS on the Mormon Bible are Spaulding's brother, John, and a close friend, Joseph Miller. Describing his brother's MS, John said, "It was an historical romance of the first settlers of America, endeavoring to show that the American Indians are the descendants of the Jews, or the lost tribe. It gave a detailed account of their journey from Jerusalem, by land and sea, till they arrived in America, under the command of Nephi and Lehi . . . I have recently read the 'Book of Mormon,' . . . and according to the best of my recollection and belief, it is the same as my brother Solomon wrote, with the exception of the religious matter." According to Miller, "I am convinced that Spaulding's manuscript was appropriated and largely used in getting up the 'Book of Mormon.'" *Ibid.*, pp. 53-55.
7. *Ibid.*, p. 87.
8. *Ibid.*, p. 297.
9. James E. Talmage, *Articles of*

Faith (Salt Lake City: Church of Jesus Christ of Latter-Day Saints, 1952), p. 2.

10. *The Book of Mormon* (Salt Lake City: Church of Jesus Christ of Latter-Day Saints, 1921), Introduction, p. i.
11. Talmage, *op. cit.,* p. 311.
12. *Ibid.,* p. 48.
13. *Ibid.,* p. 475.
14. *Ibid.,* p. 443.
15. *Ibid.,* p. 445.
16. *Ibid.,* p. 446.
17. *Book of Mormon,* p. 516.
18. *The Doctrine and Covenants* (Salt Lake City: Church of Jesus Christ of Latter-Day Saints, 1926), chap. 20, vv. 72-74.
19. Talmage, *op. cit.,* p. 145.
20. *Ibid.,* p. 175.
21. *Ibid.,* p. 176.
22. *Ibid.,* pp. 176-177.
23. *Ibid.,* p. 490.
24. Linn, *op. cit.,* pp. 284-285.
25. *Ibid.,* p. 590.
26. *Ibid.,* p. 595.
27. *Loc. cit.*
28. *Loc. cit.*
29. *Ibid.,* p. 596.
30. *Ibid.,* p. 603.
31. *Loc. cit.*
32. *Ibid.,* p. 607.
33. Talmage, *op. cit.,* pp. 424-425.
34. J. Cary, "Untold Story of Short Creek," *American Mercury,* LXXVIII (May, 1954), pp. 119-123.
35. Talmage, *op. cit.,* p. 205.
36. *Ibid.,* p. 207.
37. *Ibid.,* p. 206.
38. Linn, *op. cit.,* p. 194.
39. Talmage, *op. cit.,* pp. 447-448.
40. Richard L. Evans, "What Is a 'Mormon'?", *A Guide to the Religions of America* ed. by Leo Rosten (New York: Simon and Schuster, 1955), p. 100.
41. Smith, *Essentials in Church History,* p. 652.

10. Presbyterians

UNLIKE THE Baptists, whose name is derived from the stress on a single ritual practice, or the Lutherans, who are named after their founder, the Presbyterians are called after the principal characteristic of their form of Church government. Their name is a doctrinal synthesis in one word, born of the historical conflict out of which the church arose as a distinct denomination.

In opposition to other churches, Presbyterianism is an ecclesiastical system in which ultimate authority on earth is not vested in one person, the Pope, as in Roman Catholicism; or in the bishops, as in Episcopalianism; or in the local congregation, as in Congregationalism—but in a group of persons representing a number of churches, and called the presbytery. This approach denies that Christ founded the Church as a visible institution; Church government is entrusted to a purely human organization, quasi-democratic in structure, in which delegates from the various congregations represent the highest authority in spiritual matters.

HISTORY

John Calvin is commonly regarded as the founder of Presbyterianism. However, it would be more correct to say that he originated a theological system out of which de-

veloped the Huguenots in France, the Dutch Reformed
Church in Holland, and the Presbyterians in Scotland and
America. Calvin was born at Noyon in Picardy, France,
July 10, 1509, and died at Geneva, May 27, 1564. Contrary
to popular opinion, he never met Luther, although Lu
theran books and teachers undoubtedly influenced his defection from the Catholic faith in 1533, after he had given
up the study of law to prepare for the ministry. In 1536,
Calvin published the *Institutes of the Christian Religion,*
which to this day remain the most authoritative exposition
of Protestant theology. The same year he went to Geneva
where he stayed two years until banished for attempting
to exclude public sinners from the Communion table.
After three years' exile, he returned to establish in Geneva
a stronghold of moral rigorism. Here in 1553 Michael
Servetus was executed for denying the Trinity, and within
sixty years, 150 people were burnt for witchcraft. Calvin's
attitude toward his former co-religionists is summarized in
a letter he wrote to Somerset, the English Regent during
the minority of Edward VI. "From what I understand," he
recommended, "you have two kinds of rebels who have
risen up against the King and the state of the realm. The
one are fantastic people, who under color of the Gospel
would cast all into confusion; the other, obstinate adherents of the superstitions of the Roman Antichrist. Both
alike well deserve to be suppressed by the sword." [1]

The link between Calvin and American Presbyterianism is John Knox (c. 1515-1572), an apostate priest who,
because of his implication in the murder of Cardinal
Beaton, was a prisoner on the galleys for nineteen months.
After release, during his travels on the continent, he met
Calvin and lived at Geneva under his direction for three
years. Returning to Scotland, he was instrumental in having Queen Mary Stuart dethroned and Presbyterianism established as the state religion by an act of the Scottish

Parliament in 1560. Meantime the Puritans in England had adopted Calvinist principles, while favoring a congregational form of government. In 1643, the Westminster Assembly of divines, called by a Puritan English Parliament, met to resolve the struggle over the compulsory use of the Anglican *Book of Common Prayer*. After five years' session, the Assembly produced a Larger and Shorter Catechism, a Directory of Worship, a Form of Government and, most important, the Westminster Confession of Faith, which became the doctrinal standard of Scottish, British and American Presbyterianism.

Presbyterianism in the United States had three beginnings, all due to migrations from Europe. In 1620 the Puritan refugees from England landed in Massachusetts at Plymouth, and although they first merged with the Pilgrims to form the Congregational Church, eventually many of them changed allegiance and became Presbyterians; in 1623 the Dutch settled in New York as members of the Calvinist Reformed Church; and in 1685 Ulster men, or Scotch-Irish, arrived in New Jersey and Pennsylvania under the leadership of Francis Makemie, "the father of American Presbyterianism." Before Makemie's time, Presbyterians were to be found scattered throughout the colonies, but without having over them any presbytery, which is essential to the Calvinist ecclesiastical system. To Makemie goes the credit of organizing in 1706, at Freehold, New Jersey, the first presbytery, and thus establishing the church as a corporate entity in America. Between 1705 and 1775, about 500,000 Scotch-Irish arrived in America to swell the ranks of American Presbyterianism in New Jersey, Pennsylvania, Maryland, Virginia, and the Carolinas.

The first milestone in American Presbyterianism was the Adopting Act of 1729, which decided that every minister and candidate for the ministry had to declare the Cal-

vinist Westminster Confession and the Larger and Shorter
Cathechisms "in all essentials and necessary articles, good
forms of sound words and systems of Christian doctrine." [2]
This was approved over the protests of those who questioned the Trinity and the divinity of Christ. To satisfy
the latter, the concession was made that if any minister
had scruples about any parts of these standards, he should
propose them to the Synod who would then decide
whether his difficulties involved anything "essential" that
would warrant his exclusion.

There was a temporary break in Presbyterian unity
from 1741 to 1758 over conflicting interpretations of "essential and necessary articles" of faith in the Westminster
Confession. The matter was settled by expunging the controversial phrase, "essential and necessary articles." Instead,
candidates for the ministry were to be examined as to
their "experimental acquaintance with religion." [3] This
amity lasted until 1810, when the Cumberland Presbytery
seceded to form a separate denomination, known as the
Cumberland Presbyterian Church. Its grievance was the
Calvinist doctrine on predestination, which was rejected
as "fantastic." Although a partial reunion took place in
1906, the Cumberland Presbyterian Church continues its
autonomous existence in two segments: the Cumberland
Presbyterian Church for the whites, and the Colored Cumberland Presbyterian Church, with a combined membership in 1954 of 114,776 communicants.

Another temporary schism, lasting thirty years (1837-
1869), divided the Presbyterian Church into the Old
School and the New School, the former rejecting the Plan
of Union with the Congregationalists. The issue at stake
was acceptance or rejection of "the novelties of New England (Congregational) theology."

Meantime, in 1857, a more serious and lasting split
took place over the slavery question. In that year several

southern synods withdrew to form the United Synod of the Presbyterian Church. They were joined eight years later by forty-seven southern presbyteries, called the General Assembly of the Presbyterian Church in the Confederate States of America. The new merger (1865) became known as the Presbyterian Church in the United States, and has remained separated from the parent body to this day. Frequently called the Southern Presbyterian Church, its doctrinal position is notably conservative and the membership is mostly urban. Efforts have been made to reunite this body with the northern segment, one as late as 1955, but the merger failed of adoption. The church has four theological seminaries: Austin (Texas), Columbia (Georgia), Louisville (Kentucky)—operated jointly with the Presbyterian Church in the U.S.A.—and Union Seminary in Richmond, Virginia. In 1954 there were 780,837 church members. Following the general pattern in the south, the Presbyterian Church in the U.S. has segregated Negro churches; these are organized into separate presbyteries, and are made up exclusively of Negro clergy and laity.

The northern denomination retained the name of the Presbyterian Church in the U.S.A., adopted in 1821, and has the reputation of being more tolerant of theological liberalism. In 1954 the church had nine seminaries, including Princeton and McCormick (Chicago), and forty-one officially endorsed colleges. The semi-monthly *Presbyterian Life* has a circulation in excess of 800,000. Current (1956) membership is two and a half million.

Parallel with the above developments, an independent group of Calvinists, set up by secessionist missionaries from Scotland, gradually evolved into the present-day United Presbyterian Church of North America. Officially organized in 1858 at Pittsburgh by a union of the Associate Synod of North America and the Associate Reformed Church, it maintains the Pittsburgh-Xenia Theological Seminary, and a seminary each in Egypt and Pakistan. There were 827 churches and 237,233 members in 1954.

All the major branches of American Presbyterianism carry on active missionary work in more than thirty foreign countries, with concentration in Africa, which has an estimated 1,300,000 Presbyterians, and Asia, with 900,000. Indicative of the evangelistic zeal on the home front, the Presbyterian Church in the U.S.A. in 1955 showed a per capita contribution of $3.43 for the missions, totalling over $8,500,000 for one year from this single body.

DOCTRINE

It is comparatively easy to analyze Presbyterian doctrine because the church professes to have a creed. "Some denominations have none; but Presbyterian elders, ruling or teaching, accept at ordination the Westminster 'Confession of Faith' as 'the system of doctrine taught in the Holy Scriptures.' " [4] An appraisal of the Westminster Confession, therefore, will give us a substantially accurate picture of the doctrinal mentality of American Presbyterians, with one important reservation since the Presbyterian Church in the U.S.A. has considerably modified the Westminster formulary. These modifications will be noted, while omitting such doctrines as the Trinity and the Incarnation which are substantially the same as in the Catholic Church. Of special significance are the changes which involved the removal of objectionable references to Roman Catholicism, some of them altered as recently as 1953.

The Church is conceived in two ways. As "the catholic or universal Church, which is invisible, (it) consists of the whole number of the elect," whereas "the visible Church, which is also catholic or universal under the gospel—not confined to one nation, as before under the law—consists of all those throughout the world that profess the true religion, together with their children, and is the Kingdom of the Lord Jesus Christ." [5] Then to make a clear distinction between itself and the Roman Catholic Church, it is stated that, "There is no other head of the Church but the Lord Jesus Christ. Nor can the pope of Rome in any sense be head thereof; but is that anti-christ, that man of sin, and son of perdition, that exalteth himself, in the Church, against Christ, and all that is called God." [6] This passage was revised by the northern Presbyterians in 1903 during the pontificate of St. Pius X; the direct reference to the Pope was deleted and the new version reads: ". . . the claim of any man to be the vicar of Christ and the head of the Church, is unscriptural, without warrant in fact, and is a usurpation dishonoring to the Lord Jesus Christ." [7]

Predestination, regarded as the keystone of Calvin's theology, has been the focus of practically every doctrinal schism since the origin of Presbyterianism. We should therefore expect radical changes in the expression of this doctrine. Actually, a compromise has been reached, as in the Presbyterian Church in the U.S.A., which retained Calvin's teaching verbally intact in the body of the Confession, and then added an appendix to soften its harshness. As found in the Confession, we read that, "By the decree of God, for the manifestation of his glory, some men and angels are predestined unto everlasting life, and others foreordained to everlasting death." [8] Lest there be any doubt about the latter, it is further declared that no others are "redeemed by Christ, effectually called, justified, adopted, sanctified, and saved but the elect only. The rest of mankind, God was pleased, according to the unsearchable counsel of his own will . . . to ordain them to dishonor and wrath for their sin, to the praise of his glorious justice." [9] But in 1903 the Presbyterian Church in the U.S.A. added an interpretation which quite negatives the foregoing rigid predestinarianism. "Concerning those who perish," it is said, "the doctrine of God's eternal decree is held in harmony with the doctrine that God desires not the death of any sinner, but has provided in Christ a salvation sufficient for all . . . men are fully responsible for their treatment of God's gracious offer . . . his decree hinders no man from accepting that offer . . . no man is condemned except on the ground of his sin." [10]

Sacraments are defined as "holy signs and seals of the covenant of grace," but not in the Catholic sense of conferring grace by their intrinsic efficacy.[11] Only two Sacraments are recognized: baptism and the Lord's Supper. The first is administered by immersion, pouring or sprinkling, together with the invocation of the Trinity. Unlike Baptists, Presbyterians hold that "infants of one or both believing parents are to be baptized." [12] And though it is regarded a sin to contemn this sacrament, "yet grace and salvation are not so inseparably annexed unto it as that no person can be regenerated or saved without it." [13] To clarify the lot of those who die without baptism before reaching the age of reason, the Presbyterian Church in the U.S.A. added the following: "We believe that all dying in infancy are included in the election of grace, and are regenerated and saved by Christ, through the Spirit, who works when and where and how he pleases." [14] Without giving any proof for this insight into God's providence, it is assumed that death in infancy is an infallible sign of salvation, whether the child is baptized or not.

The concept of the Lord's Supper is the same as Calvin's, with no modification in any of the modern Confessions. Christ is said to be only represented in the sacrament, so that even after the "prayer of consecration" the elements, "in substance and nature . . . still remain truly and only, bread and wine, as they were before." [15] In keeping with the Calvinist tradition, the Sacrifice of the Mass, as offered by the Catholic Church, is called "most abominably injurious to Christ's one only sacrifice." [16]

Marriage is not considered to be a sacrament. Nevertheless Christians are reminded they have a duty "to marry in the Lord." Consequently, "such as profess the true reformed religion should not marry with infidels, Papists, or other idolaters." [17] In 1953, the Presbyterian Church in the U.S.A. completely modified the Westminster Confession on marriage, removing all reference to "infidels, Papists and idolaters."

In the basic Westminster creed, divorce with remarriage is allowed for "adultery, or such willful desertion as can in no way be remedied by the Church or civil magistrates," which are considered "sufficient of dissolving the bond of marriage." [18] The Presbyterian Church in the U.S.A. professed this doctrine as late as 1939. But in 1953 a revision was made, laying down no restrictive conditions beyond declaring that, ". . . remarriage after a divorce granted on grounds explicitly stated in Scripture or implicit in the gospel of Christ may be sanctioned in keeping with his redemptive gospel, when sufficient penitence for sin and failure is evident, and a firm purpose of an endeavor after Christian marriage is manifest." [19]

FORM OF GOVERNMENT

The organizational system of the Presbyterian Church most clearly distinguishes it from other Protestant denominations. And just as the doctrines of faith are substantially embodied in the Westminster Confession, so the essentials of the church's juridical structure are specified in the Form of Government, which was drawn up, along with the Confession by the Westminster Assembly in 1647. Since all Presbyterian bodies follow the same general pattern, our analysis will be confined to the Form of Government presently in use by the Presbyterian Church in the U.S.A.

Officers in the Church. Three grades of church officials are recognized: bishops or pastors, ruling elders, and deacons. First in dignity is the pastor, who is given no less than eight titles, depending on the aspect from which his office is considered. "As he has the oversight of the flock of Christ, he is termed bishop. As he feeds them with spiritual food, he is termed pastor. As he serves Christ in his Church, he is termed minister. As it is his duty to be grave and prudent, and an example of the flock, and to govern well in the house and Kingdom of Christ, he is termed presbyter or elder. As he is the messenger of God, he is termed the angel of the Church. As he is sent to declare the will of God to sinners, and to beseech them to be reconciled to God through Christ, he is termed ambassador. And, as he dispenses the manifold grace of God, and the ordinances instituted by Christ, he is termed steward of the mysteries of God." [20] Under all these names, however, the pastor has only one essential function, that of *teaching* the word of God.

Next in dignity are the ruling elders, who are "properly the representatives of the people, chosen by them for the purpose of exercising government and discipline." [21] Thus the Presbyterian Church has two kinds of elders, the teaching and the ruling, so that every congregation duly constituted has a pastor, or teaching elder, and a group of ruling elders. Both types are specially ordained to their office. However the essential element is their previous election to this office by the laity of the congregation, and, "a Presbyterian church" may be defined as "a church with a representative form of government by elders elected by the people." [22]

Last in rank are the deacons, "whose business it is to take care of the poor and to distribute among them the collections which may be raised for their use. To them also may be properly committed the management of the temporal affairs of the Church." [23] Deacons must also be elected before ordination.

In order to provide workers in the ministry who are not forthcoming from the ordained, Presbyterian polity allows the laity to become preachers in the local churches, normally for a period of three years which may be renewed, and without the duty of ordination. Both men and women are eligible for lay preachership, the sole condition being their acceptance by the presbytery after declaring, among other things, that they "believe the Scriptures of the Old and New Testaments to be the Word of God, the only infallible rule of faith and practice." [24]

Governing Bodies. There are four hierarchical levels in the church organization: session, presbytery, synod and general assembly, each with clearly defined functions and specific directors.

The local church, in Presbyterian parlance, is called a session, and "consists of the pastor or co-pastor and ruling elders of a particular congregation." [25] Ordinarily the pastor is moderator of the local session, which has the right to admit and dismiss members, "to admonish, to rebuke, to suspend or exclude from the sacraments," and, in general, "to concert the best measures for promoting the spiritual interests of the congregation." [26]

Next in authority and so distinctive that it denominates the whole church is the presbytery, "which consists of all the ministers, in number not less than five, and one ruling elder from each congregation, within a certain district." [27] Presbyteries are usually organized on a geographical basis, but some exist to take care of separate language groups or racial minorities within a larger area. Although there are still two grades of jurisdiction technically higher than the presbytery, the latter is, for practical purposes, the principal governmental body in Presbyterianism, having "power to receive and issue all appeals, complaints and references that are regularly brought before it from church sessions . . . to examine and license candidates for the holy ministry; to ordain, install, remove, and judge ministers; to examine and approve or censure the records of church sessions; to resolve questions of doctrine or discipline seriously and reasonably proposed; to condemn erroneous opinions which injure the purity or peace of the Church; to visit particular churches, for the purpose of inquiring into their state and redressing the evils that may have arisen in them; to unite or divide congregations, at the request of the people, or to form or receive new congregations, and, in general, to order whatever pertains to the spiritual welfare of the churches under their care." [28]

As presbyteries grow in number, they are united into synods, including at least three to each synod. Membership in the synod is by election among the presbyteries, with equal representation of pastors and ruling elders. In general, the function of the synod bears the same relation to the presbytery as the latter does to the session. It meets at least once a year to decide on such varied issues as erection of new presbyteries, passing judgment on appeals and complaints and settling all questions submitted to it "that do not affect the doctrine or constitution of the Church." [29] In 1951, there were 350 presbyteries and 57 synods in the two largest denominations: 265 and 40 in the Presbyterian Church in the U.S.A., 85 and 17 in the southern, Presbyterian Church in the U.S.

At the highest juridical level stands the General Assembly, which consists of an equal delegation of pastors and elders from each presbytery. Like the synod, it meets once a year to decide "in all controversies respecting doctrine and discipline," in any church, presbytery or synod. It may erect new synods, divide old ones, and especially has the right of "corresponding with foreign Churches (and) of suppressing schismatical contentions and disputations." [30] Among the important "correspondence" currently handled by the Assemblies of the three major groups (U.S.A., U.S., and United Presbyterian) are plans for their eventual merger. To date (June, 1956) the southern Presbyterians have turned down the offer, while ratification seems certain for a union between the U.S.A. and the United Presbyterian Church, first in their respective Assemblies and then in the presbyteries. "When the united church is formed, its members will hope that it will generate enough powers of attraction to cause the southerners to change their minds." [31]

A striking example of the Assembly's suppression of schismatical contentions was the action which the Presbyterian Church in the U.S.A. took in 1936 against two of its ministers, Carl McIntyre, now president of the International Council of Churches, and J. Gresham Machen, founder of the Presbyterian Church in America, a sect whose 9,000 members now call themselves Orthodox Presbyterians after an injunction was brought against their use of the former name. According to his account, McIntyre was ousted by the General Assembly for opposing his church's theological liberalism and compromise with Christian fundamentals. The Assembly declared it found him guilty of "advocating rebellion against the constituted authorities of the Church." [32] After a series of legal battles, McIntyre lost his parish property, but the 1,200 parishioners sided with their pastor and renounced the jurisdiction of the denomination. Machen, since dead, established his church with a strong emphasis on the infallibility of the Bible, original sin, the virgin birth, divinity, sacrificial atonement and resurrection of Christ. Doctrinal disputes with Machen led McIntyre to split with his former professor and found a sect of his own, the Bible Presbyterian Synod, which has no available record of its membership.

RITUAL AND WORSHIP

The ritual of the Presbyterian Church, in all sects, is fundamentally the same, and is founded on the Directory for the Worship of God composed by the Westminster Assembly in the seventeenth century. In keeping with the spirit of Calvin and Knox, and their theological presuppositions, the Presbyterian order of worship is markedly grave and restrained. Thus, says the Directory, "in time of public worship, let all the people attend with gravity and reverence." [33] When beginning public worship, it is declared fitting to adore "the infinite majesty of the living God, expressing a sense of our distance from him as creatures, and unworthiness as sinners, and humbly imploring his gracious presence." [34]

However, a liturgical revival is taking place, with a growing sense of the need of reform, if not to restore the severed connection with the Church of antiquity, at least to introduce many elements that are contrary to the Calvinistic tradition. Accordingly a new Book of Common Worship was drawn up in 1944 for the Presbyterian Church in the U.S.A., after years of sifting and compilation from many sources. Looking to the improvement of Presbyterian worship, the liturgical movement "seeks . . . not only to provide the minister with the treasures in thought and expression that are the inheritance of the Church, but to encourage Christian congregations to more active participation in Christian worship, which was the custom in the Early Church." [35] The whole ritual set-up of the Presbyterian Church in the U.S.A. has been recast. Following the Anglican tradition, a lectionary was added, giving two sets of readings from Scripture, for the morning and evening of each Sunday and feast day of the year: from the Psalms, the Old Testament, Gospels and Epistles.

Four new forms of public worship for morning and evening were added. Three orders (rites) for Holy Communion are now provided. An order for giving communion to the sick has been included. Important changes were made in the ritual for baptism of infants and adults, though retaining the Trinitarian formula in each case. An alternate ritual for administering the Lord's Supper was provided, removing the repetition of the words of institution and only once, as in the Roman Missal, pronouncing over the bread and wine the prayer of consecration: "This is My Body . . . This cup is the New Covenant in My blood." [36] However, both services still enjoin that "after the celebration, reverent disposition of the Elements which remain shall be made by the Minister and Elders." [37]

Along with a comprehensive change in the ritual there has been a revision in congregational singing, always an essential part of Protestant worship. In October, 1955, a cooperative Hymnbook was published by the northern and southern Presbyterians, the United Presbyterian and the Reformed Churches, representing 95 per cent of American Presbyterianism. Although "there is some question whether the melange has the integrity of any one of the participants' own tradition," the hymnal is looked upon as a "portent" of greater unity among Presbyterian denominations.

STATISTICS

Membership in the World Presbyterian Alliance, including both Presbyterian and Reformed Churches	13,330,000
— in Europe	3,816,000
— in British Isles	1,662,000
— in Asia	899,000
— in Africa	1,298,000

— in Australia	171,000
— in South America	100,000
— in North America	5,584,000
Presbyterians, technically so-called, in the United States	3,703,021
Churches in the United States	14,352
Ordained Clergy in the United States	15,217

REFERENCES

1. William R. Inge, "Calvin," *Protestantism* (New York: Doubleday-Doran, 1928), pp. 30-31.
2. Lefferts A. Loetscher, *Brief History of the Presbyterians* (Philadelphia: Board of Christian Education of the Presbyterian Church in the U.S.A., 1938), p. 41.
3. *Ibid.*, p. 45.
4. Cleland McAfee and Eliot Porter, *Why a Presbyterian Church?* (Philadelphia: Presbyterian Board of Christian Education, 1930), p. 12.
5. *The Constitution of the Presbyterian Church in the United States of America* (Philadelphia: Office of the General Assembly, 1955), p. 69.
6. *Ibid.*, p. 71.
7. *Ibid.*, pp. 70-71.
8. *Ibid.*, p. 12.
9. *Ibid.*, p. 13.
10. *Ibid.*, p. 90. Presbyterian theologians are embarrassed by the inclusion of a patent contradiction within the same statement of doctrine. Chapter III, which quotes Calvin's predestinarianism, "is left to stand as grim as ever." One commentator admits he "has never been able to see . . . by what logic it is said to be 'in harmony with' the doctrine as given in the Declaratory Statement," adopted in 1903. Kenneth J. Foreman, *God's Will and Ours* (Richmond, Va.: Outlook, 1954), p. 24. In 1938-1939 the U.S. Presbyteries were asked to vote on the excision of the obnoxious predestinarianism in Chapter III; two-thirds wanted the doctrine eliminated, but the number was three short of the constitutional requirement; so the statement remained.
11. *Constitution*, p. 72.
12. *Ibid.*, p. 75.
13. *Loc. cit.*
14. *Ibid.*, p. 90.
15. *Ibid.*, p. 77.
16. *Loc. cit.*
17. Philip Schaff, "The Westminster Confession of Faith," *The Creeds of Evangelical Protestant Churches* (London: Hodder and Stoughton, 1878), p. 655.
18. *Ibid.*, pp. 456-457.
19. *Constitution*, pp. 68-69.
20. *Ibid.*, pp. 242-243.
21. *Ibid.*, p. 243. Technically the relation of elders to pastor is that of counselling assistants. "But he and they need to remember that he is responsible under God . . . not to the particular church of which he is pastor, but to the whole Church through the presbytery, which made him pastor." *Presbyterian*

Law for the Local Church, ed. by Eugene C. Blake (Philadelphia: Westminster, 1954), p. 66.

22. Walter L. Lingle, *Presbyterians, Their History and Beliefs* (Texarkana: Presbyterian Committee of Publication of the Presbyterian Church U.S., 1950), p. 11. One of the unsolved problems among Presbyterians is the precise status of the ruling elder. In 1943, when the Episcopalians were considering a possible merger with the Presbyterians, "They noted the grave uncertainty among Presbyterians as to whether the ruling elder is a layman or a clergyman." When the merger was voted down, this point was one of the determining factors. George E. DeMille, *The Episcopal Church Since 1900* (New York: Morehouse-Gorham, 1955), pp. 147-148.

23. *Constitution,* p. 243. There are also deaconesses in the Presbyterian Church.
24. *Ibid.,* p. 262.
25. *Ibid.,* p. 246.
26. *Loc. cit.*
27. *Ibid.,* p. 248.
28. *Ibid.,* p. 249.
29. *Ibid.,* p. 252.
30. *Ibid.,* p. 254.
31. *Christian Century,* LXXII (Dec. 14, 1955), p. 1451.
32. Ralph L. Roy, *Apostles of Discord* (Boston: Beacon Press, 1953), p. 188.
33. *Constitution,* p. 340.
34. *Ibid.,* p. 341.
35. *The Book of Common Worship* (Philadelphia: Board of Christian Education of the Presbyterian Church in the U.S.A., 1951), p. vi.
36. *Ibid.,* pp. 173-174.
37. *Ibid.,* p. 175.

11. Quakers

For three centuries the Society of Friends, or Quakers, has exerted an influence on American thought out of all proportion to its numbers—less than 200,000 in 1956. It is not sufficient to explain this influence superficially by pointing to outstanding Quakers like William Penn, John Greenleaf Whittier, Herbert Hoover or Whittaker Chambers. A more likely explanation was suggested by the philosopher, William James, who considered the Quaker religion "something which it is impossible to overpraise" because it is rooted in "spiritual inwardness." So that, "as our Christian sects are evolving, they are simply reverting in essence to the position which . . . the early Quakers so long ago assumed." [1]

More than any other offspring of the Reformation, the Quakers have consistently applied the principle of private interpretation and independence of ecclesiastical authority. There is even a question of whether they should properly be called Protestants. They prefer to call themselves "a 'third way' of Christians' emphasizing fundamentals differently from Roman Catholics and Protestants. Roman Catholics emphasize Church authority, the hierarchy, and an absolute creed. Protestant denominations emphasize one or another interpretation of religion as found in the Holy Bible. But the Society of Friends puts its mark on religion as a fellowship of the Spirit." [2] It is this emphasis on responsibility to God alone which is so appealing to non-Catholic Christians, who see in Quaker theology "the most protestant form of Protestantism" and the ultimate of religious autonomy.

HISTORY

The Religious Society of Friends was founded in England by George Fox (1624-1691), a "restless seeking spirit" who reacted against the prevalent Anglican emphasis on ceremonial. Fox was an earnest young man whose trials and temptations disturbed his peace of mind. He sought counsel from the official guides in the Church, but without success. Finally, he records in his *Journal*, "when all my hopes in men were gone, so that I had nothing outwardly to help me, nor could I tell what to do, then, O then, I heard a voice which said, 'There is One, even Christ Jesus, that can speak to thy condition.' And when I heard it, my heart did leap for joy." [3]

Enthusiastic over the discovery of this Inner Light, in 1647 Fox began to preach to others and gradually organized a group of followers who called themselves "Children of the Light," "Friends of the Truth," or simply "Friends." Hailed into court for his opposition to the Established Church, Fox warned the judge to "tremble at the Word of God." The judge called him "Quaker" in derision at his agitation over religious matters; but the name caught the popular fancy and eventually was accepted, though never formally adopted, by the Friends.

Persecution, imprisonment and in some cases death only served to increase the prestige of the Society and swell its numbers. Quakers came to America as early as 1655, and by 1661 were sufficiently organized to hold their first Yearly Meeting in Rhode Island. Fox's visit to the Colonies (1671-1673) helped encourage the Friends to remain steadfast in spite of pressure from the churches and the civil power. Four were hanged at Boston. In the 1680's and 90's, West Jersey and Pennsylvania were established as Quaker settlements. "Here Friends, under the leadership of William Penn, undertook to carry out 'a holy experiment' in conducting a government on New Testament principles." [4] Faithful to their convictions, they remained in political control in Pennsylvania until 1756, when they preferred to give up their seats in the Assembly rather than vote in favor of war against the Shawnee and Delaware Indians.

The same pacifist spirit kept most Quakers from active participation in the American Revolution. As early as 1800, their hatred of "traffic in the bodies of men" forbade membership in the Society to sellers or purchasers of slaves. Since the Civil War, they have taken a leading part in protecting and promoting the education of Negroes. During the first and second World Wars, and since, the American Friends Service Committee has been doing welfare and reconstruction work on a wide scale, including the staffing of hospitals, plowing fields and driving ambulances in war time, famine relief and child feeding programs in Serbia, Poland and Russia, allocation and housing of refugees. In 1947 the American Friends Service Committee and the Friends Service Council (London) were jointly awarded the Nobel Peace Prize.

Along with these external labors of charity, "outreaching" in Quaker terminology, there has been an internal disunity that is not surprising in view of the creedal freedom professed by the Society of Friends. Though all Quakers look upon George Fox as their founder, they have about the largest variety of sects of any comparable religious group in America. To avoid ecclesiastical terminology, two generic synonyms are used for church: the term "Meeting" designates a particular Quaker body, which is qualified as "Yearly" or "Five Years," depending on the frequency of its General Conference; or a group is called "Religious Society of Friends," with an added name to distinguish it from other Friends in a different denomination.

The largest Quaker body in the United States is the "Five Years Meeting of Friends," which was formed in 1902 by the loose federation of eleven Yearly Meetings. Headquarters are located in Richmond, Indiana. Current membership is about 70,000, which includes affiliated groups in Africa and the West Indies.

Next in size is the Religious Society of Friends, General Conference, nicknamed the Hicksites, with a central office in Philadelphia. It came into existence in 1827 as a modernist party within the Quakers under the leadership of Elias Hicks, a liberal, whose disciples were accused of denying the Trinity. There are 20,000 members, concentrated in the eastern and mid-western States.

There are six Yearly Meeting denominations, identified by the state or region in which they are localized: Central in the central States, Kansas, Ohio, Oregon, Pacific and Philadelphia. All told they number some 28,000 adherents. Until recently there were two Philadelphia Yearly Meetings, distinguished by the street on which their headquarters were located: Arch Street and Race Street. In 1955 they joined forces "in a single Yearly Meeting (as) an outward and visible embodiment of inner unity." [5]

DOCTRINAL POSITION

Quaker teaching is fluid and unpredictable. While broad doctrinal differences are generally determined by the spirit of a particular sect, individual Quakers enjoy a maximum of freedom in matters of faith as the logical consequence of the Inner Light theory of George Fox. To know what they mean by this Light is to understand something of the essence of Quakerism which, in spite of appearances, is only peripherally interested in social welfare and primarily concerned with man's personal relations with God.

In the writings of Quaker leaders, the Inner Light is variously called the Light Within, the Seed, the Christ Within, the Eternal Christ, the Divine Principle, the presence of God in man. Used indiscriminately, these titles are drawn from the New Testament, mostly from Sts. John and Paul, and radically based on the reference in John's Prologue to "the true Light, which enlightens every man that comes into this world." [6]

No Quaker has improved on the description of this Light given by George Fox, and all Quakers subscribe to his definition:

> The Lord God hath opened to me by His invisible power how that every man was enlightened by the divine Light of Christ; and I saw it shine through all; and that they that believed in it came out of condemnation and came to the Light of Life, and became the children of it; but they that hated it, and did not believe in it, were condemned by it, though they made a profession of Christ. This I saw in the pure openings of the Light, without the help of any man, neither did I then know where to find it in the Scriptures, though afterwards, searching the Scriptures, I found it. For I saw in that Light and Spirit which was before Scripture was given forth, and which led the holy men of God to give them forth, that all must come to that Spirit—if they would know God or Christ or the Scriptures aright—which they that gave them forth were led and taught by.[7]

According to Fox, therefore, all men are naturally endowed with a divine Light which they have only to recognize and follow to be saved. Profession of faith in Christ is meaningless, says Fox, unless a man believes in this Light; and given such faith, it matters little what else he professes to believe. The first function of the Light is to emancipate a person from adherence to any creed, or obedience to ecclesiastical authority, or submission to any prescribed form of worship.

Quakers are divided on the exact nature of the divine Light. They are agreed, however, that "the Light Within is not to be identified with conscience, which is the human faculty, imperfect because human, through which the Light shines."[8] It is something divine. An English contemporary of Fox described it as "a free grace of God . . . that comes from Christ."[9] More recently, a Quaker Commission reported to the World Conference on Faith and Order that, "The main differences between ourselves and most other bodies of Christians arise from the emphasis we place on the Light of God's Holy Spirit in the human soul. . . . This direct contact between the Spirit of Christ and the human spirit we are prepared to trust to, as the basis of our individual and corporate life."[10]

Over the years, Quaker belief in the Inner Light has come into conflict with practically every doctrine of traditional Christianity. As a result, many Christian concepts had to be revised, others were adapted, and not a few were simply discarded as incompatible with divine illumination.

Sacred Scriptures are highly respected. Yet "because they are only a declaration of the fountain and not the fountain itself, therefore they are not to be esteemed the principal ground of all truth and knowledge, nor yet the adequate, primary rule of faith and manners."[11] This is the individual Light of Christ in the soul.

The Church is wholly invisible, conditioned only on acceptance of the Light, and transcending the barriers of sectarian belief. It is a "great error," consequently, to "set up an outward order and uniformity and to make men's consciences bend thereto," when "the true Church government is to leave the conscience to its full liberty . . . and to seek unity in the Light and in the Spirit, walking sweetly and harmoniously together in the midst of different practices." [12]

Christ's Divinity and the Trinity are understood in various ways. An early English Quaker, Barclay, spoke of Christ as "the Mediator betwixt God and man, being Himself God, and partaking in time of the human nature." [13] The poet, John Whittier, regarded Christ as "the highest possible manifestation of God in man." [14] More vaguely, Rufus Jones, the prophet of American Quakerism, held that "Christ was divine" in the sense that we see "the divine possibilities of man revealed in Christ." [15] At the other extreme, there is a Quaker tradition of anti-trinitarianism, at least in the States, which goes back to William Penn who attacked the doctrine of the Trinity in his *Sandy Foundation Shaken* and was imprisoned as a consequence. Modern followers of Elias Hicks, in the General Conference Quakers, are openly Unitarian.

WORSHIP AND PRACTICE

Acceptance of the Light of Christ as the unique source of religious experience would seem to eliminate the need of a ministry. In practice, however, there is a ministerial office among Quakers, with two limitations: it is not a "monopoly of priestly caste through whom alone (divine grace) can be ministered to others"; and "anyone may experience 'the anointing' and, if that is known, may be called to minister to others of what God has given." [16] Hence there is no real distinction between the clergy and laity, and no ordination of ministers.

Quakers admit they are compelled "to stand apart from other communions in such matters as . . . forms of pub-

lic worship, and the use of outward sacraments." [17] They
do not "make use of the outward rites of Baptism and the
Lord's Supper, but . . . believe in the inward experiences
they symbolize." The underlying claim is "to actuality of
this experience even without the external rite." [18] The
usual practice is to dispense with any formal program for
the Worship Meeting. Nothing is pre-arranged. Worshipers gather at the appointed time and just wait silently until the Spirit moves someone to speech or action. Out of
this inspiration come divine communications, individual
or community prayer, reading the Scriptures, testimonies
of faith in the form of sermons, and even bodily healing—
from anyone in the congregation. After about an hour of
such worship, the assembly is closed by a general shaking
of hands with one's neighbor, following the lead of the
overseers who sit on a bench facing the people during
the meeting. In some Quaker sects there is a fixed program
for worship, which is called a Pastoral Meeting. But this
is an exception to the traditional custom.

Marriage among Quakers is a concern of the whole
Society. In the ideal situation, where bride and groom are
members of the same congregation, they write a letter to
the church officials stating their intention of getting
married. This letter is presented to a session of the
Monthly Meeting, at which a Committee on Clearness or
Family Relationships takes up the matter. Since the committee's report is normally approved at the next session, a
minimum of two months is required before wedding invitations may be sent out. The actual ceremony is "a meeting of worship within which a marriage takes place. In an
atmosphere of quiet and reverence, the promises of the
bride and groom are made without the help of a third person. Thus they enter into a binding relationship before
God and in the presence of their friends." [19]

Quaker simplicity is said to begin "inside, with the

quality of the soul. It is first and foremost the quality of sincerity, which is the opposite of duplicity or sham." [20] In effect it extends to all the details of daily life. A conscientious Quaker avoids luxury in dress and living quarters; he does not gamble or trade in the stock market, abstains from tobacco and intoxicating drinks, and is restrained in his speech and recreation. The use of "plain language" is confined nowadays to conversation among Quakers and in family life. It means avoiding the pronoun "you," in plural, when referring to one person, and using "thee" and "thou" instead. Also, instead of saying Sunday, Monday, etc., they use "First-day, Second-day," and for January, February and the other months, they substitute "First-month, Second-month . . . , on the principle that the names of days and months are pagan in origin and hence not to be employed by those who profess Christianity. Opposition to judicial oaths is "not merely a negation but is a positive affirmation of an ideal of sincerity for the regulation of life. A man's word should be as good as his sworn statement." [21] Quaker agitation from colonial times has contributed to the change in federal law in most states, which permits a simple statement instead of sworn testimony in legal processes.

GOVERNMENT AND ORGANIZATION

Quaker organization is necessarily very simple. Since all members are considered priests or ministers, there is no hierarchy of jurisdiction and no recognized superiority of clergy over lay people. Contrary to popular belief, there are church officers, called elders or ministers. They are not ordained but chosen "by acclamation" for their ability in leadership.

The governmental structure is an adapted form of congregationalism, in which four strata of authority are distinguished. At the bottom level is the Preparatory or

Congregational Meeting, whose only function is to prepare and digest business for the Monthly Meeting. Except
in large "parishes," the Preparatory Meeting is absorbed
by the Monthly Meeting, which is the fundamental unit
of Quaker polity, receiving and recording members, extending spiritual care and, if necessary, material aid to its
adherents. "It provides for the oversight of marriages and
funerals; for dealing in a spirit of restoring love with those
who fail to live in accordance with Friends' principles and
testimonies; for the collection of funds required to carry
on the work of the Meetings; for holding titles to property
and for the suitable administration of trust funds." [22]
Three officers, a Clerk, Treasurer and Recorder, are appointed for definite terms.

Above the Monthly Meeting is the Quarterly Meeting,
which is "designed to bring together a larger group for
inspiration and counsel and to consider more varied interests than a Monthly or Preparative Meeting can undertake.
It is composed of constituent Monthly Meetings, each of
which shall appoint representatives to attend it." [23]

Finally, in most Quaker groups, "the Yearly Meeting
is composed of the entire membership of its constituent
Monthly and Quarterly Meetings, members of which have
both the privilege and the responsibility to attend all sessions and to participate in the deliberations. Members of
other Yearly Meetings and any interested persons are wel-
come." [34] The few sects that operate on a five year plan add
one juridical unit to the previous three, in which case the
Yearly Meetings are self-sustaining, but they meet every
five years in a given locality for advisory purposes and
without the authority enjoyed by the lesser bodies.

Among the important sub-meetings used by Quakers,
the best known is the Meeting for Sufferings, established
in 1756 as a standing committee of the respective Yearly
Meetings. Its name was derived from a similar organization founded in England, "to care for and relieve members

and their families suffering persecution for their testimonies." Because the name was misunderstood, it was changed in 1955 to the Representative Meeting. Its purpose is manifold, notably to popularize the Quaker way of life, defend it against opposition, and assist "any individuals suffering because of maintaining Friends' testimonies." A recent outlet for this phase of Quaker piety was to provide moral and financial help for conscientious objectors during World War II. Quaker camps were organized for pacificists of all denominations. When a national board for religious objectors was set up by the Friends, it was generally accepted as the co-ordinating agency for this kind of work.

While there is no organic unity among the Quaker sects, they collaborate in social activities on a fairly large scale. For example, all Societies of Friends contribute to the American Friends Service Committee. They all support Pendle Hill, "an educational community (outside Philadelphia) for religious and social study, open to persons who are sufficiently mature to use their time profitably without the incentive of grades, examinations and degrees." [25] Lecturers in the summer of 1956 included Dorothy Day of the *Catholic Worker,* and the religion editor of *Time* magazine.

Not surprisingly, the Friends are prominent members of the National and World Councils of Churches, where they "testify to the same experience through corporate silent worship and lay ministry arising therein." [26] But the inclusion of the very liberal General Conference Quakers is a reflection on the Christian orthodoxy of the whole ecumenical movement.

STATISTICS

Quaker World Membership	200,000
Quakers in England	21,969
Ireland	2,000

U.S.A. Quaker Membership	119,415
Quaker Churches (Meeting Houses)	981
Non-Ordained Clergy (4 Sects)	961
Pastors Having Charges (4 Sects)	517
Organized Sects	9
Sunday Schools	753
Enrollment	59,907

REFERENCES

1. William James, *The Varieties of Religious Experience* (London: Longmans-Green, 1903), p. 7.
2. Richmond P. Miller, "What Is a Quaker?", *A Guide to the Religions of America*, ed. by Leo Rosten (New York: Simon and Schuster, 1955), p. 122.
3. Quoted in *Faith and Practice of the Philadelphia Yearly Meeting* (Philadelphia: 1955), p. 1.
4. *Ibid.*, p. 3.
5. *Ibid.*, p. 6.
6. John 1:9.
7. George Fox, *Journal*, ed. by John L. Nickalls (Cambridge Univ. Press, 1952), p. 33.
8. *Faith and Practice*, p. 11.
9. *Ibid.*, p. 166.
10. *Ibid.*, p. 168.
11. *Ibid.*, p. 174. Quoted from Robert Barclay, *Apology*, Proposition III.
12. *Ibid.*, p. 152. Quoted from Isaac Penington, *Works*, Part I, pp. 240-241.
13. Quoted from Barclay's *Apology*, Proposition II, in F. E. Mayer, *The Religious Bodies of America* (St. Louis: Concordia Publishing House, 1954), p. 409.
14. Howard M. Jenkins, *Religious Views of the Society of Friends*, Paper read at the World's Congress of Religions, Chicago, 1893. Quoted in *Faith and Practice*, p. 155.
15. Rufus M. Jones, *A Call to What is Vital* (New York: Macmillan, 1948), p. 109.
16. *Faith and Practice*, p. 167.
17. *Ibid.*, p. 168.
18. *Loc. cit.*
19. *Ibid.*, p. 78.
20. Rufus M. Jones, *The Faith and Practice of the Quakers* (New York, Harper, 1927), p. 90.
21. *Faith and Practice*, p. 24. Quaker opposition to oaths is based on the words of Christ, "Do not swear at all. . . . Let what you say be simply 'Yes' or 'No'; anything more than this comes from evil" (Matt. 5:33-37).
22. *Faith and Practice*, p. 46.
23. *Ibid.*, p. 50.
24. *Ibid.*, p. 51.
25. *Twentieth Century Encyclopedia of Religious Knowledge* (Grand Rapids: Baker Book House, 1955), Vol. II, p. 862.
26. *Third World Conference on Faith and Order* ed. by Oliver S. Tompkins (London: Camelot Press, 1953), p. 40.

12. Salvationists

A COMMON misunderstanding is to regard the Salvation Army as only a social welfare organization which is sponsored by non-Catholics for the purpose of relieving poverty and other temporal necessities. In reality the Army is a Protestant sect in the fullest sense of the term, with a mandatory body of doctrine, following a prescribed ritual and worship, and governed by a well-defined ecclesiastical authority.

It is not detracting from the creditable work of the Salvation Army in feeding the hungry and comforting the sick to say that this phase of its ministry is purely secondary. "Its primary aim," according to an official declaration, "is to preach the gospel of Jesus Christ to men and women untouched by ordinary religious efforts." [1]

HISTORY

First known as the East London Revival Society and later as the Christian Mission, the Salvation Army was organized in 1865 by William Booth (1829-1912), an ordained minister of the Methodist Church in England. "Filled with compassion for the wretched multitudes outside the influence of the religious agencies of the time," Booth left the pulpit of the Methodist New Connection Body to preach to the people on the street corners in the slum district of East End, London. His original plan was to supplement the work of the churches, but when the latter refused to accept his converts into active membership, Booth decided to establish a religious society of his own. He was moved to this decision by the appalling indifference of the existing religious bodies to care for the dregs of humanity, numbered in the thousands, living in the heart of a supposedly Christian capital. "Drunkenness and all manner of uncleanness," he wrote, "moral and physical, abound. . . . A population sodden with drink, stupid in vice, eaten up by every social and physical malady, these are the denizens of Darkest England (analagous to Darkest Africa) amidst whom my life has been spent, and to whose rescue I would now summon all that is best in the manhood and womanhood of our land." [2] What a cruel satire, he complained, that the existence of these colonies of heathens and savages should attract so little concern. To his mind, "it is no better than a ghastly mockery to call by the name of One who came to seek and save that which was lost those Churches which in the midst of lost multitudes either sleep in apathy or display a fitful interest in the chasuble. Why all this apparatus of temples and meeting-houses to save men from perdition in a world which is to come, while never a helping hand stretched out to save them from the inferno of their present life?" [3]

Consistent with this attitude toward the churches, Booth changed the original Methodist structure of his movement into a quasi-military organization. Instead of being a church, the society should be called an army; from superintendent, Booth became general; the traditional articles of faith became "Articles of War"; converts from sin became recruits and then cadets; after a period of training they rose to the rank of lieutenants, captains and finally majors. Mission houses were changed into "citadels," and prayer meetings were transformed into "knee drills."

Within a decade, the Army spread to other countries, Ireland, Scotland and Wales, coming to the United States in 1880. Booth personally nurtured the American foundation in four visits that he made to the States, and in 1904 appointed his daughter, Evangeline, the first American commander.

The variety and scope of the Army's work of social rehabilitation in the United States is unique among the Protestant sects. Certainly no other denomination with comparable numbers has a greater reputation for being the friend of the poor and homeless or of more effectively dealing with the problems of moral degradation, especially those of alcoholism. Salvation Army hotels for homeless and transient men and women, maternity homes, general hospitals, children's homes and nurseries add up to an aggregate of more than 250 institutions, besides summer camps, missing persons' bureaus and prison-gate homes; sympathetic observers have been prompted to call the Salvationists "the most powerful minority in the world." [4] Their work is not only extensive, it is highly efficient. As Secretary of Health, Education and Welfare, Mrs. Oveta Culp Hobby declared she had met with "many of our great voluntary social welfare organizations. None has impressed me more than the Salvation Army . . . . They get things done for people. I think they talk less and do more than almost any group I know." [5] In 1954, both Houses of Congress passed a complimentary resolution which proclaimed the week of November 28 through December 4, 1954, as National Salvation Army Week. President Eisenhower added an official proclamation to the nation urging citizens to honor the Salvation Army because of its work and principles.

DOCTRINE ON FAITH AND MORALS

The basic tenets of the Salvationist creed are set forth
in a series of eleven propositions, first elaborated by William Booth in 1878, and since then accepted as "the principal doctrines held and taught by the Salvation Army
. . . extending to all enactments and settlements throughout the world under which its property is held." [6] However, a bare examination of this creed would not reveal
much of its inner meaning, which is supplied by the *Orders and Regulations for Officers of The Salvation Army*
and the *Handbook of Doctrine,* containing "an exposition
of the principal Doctrines" obligatory on the "officers of
all ranks." Unlike other denominations, the Army allows
a minimum of freedom in the interpretation of its articles
of faith.

Jesus Christ. The divinity of Christ is professed unam-
biguously, for "Jesus Christ has been God from all eternity: He is God and will be God for evermore." [7] Among
the proofs offered for the deity of Christ, Salvationists
learn that, "the Bible repeatedly calls Him God . . .
ascribes to Him those wonderful powers and perfections
which belong only to God . . . shows that Jesus made
claims so tremendous that they could rightly have been
made only by God." [8] While developing this theme, the
Handbook is strangely silent on Christ's appeal to miracles
to prove His claim to divinity. Also a characteristically
revivalist attitude is betrayed in saying that, "the experience of those who are truly saved shows that Jesus must
be God," when they realize that forgiveness comes only
through the merits of Christ and no one less than God
could atone for their sins.[9]

Redemption and Salvation. The Salvationist concepts
of original sin and redemption are considerably removed
from those of Luther and Calvin. Through Adam's sin,
"all men are born with a sinful nature, which early leads

to actual wrongdoing." [10] Nevertheless, ". . . although prone to evil, man is a free agent. His spiritual powers were marred but not destroyed by the Fall." [11] Also contrary to the Protestant idea of redemption as a mere "covering over of sin," the Salvationists believe that forgiveness of sin is the first and greatest blessing of Christ's death on the cross. "God," they say, "forgives or justifies a sinner completely," with consequent "regeneration (which) is of the nature of a new birth," whereby man is "brought into a new spiritual world and has a new spiritual force within him." He thus becomes an adopted son of God, who "receives into His family the pardoned and regenerated sinner and makes him His own child." [12] Unlike many Protestants, the Army teaches that, "persons who are truly saved may backslide entirely and be eternally lost." [13] The opposite opinion is branded as "contrary to the general teaching of the Bible. It is based upon (a misinterpretation of those) passages which speak of the security of God's faithful people, especially: 'My sheep . . . shall never perish' (John 10:27-28)." Basically, the possibility of a relapse even after conversion arises from the fact that "otherwise we should not be free agents." [14]

Entire Sanctification. Quite different from most sectarians who are preoccupied with sin, the Salvationist religion offers prospects of spiritual perfection or "entire sanctification," which is described as a "complete deliverance from sin, and dedication (or consecration) of the whole being, with all its gifts and capacities, to the love and will of God." [15] From God's point of view this is to be regarded as being "overpowered by divine grace." [16] From man's side it means having "a clean heart . . . freedom from sin . . . perfect love . . . rest from inward conflict and from anxious care." [17] It is not to be expected, however, that perfect sanctity will take place at the moment of conversion. "It is only later, when (people) discover the

true nature and power of inborn sin, that they realize further need; then they earnestly seek deliverance and God
sanctifies them." [18] This ideal of Christian perfection is
held up to the officers of the Army as a goal to be attained
already in this life and well before eternity. Hence "the
idea that sanctification cannot take place at or near the
time of death is contrary to the teaching of the Bible." [19]
The secret lies in understanding that perfection, like every
gift of God, is conditional. Four conditions are laid down:
conviction of the malice of sin and that holiness is possible; consecration to God of oneself and of all that one has
"to live only to please Him"; faith, which is "the act of
simple heart-trust by which a soul commits itself to God
and believes that He does now sanctify according to His
promise"; and most practically, renunciation, which is
"giving up everything opposed to the will of God," forever
and entirely.[20] Renunciation will affect many common
habits to which other people are accustomed, but which a
consecrated soul will sacrifice to the glory of God. A faithful Salvationist must give up "the use of strong drink,
even in moderation . . . because the practice is wasteful,
injurious, and productive of misery, wickedness and ruin;
because the influence of a moderate drinker may lead
weaker people to drunkenness." He should also abandon
"the use of tobacco . . . because the practice is wasteful,
injurious, dirty, often selfish and annoying to others." He
must discontinue "the wearing of fashionable dress and
worldly adornment . . . because it tends to gratify and
encourage pride; it absorbs time, thought and money
which could be better employed." He should avoid
"worldly amusement and selfish indulgence . . . it being
realized that attendance at gatherings with associations of
an unworthy kind, also frivolous conduct and the reading
of trashy literature are detrimental to spiritual life." [21]

The Sacraments. A sad feature of Salvation Army teaching is its repudiation of the sacramental system, inherited from William Booth. "Various opinions are held," it is said, "as to how many Sacraments there are. Roman Catholics observe seven, many Protestants only two, namely, Baptism and the Lord's Supper." However, ". . . as it is the Salvation Army's firm conviction that these ceremonies are not necessary to salvation nor essential to spiritual progress, we do not observe them." [22]

Various arguments are given to support this negativism: isolated scriptural texts which describe Christianity as interior are quoted and "the religion of Jesus Christ" is said to be wholly "a spiritual religion." [23] The ritual practices of Christ and the early Church, *e.g.,* the Eucharist, are dismissed as "carried over from the Jewish dispensation." [24] And most arbitrarily it is argued that some people "who observe the Sacraments give no evidence of a spiritual change, while others who do not observe Sacraments give definite evidence of such a spiritual change." Moreover, since the "Sacraments are sometimes a hindrance to spiritual life, in that many people rely upon them rather than upon Christ," they have no essential function in the spiritual life of a Christian.[25]

This doctrinal position was determined by Booth, who in the early days of the Army baptized infants and administered the Lord's Supper at all Salvationist stations. Gradually he gave up both practices, and eventually legislated against them. He was moved to this decision by the Society of Friends (Quakers), "which came into being and exercised so mighty an influence when England was full of the practise of external religion, but almost dead in respect of vital Christian experience. George Fox and his followers, being convinced that the Church Sacraments were merely symbols of spiritual truth, had laid them aside and sought after the experience which these symbols represented." [26]

Booth was willing to retain the Lord's Supper except
for certain practical considerations. Many of his converts
"had been slaves of strong drink, to whom the taste, even
the odour, was a danger." [27] Should he expose them to
temptation by placing in their hands "the cup of remembrance" of Christ's Passion? He was also determined to
have women enjoy perfect equality with men in his Army.
But the prevalent attitude was against the administration
of the sacraments by women. He therefore chose to eliminate the Eucharist rather than deprive his wife and other
women of the privileges of the ministry. A final explanation lay in the conciliatory nature of the founder of the
Salvation Army, who "wished to avoid anything that might
cause disorder." [28] Since the Lord's Supper had been the
cause of so much controversy over the centuries, Booth
decided to drop it rather than stir up dissension.

Divorce and Remarriage. As marriage is not recognized
as a sacrament, divorce with remarriage is permitted to
Salvationists, though with some qualifications. Officers
contemplating divorce or legal separation must notify the
Commander and relinquish their office before the com-
mencement of divorce proceedings. Reinstatement is not
encouraged, although the innocent party is given every
consideration for readmission to his rank in the Army.
"In the event of the re-acceptance of a divorced person, or
one whose marriage has been annulled, the Chief of Staff
will, at the same time, give a ruling in regard to the time
which must elapse before re-marriage can be considered." [29]
But not even these mild regulations apply to the Army
privates, who have no official rank in the society.

RITUAL AND WORSHIP

Although he deprived his followers of the sacraments,
Booth did not leave them without a complicated ceremonial. Salvationists are now told that "too much impor-

tance cannot be attached to ceremonies . . . in which
vows are registered and covenants entered into between
the soul and God." [30] Five principal kinds of ceremonies,
in addition to Salvation Meetings, are prescribed by the
Army manuals.

The Swearing in of Soldiers is the solemn installation
of Salvationists when they sign the "Articles of War," professing their faith in "the truth of the Army's teaching,"
promise to abstain from intoxicating liquors, anything low
or unclean, and pledge to support the Salvation War in
obedience to their officers.[31]

The Presentation of Colours, or the Army Flag, is "em-
blematical of the aggressiveness of Salvation warfare." The
principal feature of the ceremony is a homily on the meaning of the flag: red standing for the Blood of Christ, yellow
for the fire of the Holy Spirit, and blue for the purity of
God.[32]

Covenant Services are of two kinds, referring to holiness or to the Salvation war, in which the candidate makes
a solemn promise to God, vowing to maintain holiness of
life and promote the work of the Army until death, asking
that "the promises I make on earth be ratified in heaven." [33]

The Dedication of Children is a substitute for baptism
and consists in the officer accepting a child while pronouncing the formula: "In the name of the Lord and of
the —— Corps of the Salvation Army, I have taken this
child, who has been fully given up by his (her) parents for
the Salvation of the world. God save, bless, and keep this
child. Amen." [34]

Marriages are governed by detailed regulations, which
increase in number and severity with the rank of the Salvationist. Officers, *e.g.,* may not have courtships during
training, the men must have served at least two years and
be twenty-three years of age, they may marry only another
Salvationist, and the woman partner must be younger than

the man. The marriage ceremony is prescriptive and includes a profession of the "Articles on Marriage," among them a solemn promise that "we will not allow our marriage in any way to lessen our devotion to God, our affection for our comrades, or our faithfulness in the Army." [35]

While upwards of thirty types of meetings are provided by the *Orders and Regulations,* the most familiar is the Ordinary Meeting, "at which a determined and usually a prolonged effort is made for the Salvation of sinners." [36] A typical program begins with "a united Salvation song, to enlighten and cheer everyone," followed by prayer, a chorus, Bible reading and a brigade or united song. Then "testimonies, or short address, with singing interspersed, collection and Band music, announcements" and a solo or chorus to introduce the main function which is an appeal for sinners. One method of procedure is to preach a sermon, after which "a call may be given to silent prayer, during which the leader should gently urge the unsaved to tell God there and then whether or not they will accept His salvation." [37] The appeal for sinners to repent is made over and over again, "as long as any unsaved remain in the Meeting." Every possible motive is presented: "the claims of God, the uncertainty of life, the terrible condition of the lost . . . the blessedness of the saved both here and hereafter, the thraldom and disappointment of sin even in this life . . . should all in turn be brought forward as reasons for immediate decisions." In addition to these verbal appeals, "the singing is highly important. The Officer should consider what songs are best calculated to help sinners to the Mercy Seat, and when there, to lead them to commit themselves to the Saviour." A further suggestion is, "bombarding a sinner or backslider, (which) if wisely, earnestly, and believingly done, frequently helps the person concerned to yield. For instance . . . it may be very helpful for a few praying Salvationists to surround him, and while one pleads with him directly the others pray for his Salvation. Some of the best Salvationists have been literally 'compelled' into the Kingdom after this fashion." [38]

ORGANIZATION AND GOVERNMENT

The organizational structure of the Salvation Army is rigidly military. "Without any intention, in the first instance, on the part of its leaders to adopt military organization, the Salvation Army government has come to resemble the military form. Experience has proved this system of administration to be best adapted for preserving order and conducting aggressive warfare, and is, as all who have practical acquaintance with the management of men know, more prompt, forcible, and energetic than any other." [39]

Accordingly the governing personnel is strictly hierarchical. At the head of the Army stands the General who is elected by the High Council, and may be removed from office by the same authority. "The control of the General extends to every part of the Salvation Army, and to every phase of its operations throughout the world." [40] Under the General are the officers, divided into two classes: the field and staff officers. The first group, in turn, are variously ranked, from Probationary Lieutenant to Brigadier; the second from Lieutenant Colonel to Commissioner. All positions of authority are held by the officers, under whom serve the rank and file of the Army, called the Soldiers.

The basic juridical unit of the Army is the corps, of which there are over 17,000 in the world. Each corps is commanded by an officer, from Lieutenant to Brigadier, who is responsible to divisional headquarters which direct larger areas, corresponding to the whole or part of a State, *e.g.,* Indiana, Iowa and Eastern Michigan. Divisions are further organized into territories, the Eastern, Western, Southern and Central, with headquarters in New York, San Francisco, Atlanta and Chicago, each governed by a territorial commander and all united under a secretary at the national headquarters in New York.

Ultimate control of the organization, however, is vested in the General, who directs the Army's activities from the International Headquarters in London. Immediately under the General are the Chief of Staff and the heads of all the Departments—finance, audit, literary and translation, overseas, public relations, youth and education. "The work of all officers at International Headquarters is inspired by our Lord's command: 'Go ye into all the world, and preach the gospel.' " This ideal is implemented through a number of corporations, like the Salvation Army Trustee Company and the Reliance Bank, which offers "varied types of banking services." Not more than 1,000 pounds may be deposited in any one year and no fees are paid to directors; the profits, after providing for reserves, are paid over to the Salvation Army. The Salvation Army Assurance Society operates on the same non-personal profit basis. Currently handling 2,000,000 policies and having a premium income of 2,500,000 pounds, it is an insurance company with a "fundamental difference," where "the policyholder is not only a client, but a friend of the Salvation Army, and the Salvation Army assurance agent or officer is the 'padre of the people.' "[41]

Indicative of the complete dependence on the International Headquarters are the rules governing property and finance. "All Army property in any Territory is dealt with by the Headquarters of that Territory, under the direction of the General." Again, "The Headquarters concerned is responsible to the General for the oversight and care of all property, receiving the rents (where rent is payable), and paying the charges due in respect of it."[42] Correlative to this dependence are the "chief means by which the General controls the world-wide operations of the Army," namely, "by Orders and Regulations, which all Officers and Soldiers are under obligation to obey . . .

by appointing Officers to represent him . . . by the administrative control of the property of the Army . . . by having reports of the Salvation War regularly presented to him (and) by personal inspections and visitations." [43]

Such responsiveness to Superiors implies a training in discipline from the dawn of reason. "As a soldier under authority, which with all its human limitations he broadly accepts as from God, the Salvationist is a disciplined citizen of heaven (whose) conscience is instructed from childhood upward." [44] Behind this "outward man" of obedience, the Army professes to follow an "inner law," which it calls its faith in the redeemability of human nature and in the power of divine help. Opposed to the main stream of Protestant thought, it believes that "there is salvation for all who will come to Christ in sincere repentance." It will ". . . not countenance any restrictiveness in the grace of God (and) doctrines which deny the universality of redemption." [45] The result has been "the most widespread social program" in Protestant Christendom, based on the "Catholic" principle of William Booth's Methodism, which he borrowed from John Wesley and which denies man's utter depravity while affirming his power of free cooperation with the grace of God.

STATISTICS

International

Countries and Colonies where Salvation Army is Established	85
Officers	133,028
Social Institutions and Agencies	1,758
Periodicals Published	136
Circulation per Issue	1,959,250

United States

Total Membership	240,130
Meeting Halls (Legally called Churches)	1,327
Officers	28,163

Welfare Institutions (Not Including Stores or
Warehouses)   423
U.S.O. Stations   34
Hospitals (Including U.S.A. Possessions and
Mexico)   41
Sunday Schools   1,150
Total Enrollment   133,504

REFERENCES

1. *The Salvation Army Year Book, 1956* (London: Salvationist Publishing, 1956), p. 50.
2. William Booth, *In Darkest England and the Way Out* (Atlanta: Southern Territorial Headquarters, U.S.A., 1942), p. 21.
3. *Ibid.,* p. 23.
4. Alfred J. Gilliard, *The Faith of the Salvationist* (London: Salvationist Publishing, n.d.), p. 3.
5. *Salvation Army Year Book,* p. 135.
6. *The Salvation Army Handbook of Doctrine* (London: International Headquarters, 1955), p. 1.
7. *Ibid.,* p. 31.
8. *Ibid.,* pp. 32-35.
9. *Ibid.,* p. 35.
10. *Ibid.,* p. 47.
11. *Ibid.,* p. 49.
12. *Ibid.,* pp. 96, 99.
13. *Ibid.,* p. 112.
14. *Ibid.,* p. 115.
15. *Ibid.,* p. 118.
16. *Ibid.,* p. 116.
17. *Ibid.,* pp. 119, 120, 122.
18. *Ibid.,* pp. 118-119.
19. *Ibid.,* p. 127.
20. *Ibid.,* pp. 131, 135.
21. *Ibid.,* pp. 132-133.
22. *Ibid.,* p. 160.
23. *Loc. cit.*
24. *Ibid.,* p. 161.
25. *Ibid.,* p. 162.
26. M. L. Carpenter, *Salvationists and the Sacraments* (London: Salvationist Publishing, 1945), p. 4.
27. *Ibid.,* pp. 4-5.
28. *Loc. cit.*
29. *Orders and Regulations for Officers of the Salvation Army* (London: International Headquarters, 1950), pp. 121-122.
30. *Salvation Army Ceremonies* (London: Salvationist Publishing, 1947), p. 1.
31. *Ibid.,* p. 3.
32. *Ibid.,* pp. 6-7.
33. *Ibid.,* p. 11.
34. *Ibid.,* p. 16.
35. *Ibid.,* p. 21.
36. *Orders and Regulations,* p. 279.
37. *Ibid.,* p. 287.
38. *Ibid.,* p. 291.
39. *Ibid.,* p. 6.
40. *Ibid.,* p. 11.
41. *Salvation Army Year Book,* p. 65.
42. *Orders and Regulations,* pp. 30-31.
43. *Ibid.,* p. 12.
44. Gilliard, *op. cit.,* p. 14.
45. *Ibid.,* p. 18.

13. Unitarians

JUDGED BY Catholic standards, the Unitarians are not really Christians because they deny the divinity of Christ. And even among Protestants they are ostracized by professedly Christian societies, like the National Council of the Churches of Christ. But Unitarians have their own definition of Christianity. They argue that, "If to be a 'Christian' is to profess and sincerely seek to practice the religion of Jesus, so simply and beautifully given in the Sermon on the Mount, then Unitarians are Christians." [1] In fact, they are more Christian than their critics, since "the orthodox Christian world has forgotten and forsaken the real, human Jesus of the Gospels, and has substituted a 'Christ' of dogmatism, metaphysics, and pagan philosophy." [2]

Behind this militant opposition to dogma is the real spirit of Unitarianism as an ecclesiastical institution built on the foundations of anti-supernaturalism. Substantially negative, its corporate existence is a symbol of the limits to which Protestant liberalism can go and still call itself Christian.

HISTORY

Although Unitarians as individuals or groups denying the Trinity may be found in the first century of the Chris-

tian era, the actual beginnings of the denomination go
back less than two hundred years. Theologically the genesis of Unitarianism can be traced to the liberal reaction
against Calvinism as understood by the Congregational
churches in colonial New England. Under the influence of
deistic ideas imported from England, liberal-minded Congregationalists began publicly to preach doctrines that contradicted the Calvinist elements in their church's confession. "The doctrine that Jesus is God, the principle of
predestination, the belief in the depravity of human nature, the dogma of the atonement, the conception of Deity
as a God of wrath, damnation and hell-fire—all these teachings were challenged." [3]

American Unitarianism was consequently born as a
secessionist movement in the Congregational Church,
though the first church to profess Unitarian teaching was
the Episcopalian King's Chapel, Boston, which in 1785
modified its liturgy by eliminating the Athanasian and
Nicene Creeds and all references to the Trinity. In 1802
the oldest Pilgrim church, founded at Plymouth in 1620,
became Unitarian. Within a short time, twenty out of the
twenty-five original churches in Massachusetts became
Unitarian, until approximately 125 churches broke with
the conservative Congregational body or were forced to
resign as unorthodox and essentially unchristian. Drawing
from the intelligentsia among the liberals and lacking
creedal cohesion, it was felt that an official Unitarian publication would help to unify the secessionists. Thus in 1821
the *Christian Register* was founded, which is reputedly the
oldest religious journal of continuous publication in
America.

Two landmarks in Unitarian history which laid down
the principles for future development were the Baltimore
Sermon in 1819 of William Ellery Channing, outstanding
Congregationalist preacher, and the address delivered by

Ralph Waldo Emerson at the graduation exercises of Harvard Divinity School in 1838. Channing proclaimed that the liberal position is more soundly based on Scripture than traditional Calvinism. Emerson's speech was more radical. He proposed to change the foundation of religion from historical documents and external events, *i.e.*, from the Scriptures and miraculous phenomena, to the subjective life within man. "Jesus Christ," for him, "belonged to the true race of prophets. . . . Alone in all history he estimated the greatness of man. One man was true to what is in you and me. He saw that God incarnates himself in man, and evermore goes forth anew to take possession of his world. He said in the jubilee of this sublime emotion, 'I am divine.'" [4] Like his contemporary, David Strauss, Emerson thought this picture of the man Christ suffered distortion in the early Church. "The understanding caught this high chant from the poet's lips, and said, in the next age, 'This was Jehovah come down from heaven.' . . . Christianity became a Mythus, as the poetic teaching of Greece and Egypt before." [5]

Regarded as one of the founders of American Unitarianism, Emerson later left the ministry and organized a group of Transcendentalists. Eventually he replaced the Unitarian deity by a vaguely pantheistic Over-soul and rejected the idea of personal immortality.

Meantime, in 1825, the American Unitarian Association was established as a society of individuals interested in promoting the influence of Unitarianism, to be reorganized sixty years later as an association of churches. The Beacon Press, current publisher of Paul Blanshard's books, was started in Boston in 1902 as the official publishing house of the American Unitarian Association. Two years later the Starr King School for the Unitarian Ministry was founded in Berkeley, California.

In the early 1930's, the "Unitarians suddenly awoke

to the realization that a long period of neglect of organizational matters had brought the denomination to the verge of collapse." They were also under pressure from "outside forces illiberal and totalitarian in character," and "slowly made up their minds to accept the undeniable fact that they could no longer depend upon the generosity of a few men and women of great wealth to support their denominational program." [6] The result was a complete over-hauling of organization structure to make previously disparate agencies more cooperative; a new emphasis was placed on social and youth services; the United Unitarian Appeal was made into a permanent institution, drawing funds from local churches for national and corporate ventures and, perhaps most important, the Beacon Press entered on a more "bold policy in the publication field," so that between 1948 and 1953, some $2,500,000 worth of books was sold by the Press. Among the best sellers were Blanshard's trilogy: *American Freedom and Catholic Power* (1949), *Communism, Democracy and Catholic Power* (1951), and *The Irish and Catholic Power* (1953).

DOCTRINAL POSITION

The doctrinal position of the Unitarians can be defined negatively as a radical deism which denies any validity to the supernatural, whether as revelation, divine grace, or an order of reality beyond the natural, *i.e.*, beyond what is due to man as a human being. Thus, as regards revelation, the Scriptures are equated with the Moslem Koran and the Hindu Vedas, and summarily described as mythical:

> In all cultures men's keenest thoughts, deepest longings, most haunting fears, and boldest affirmations about life's meanings have been expressed in legend, folk tale, and myth. The lives of their heroes have been

told and retold. Accepted ways of getting along with one another have been preserved in precept and in codes of law. In many instances much of this material has been written down, collected, edited, and re-edited. These are the sacred literatures or Bibles of the world, often considered by the peoples that have produced them as the very word of God. The Judeo-Christian Bible is a remarkable collection of this sort.[7]

Consequent on this anti-supernaturalism, the Unitarians as a body reject all the basic dogmas of Christianity. "We neither believe," writes one of their ministers, "in the unique divinity of Jesus as the supernatural son of God nor in the human depravity which was supposed to make a supernatural savior necessary. We believe that, as he was, so are we all—as Paul said—offspring of the Eternal, 'in whom we live and move and have our being.' " Consequently, "It is not the details of Jesus' teaching, nor the doctrines about his birth and death, but the quality of the spirit in which he met his problems and lived his faith that we find inspiring. It is as an inspiration to living, not as the price paid to free us from sin and mortality, that we look to him."[8] The reference to Scripture to deny a scriptural doctrine is characteristic of Unitarian polemics and dogmatism. St. Paul's solitary quotation from a pagan poet is lifted out of context, arbitrarily combined with a perfectly irrelevant passage, and the combination used to dismiss the Christian Redemption, which is taken for granted on every page of St. Paul's epistles.

Another quality of Unitarian logic is to pit faith against faith, the Unitarian against the Christian, and deny the latter by the device of calling it unreasonable. Thus:

> The doctrines of atonement and resurrection, supposedly divinely revealed in the Christian Scriptures,

have no meaning for us, since we could not believe
that any man could by any act take from us or any
others the responsibility for our own sins, whether we
had inherited them—an obvious absurdity—or committed them ourselves. Nor does the supposed resurrection of one man prove or provide for a similar resurrection of others. Immortality could not be, we believe,
a commodity bought for us by a transaction between
God and a supposed devil, but if, as many of us believe,
there is a real immortality, it must necessarily be the
natural continuation of life *per se*. The "devil" and
"hell" have greatly enriched the vocabulary of abuse
and humor, but they add nothing to the understanding
of nature.[9]

To arrive at this expression of Unitarian faith, however,
it was first necessary to confuse bodily resurrection, restored to us as a grace by Christ, with the immortality
which is natural to the soul as a spiritual substance; it was
further necessary falsely to attribute to Christians the notion that Christ takes away the responsibility for our sins,
rather than guilt for sins honestly repented; and finally to
posit the blasphemy that God and the devil had to bargain
over the price of man's redemption.

   While Unitarianism as an institution is conveniently
identified with a kind of deism, individual Unitarians, including leaders in the church, go beyond the mere denial
of the supernatural. Their concept of God and the real
distinction between Creator and creature can be very
vague. "All Unitarians would agree," for instance, "that
there is something within the range of human experience
—whether in the reality of God or in what Wordsworth
called 'the still sad music of humanity'—that properly calls
forth the responses of reverence, wonder, appreciation

and humility. It is known by many names and expressed in many ways." [10] Less vague and more nearly monistic is the declaration that, "The Cosmos (Nature, Universe) is the highest unity that we know. Many and varied are the things and beings of the world; yet all are parts of one vast and enduring Whole or Cosmos. . . . The Cosmos . . . is creative. This does not mean making something from nothing, but rather making the new out of the old. . . . Since the Cosmos is the highest known unity and is creative, we call it God. God and the Cosmos are one." [11]

WORSHIP AND LITURGY

Unexpectedly, the Unitarian churches have an elaborate system of corporate worship, sufficiently uniform to be compiled in an official *Services of Religion*. Liturgical functions, orders of service, with hundreds of prayers and hymns have been edited by the Unitarian and Universalist Commission on Hymns and Services, to be used by the member churches as "a sound norm which can be followed to advantage." Sources from which the formularies are drawn are mostly Roman Catholic and Protestant, with additions and alterations from "the religious ideals of our own day." [12] The editors' apology for using sectarian material is that, "Although the theological content of those traditional forms, whether of the Roman Catholic Church or of the older branches of Protestantism, frequently expresses a way of thinking about religion which is far removed from that of the modern man, the pattern upon which the older services have been built up is often beautifully and nobly devised, and offers a norm which may well be followed." [13] Thus we find among the 576 hymns in the Service Book, such familiar pieces as *Adoro Te Devote* (words changed), *Adeste Fideles* (words retained), *Tantum Ergo* (words changed), *O Salutaris Hostia* (three melodies, words changed in each), *Stabat Mater* (no words), *Magnificat* (words retained), *Lead Kindly Light* (words retained).

To provide for every taste, sixteen Orders of Services are offered by the Manual, five for festive occasions, and eleven for the regular Sunday and occasional functions. The First Order of Service, in sequence, covers twenty different acts of worship, including:

Litanies, with the minister and people alternating in such petitions as: "From all ambition and greed, which bring want and distress to multitudes and debase the bodies and souls of men, shutting them from the fulness of life . . . O Lord deliver us." [14]

The *Offertory,* which consists of sentences from the Scriptures with corresponding prayers, such as: "We give thee, Lord, what is thine own, for all we have comes from thy bounty to enrich our lives. Grant us thy grace with these outward offerings to present ourselves willingly before thee, dedicated anew to thy service in the spirit of Jesus Christ." [15]

The *Benediction,* which means the reading of selections from the Scriptures, frequently described as "adapted." Thus II Corinthians 13:14 reads: "The grace of the Lord Jesus Christ . . . and the love of God, and the fellowship of his Holy Spirit be with us all, this day and forevermore. Amen." [16]

Two kinds of invitation to the Communion Service are provided, one at which the elements are distributed, and another in which, "The bread and wine will not be passed, the communion being wholly symbolic." [17] Corresponding provision is made in the ritual when the elements are not given to the people. After the words of institution, the minister says: "Let us partake in spirit with those who, remembering him, have shared the bread of life and the wine of sacrifice." Then lifting up the plate with the bread and also the cup, tasting a little of each, he says to the people: "We take and eat this in remembrance of Christ. . . . We drink this in remembrance of Christ." [18]

ORGANIZATIONAL STRUCTURE

Unitarian Churches in the United States are always congregational, which means that the local church is juridically independent. Each church has its own set of by-laws and statement of purpose. It chooses its own minister, who "is given a position of leadership, not in order that he may dogmatically instruct the congregation in beliefs and practices, but in order that he may stimulate the members in their own free development of religious belief and action. The minister holds no ecclesiastical authority given to him by external agencies." [19]

As Unitarian churches became more numerous, they took on the organizational form of the Congregational Church from which they seceded, so that, at present, the administrative set-up is not unlike that of the parent denomination: Local churches are organized into Conferences, which form natural geographical associations, and vary in size from seven or eight to twenty member churches. "The projects initiated by the Conferences vary greatly, from the founding of new churches to the establishment of homes for aged people. But the major purpose of the Conference usually is to help churches and church members to become acquainted with one another and to promote more effectively the cause of Unitarianism in their area." [20]

As Conferences grow, they unite into regional bodies, largely the outgrowth of a study by the Commission on Appraisal (1934-1936), which recommended a decentralization of administrative functions. Eight regional units are now operating in the States. The Southern Unit is called the "Thomas Jefferson Conference Region" in trib-

ute to that historical figure's avowed Unitarianism.[21] Leading the Regions are elected Council boards, "charged with
policy decisions, with the employment of executive directors, and with the budgeting of funds which are secured,
in the main, from the United Unitarian Appeal." [22]

At the top level is the American Unitarian Association,
founded in 1825, and reorganized in 1844 as a voluntary
association designed "to undertake such functions on behalf of the entire body of associated churches as these
churches, by delegates assembled, may at any time commit
to it." [23] The American Unitarian Association may in no
way infringe on the autonomy of the local churches, while
performing "many functions that are of the greatest importance but that individual churches could not carry out
alone." [24] Such, among others, are the General Alliance of
Unitarian and Other Liberal Christian Women, with 413
branches doing educational, inter-faith and lay-leadership
work; the Laymen's League, charged, besides other duties,
with recruiting for the ministry; the American Unitarian
Youth, recently merged with the youth organization of the
Universalist Church of America under the name of Liberal Religious Youth; the Service Pension Society which
administers the invested funds to provide a pension for
retired Unitarian ministers; and the Unitarian Fellowship
for Social Justice, founded in 1908, to sustain its members
"in united action against social injustice and in the realization of religious ideals in present day society." [25] In the
thirties, the U.F.S.J. opposed Father Coughlin; it is now
working with other groups "to prevent any further en-
croachment on state by church." [26] In 1953 it presented
its annual award to Mrs. Vashti McCollum, active Unitarian in Urbana, Illinois, "who so courageously took her
case on released-time religious education to the U. S. Supreme Court—and won." [27] The U.F.S.J. has 75 local chapters in America.

STATISTICS

Membership of Unitarian Churches in U.S. and Canada 92,600
Membership in the United States   90,398
     Churches   366
     Ordained Clergy   518
     Pastors having Charges   366

REFERENCES

1. Karl M. Chworowsky, "What Is a Unitarian?", *A Guide to the Religions of America,* ed. by Leo Rosten (New York: Simon and Schuster, 1955), p. 142.
2. *Loc. cit.*
3. Harry B. Scholefield, *Guide to Unitarianism* (Boston: Beacon Press, 1955), p. 36.
4. Ralph Waldo Emerson, *Nature, Addresses and Lectures* (Boston: Houghton-Mifflin, 1883), p. 128.
5. *Loc. cit.*
6. Scholefield, *op. cit.,* p. 53.
7. *Ibid.,* p. 15.
8. Robert T. Weston, *Faith Without Fear* (Louisville: Private Printing, 1949), p. 9.
9. *Ibid.,* p. 10.
10. Scholefield, *op. cit.,* p. 5.
11. John H. Hershey, "The Liberal Way for Today," *Unity,* CXLI (May-June, 1955), 31. This statement of monism is doubly significant; the author is minister of the First Congregational Church in Easton, Mass., and the publication is an official organ of the Western Unitarian Conference, with headquarters in Chicago.
12. *Services of Religion* (Boston: Beacon Press, 1953), p. vi.
13. *Loc. cit.*
14. *Ibid.,* p. 6.
15. *Ibid.,* p. 71.

16. *Ibid.,* p. 165.
17. *Ibid.,* p. 148.
18. *Ibid.,* p. 152.
19. Scholefield, *op. cit.,* p. 44.
20. *Loc. cit.*
21. Jefferson was a member of the Episcopalian Church in his community but according to a letter he wrote in 1825 to Dr. Waterhouse, ". . . the population of my neighborhood is too slender and is too much divided into other sects to maintain any one preacher well. I must therefore be contented to be a Unitarian by myself." *Ibid.,* p. 62.
22. *Ibid.,* p. 45.
23. *Loc. cit.* The present constitution of the American Unitarian Association was adopted in 1894 to heal a doctrinal schism in the denomination. It is "so broad as to satisfy both conservatives and radicals," and for fifty years has preserved peace among the churches, "for it is realized that perfect spiritual freedom has been achieved." Earl M. Wilbur, *Our Unitarian Heritage* (Boston: Beacon Press, 1954), p. 465.
24. Scholefield, *op. cit.,* pp. 45-46.
25. *Ibid.,* p. 48.
26. *Ibid.,* p. 27.
27. *Loc. cit.*

14. United Church of Christ

WHEN IT COMES into existence in June, 1957, as the result of a merger between the Congregational Christians and the Evangelical Reformed, the United Church of Christ will be the newest major addition to the family of Protestant denominations in the United States. The legal controversy which this merger occasioned has received national publicity. After years of litigation in the civil courts, certain decisions have been handed down which are deeply significant for future church and state relations in the country.

Leaders in the merger plans have tried to keep intact the doctrinal and ritual characteristics of the respective bodies. Even the ecclesiastical structure of the uniting parties will not be much altered. For this reason it seemed best to treat the Congregational Christian and the Evangelical Reformed Churches separately, in order to do full justice to the distinctive elements of each.

Congregationalists

CONGREGATIONALISM boasts of being the most ecumenically-minded of the Protestant sects. "No other ecclesiastical group has participated in a greater number of unions with other groups." Congregationalists "will cooperate with any Christian communion which will cooperate with them. In any community, they oppose religious isolationism and denominational exclusiveness." [1]

Tangible evidence of this ecclesiastical cooperativeness is the fact that twice in less than thirty years the Congregational Church will have fused with other denominations on a national scale, and altered its name to the point of obliteration. Comparable to their penchant for organic merger is the active promotion by Congregationalists of church union among other religious bodies. If they are sometimes called, "the interdenominational denomination," this title is well deserved.

HISTORY

As the name suggests, the Congregational Christian Church is a union of two denominations, the Congregational and the Christian. Actually it is the amalgamation of at least six religious bodies, going back to the late sixteenth century. The beginnings of Congregationalism are

254

commonly dated from the founding, in 1581, of a church in Norwich, England, by Robert Browne, a Separatist Anglican minister. A Cambridge graduate, Browne was demoted from the ministry for teaching "seditious doctrines," notably that the basis of church membership was not submission to episcopal authority but acceptance of a covenant, to which a group of people gave their mutual consent. Pressure from the government forced Browne's followers to move to Holland, and then to America, where, as the Mayflower Pilgrims, they landed at Plymouth, Massachusetts, in 1620.

As Separatists without a ministry, "who had broken away from the arbitrary rule of the episcopacy and from what they regarded as the empty and unchristian forms prevailing in the Church of England," the Pilgrims would probably have disappeared as an ecclesiastical body had they not been joined in 1629 by the immigrant Puritans, who made their first settlement in Salem three years before.[2] Unlike the Pilgrims, the Puritans admitted the validity of a state church in England, but they sought to reform this body from within. Basically Calvinist in doctrine, they were willing to remain in the Established Church on condition that there was "more preaching and less liturgy, fewer vestments and more well-educated clergy;" they wished to cleanse English worship "of any vestige of Roman Catholicism."[3] On August 6, 1629, the Salem Puritans united to form a church by covenant, elected and ordained a pastor and teacher, and sent their first "letter missive" to the Plymouth Separatists, asking for approbation and guidance. The Plymouth Church was happy to comply and sent delegates to Salem to extend the right hand of fellowship. "This was the real inception of American Congregationalism."[4]

In striking contrast with present-day liberalism among Congregationalists, the early days of the sect (c. 1640)

showed a fanatical intolerance of other religions, which
their own historians admit "was a blot on the escutcheon
of the Puritan colonists." [5] Quakers and Baptists especially
were maltreated and persecuted, even to death. The Salem
executions for witchcraft belong to this period.

While the Puritan element in Congregationalism gave
it a doctrinal basis of unity, the Separatist "independency"
of thought and policy slowly neutralized the Calvinist
foundation until, by 1730, the Congregationalist churches
had become quite thoroughly secularized. This induced a
reaction, called "The Great Awakening," ushered in by
Jonathan Edwards, pastor at Northampton, Massachusetts,
who was "consumed by the sovereignty of God, the fateful
brevity of life and its eternal issues." [6]

During the next century, Congregationalists were concerned with five principal developments: higher education, missions, the Presbyterian question, the Unitarian
separation, the formation of a system of government and
the formulation of a uniform statement of doctrine. In
education, the Congregational Church was a pioneer.
Harvard, founded in 1636, and Yale, founded in 1701,
were established to prepare students for the Congregational ministry. Dartmouth (1769), Williams (1793), Am-
herst (1821), Bowdoin (1794), and Middlebury (1800) were
among the first senior colleges in New England. By 1952,
fifty-one colleges and fourteen seminaries in the United
States had professedly Congregational-Christian origins or
affiliations.

The missionary zeal of the Congregationalists spread
the denomination far into the West, but also brought on
the Presbyterian crisis which threatened to dissolve Congregationalism in America. For economic reasons, the two
churches had joined forces according to the Plan of Union
(1801), but "the more authoritative and tough-fibered Presbyterians' order was better suited to loose frontier condi-

tions," with the result that in fifty years about two thousand churches became Presbyterian, many of them originally Congregationalist.[7] The Plan of Union was rejected in 1852, and Congregational-Presbyterian relations have been somewhat aloof ever since.

The Unitarian departure is an epic in American Protestantism as illustrative of the changing theological order among the denominations. Shortly after the American Unitarian Association was founded in 1825, about 125 Congregational churches seceded in favor of the liberals. Ironically, a century later Congregationalist historians regretfully observed that although the Unitarians left because they were opposed to dogmatism, especially Christ's divinity, "the position theologically of the first generation of Unitarian preachers would now hardly provoke a Congregational examining council to argument";[8] so far has Congregationalism broken through "traditional conventionalities and . . . creedal literalism."[9]

Until 1852 American Congregationalists were united largely by ties of common origin and informal cooperative efforts among the churches. In that year, however, the first general meeting of Congregational representatives was held at Albany, New York—drawn together by the need for material support of the churches and missionary enterprises in the West. Out of this initial meeting eventually grew the existing jurisdictional structure of the Congregational Christian Churches.

In 1913, at Kansas City, the National Council adopted a statement of faith, polity and fellowship that still remains the primary cohesive force in American Congregationalism. The article on faith begins: "We believe in God the Father . . ." and goes through a sizeable portion of the Apostles' Creed, ending with the words, " . . . we look with faith for the triumph of righteousness and the life everlasting."[10] Regarding polity, the full article de-

clares, "We believe in the freedom and responsibility of
the individual soul, and the right of private judgment. We
hold to the autonomy of the local church and its independence of all ecclesiastical control. We cherish the fellowship
of the churches, united in district, state and national
bodies, for counsel and cooperation in matters of common
concern." [11] The declaration on "Wider Fellowship" is a
single sentence, stating that, "While affirming the liberty
of our churches, and the validity of our ministry, we hold
to the unity and catholicity of the Church of Christ, and
will unite with all its branches in hearty cooperation, and
will earnestly seek, as far as in us lies, that the prayer of
Our Lord may be answered, that they all may be one." [12]
Among the tangible results of this doctrine on wider fellowship was the incorporation into the body of Congregationalism of two major sects, the Protestant Evangelical
in 1925, and the Christian Churches in 1931. A more significant effect is the impulse which Congregationalism has
officially given in promoting the ecumenical movement
in the United States and throughout the world. The constitutional basis of the World Council of Churches as "a
fellowship of churches," whose function is to "offer counsel and provide opportunity of united action" among its
constituents, is a paraphrase of Congregational principle
expanded to global proportions.[13]

DOCTRINE

Before attempting to make a summary of Congregationalist doctrine, it is essential to see the two sets of principles which, according to the best commentators, are the
focal points between which the whole concept of Congregationalism oscillates:

The Principle of Independency allows the greatest freedom in matters of faith and doctrine. According to the
Congregationalists, doctrinal creeds are not expressions of

stable verities which have prior importance in man's deal-
ings with God. They are merely "intellectual statements
of religious experiences (which) represent landmarks along
the pathway of religious thought." Consequently, ". . .
as experiences and intellectual capacities change . . . it is
inevitable that creeds should change." [14] Assuming that
religious doctrine is objectively fluid, Congregationalism
logically requires no subscription to any set creed as a condition for membership. "No member," therefore, "is ever
told that he must believe any specific religious tenet in
order to be a good church member." [15]

The Principle of Fellowship is a corrective and limitation of doctrinal freedom. It means that certain people
band together into a congregation, and local churches
unite into associations and councils, out of a "sense of
comity." [16] They feel they have a common purpose, not
unlike that of "the group of disciples who were gathered
about Jesus . . . to be with him and to be like him." [17]

If Congregationalist doctrine were examined only on
the principle of independency or freedom, there would be
nothing, practically, to describe, except the extremes of
dogmatic liberalism permitted within the denomination;
whereas fellowship suggests that the members and member
churches have at least some convictions in common, which
may be classified and compared with the corresponding
doctrines of the Catholic faith.

Revelation and the Bible. The Congregationalist catechism answer to the question, "What is divine revelation?"
describes it as ". . . the process by which God has helped
men to find out about Him." [18] But this is not to be understood as a supernatural communication from God,
made in times past, now closed, and to be regarded as the
inerrant and immutable word of God. The Scriptures are
only a natural, although sublime, record of the religious
sentiments of their authors, since "the Bible grew out of

the religion of a people. Originally it was not so much a guide for their living as a statement of their experience." As such experiences were conditioned by the capacity of the writer and the times in which he lived, so it is "inevitable that there should be differences of value in different parts of the Bible." To illustrate: "Belief in demons was once a part of the framework of common thought. That belief would of course creep into the record. (But) why should any sensible reader allow an outgrown category of thought to rob him of a permanent truth or cast a shadow over an abiding experience?" The experience in this case is described as a sense of evil which was so intense as to give it personality.[19]

The Church and Churches. In Congregationalist terminology, the church has two basic meanings which are not mutually exclusive. There is first the "One Holy Catholic Church" of the Apostles' Creed. This is "the Church Universal (which) includes all who accept Jesus Christ as Master, determining to do His will whatsoever it may cost. This is greater than all Churches together, for there are people who accept Jesus as Saviour who may not belong to any organization." Accordingly "the Church Universal is the whole body of Christians." [20]

While everyone who accepts Christ as Savior belongs to the Church Invisible, many Christians have banded together into separate groups, since "it is much easier to be a real Christian as a member of some congregation with which one may regularly worship, pray, study and receive the inspiration of preaching and fellowship." [21] Among these auxiliaries is the Congregational Christian Church, which is "democratic in organization. As the name 'Congregational' indicates, the *Congregation* is the final authority. Each individual church, through the action of its members, calls its own ministers, plans its own programs, regulates its own finances, determines its own policies. The principle of cooperation is recognized in that individual churches group themselves together in local associations of churches, state conferences, and the General Council of the Congregational Christian Churches. The decisions of these larger groups, however, are never mandatory unless approved by the local church." [22]

In practice, a new Congregationalist church is formed on the basis of an agreement or covenant, by which "a group of people bind themselves together in Christian fellowship 'to walk in the ways of the Lord, made known or to be made known to them.' " Here "you have the true basis of a Congregational Church. To join a church is to make a Christian confession," *i.e.,* to profess Christ as one's Savior, and "to accept the covenant." [23] In virtue of the Christian confession, a man becomes a member of the Church Universal; by reason of accepting the covenant, he becomes a Congregationalist. Verbally expressed, the covenant may be only a short formula, as, for example, "We covenant with God and one another, and do bind ourselves in the presence of God to walk together in all His ways according as He is pleased to reveal Himself unto us in His blessed word of truth." [24] But in practice it means that the members of a parish agree to believe and worship substantially alike, allowing malcontents the option of going elsewhere or forming another congregation if they so desire.

Divinity and Personality of Christ. While permitting acceptance of the Nicene Creed which declares, "I believe . . . in one Lord Jesus Christ, the only-begotten Son of God," the Congregational Christian Churches explain the divinity of Christ in terms which negative the hypostatic union. In answer to the question, "What made Jesus divine?", we are told: "To be fair with the rest of humanity, we have to suggest that it was not special privileges. . . . The divinity of Jesus was due to a complete surrender of his own will and an absolute opening up of his life until at the end, all that was human was shot through with divinity. His divinity was achieved, as well as endowed. Had he yielded to temptation, he would have weakened and ultimately destroyed his divine nature." [25] Comparable to Christ's achievement, we can become equally divine. "Our endowment of a divine nature cannot be claimed unless we deny the invitations of sin. Jesus is the source of our confidence that we can live as children of God. What God did in Jesus, He can and will do in any life which will persistently say 'No' to sin, and 'Yes' to righteousness." [26] Thus the Congregationalist idea of Christ's divinity is distinctly Arian. "Jesus had a profound and unique sense of God. To him, more than to any other man that has lived, God was real. He lived in constant fellowship with God. . . . He said that he and the Father were one in purpose and spirit," not in substance and nature.[27]

The Sacraments. Congregational Christians define sacraments as "sacred ceremonies observed from earliest times by the Christian Church, to remember Christ and to receive his spirit." [28] Two sacraments are commonly observed, baptism and the Lord's Supper. Baptism is recognized as "the Sacrament of Christian Dedication in which we dedicate ourselves or our children to God. Water is used as a symbol of the cleansing of the soul by the Holy Spirit." [29] The Trinitarian formula is used in the administration of baptism, which may be by immersion, ablution, or aspersion, depending on the person's choice; although the customary way is "to sprinkle a few drops of water on the head of the person to be baptized." [30] Infant baptism is permitted and encouraged; sponsors are optional. However, baptism is not regarded as essential for salvation, or even for membership in the Church. As expressed by a writer for the Commission on Evangelism, "Some Christians, notably the Quakers, believe only in a baptism of the spirit and do not use water baptism at all. Like many other Congregational ministers, my experience has been that our churches gladly receive members of the Society of Friends without requiring water baptism. We leave it to their conscientious choice." [31] Although the phrase, "sacrament of cleansing," occurs in the baptismal ritual, the doctrinal explanations sedulously avoid reference to the remission of sin, original or actual. Congregationalism, we are told, turns away from the external magical concept which "makes of Baptism a saving ordinance"; it regards as ". . . tragic. . . the idea that infants dying unbaptized were lost—though medieval theology modified their 'lostness' somewhat by providing for them a special compartment called 'Limbo' in the world to come, which would not be a place of torture, like hell, but not quite heaven, either!" [32]

The Lord's Supper is accorded a place of honor in the Congregationalist *Book of Worship* and generally described as a sacrament. But the real presence is admitted only in the spiritual, symbolic sense of John Calvin and Ulrich Zwingli. Erroneously attributing the Catholic doctrine of transubstantiation to a late innovation, official only "since the year 1215," [33] the Eucharistic change from bread and wine to the Lord's Body and Blood is said to consist "not in a physical change in the material properties of the elements on the altar, but in a moral and spiritual change in the ethical and religious nature of the worshipers assembled before it." [34] The "reality" in the real presence, therefore, is purely subjective. Since Christ tells us He is present where two or three are gathered in His name, then "surely he may be truly and especially present, in a spiritual sense, in the hearts of the worshipers and among them when we assemble before the table upon which are spread the symbols of his life and death, the bread and wine of the sacrament." [35] Congregationalists argue, as did Calvin, that it is not necessary "so literally" to understand Christ's words of institution. They arrive at this position as a corollary to their relativist interpretation of the Bible, and their denial of objective validity to Christian tradition which, from apostolic times, has proclaimed a corporeal presence of Christ in the Eucharist.

Life after Death. In response to the catechism question, "What is life everlasting?," the answer is that, ". . . life everlasting is the never-ending life of the soul with God." [36] Not only is life everlasting admitted for the soul, but the resurrection of the body is also accepted, at least by the authors of the Commission on Evangelism and Devotional Life. "How shall we live in (the) future state," one of the writers asks, and answers, hesitatingly, "I do not know. Jesus thought of it as a place of activity. Heaven would not mean all we want it to mean unless we could have fellowship with living personal spirits. . . . Our bodies will be different. Paul said that 'flesh and blood cannot inherit the kingdom of heaven.' But we must have some body." [37] Unfortunately no distinction is made between bodily immortality and the immortality of the soul—the first accepted on faith and the second also known from reason. Moreover, faith in an after-life is reduced to a native instinct, since Christians are simply urged to "cherish this immortal hope. You cannot and need not prove it. You are born with it. . . . You are going somewhere; you are becoming something." [38]

There is no mention of hell in the standard doctrinal treatises. In fact, a place of eternal punishment seems to be ruled out by an implicit belief in universal salvation, since ". . . what man begins here he will be given the opportunity to finish hereafter." [39] Life everlasting is univocally equated with blessedness, the "never-ending life of the

soul with God," which means, "the triumph of righteousness (in) the final victory of good over evil, which must
come because God wills it." [40]

RITUAL AND WORSHIP

Since 1948, the Congregational Christian Churches
have a *Book of Worship* that was ten years in the making
and involved the cooperative labor of a group of ministers
appointed for the task by the General Council of the denomination. This is admittedly a major departure from
the Calvinist austerity of the colonial Puritans. "Standing
as we do in the non-liturgical tradition, our Congregational Christian Churches have not commonly made much
use of symbols in their worship." [41] But under pressure
from the people, the need was felt for a re-introduction
into religious service of many things which "at the time
of the Reformation the reformed churches did away
with." [42] The result is that, while keeping the matter optional, the Ritual now provides, in detail, for the use of
an altar, covered with three white cloths; eucharistic candles which "may be present (on the altar) at all times, but
should be lighted only for the Lord's Supper"; [43] flowers
on the altar, which "are works of God's creative power
and remind us of the marvelous beauty of his natural
world"; [44] a cross, although "a crucifix (with corpus) is almost never used in a Congregational Christian Church"; [45]
following the Catholic tradition, "the church is often built
in the shape of a cross"; [46] the vestments worn by the minister now include a cassock, surplice and stole, which "is
the sign of an ordained clergyman," and which may be of
various colors.[47] While offering twenty-five pages on liturgical symbols, which "can become a language of great
potency and beauty," the Ritual is careful to point out,
"there is a grave and constant danger of losing our sense
of values in the minutiae of forms." Consequently, "it is

of the greatest importance that the congregation be ever aware of the facts or objects for which the symbols stand; that children and newcomers be instructed; and that simplicity be guarded." [48]

Among the ordinary services provided by the Congregational Ritual, the most important is the Worship with Communion. The sequence adheres closely to the Anglican formulary, modeled on the Roman Missal. Following the "Prayer of Consecration" are the "Words of Institution," verbatim from the Scriptures. But in giving communion to the people, the minister expressly says: "Ministering to you in His Name, I give you this bread. . . . I give you this cup." [49]

The ordination ceremony is the most elaborate in the Ritual, "since this is, by common consent, a most solemn and significant occasion." [50] Presiding at the functions is an ordained minister who publicly examines the candidate on his fitness for the office. Then, while the ordinand is kneeling, the officiating minister, together with the other ministers present, lays his hands on the head of the neophyte and says: "O Lord our God . . . as now in thy name, and in obedience to thy most blessed will, we do, by laying on of hands, ordain this thy servant, and set him apart to the office of the holy ministry, committing unto him authority to proclaim thy word and administer the sacraments and to bear rule in thy flock." [51] Three ritual actions follow the laying on of hands: a pulpit gown is presented, with the words, "Take thou this robe as a symbol of thine office. Wear it when thou shalt minister of the things of Christ." [52] A copy of the Scriptures is handed the newly-ordained, as he is told, "Take thou the authority of the Church of Christ to preach the Word of God and to administer the holy sacraments." [53] Finally, "the right hand of fellowship" is extended from the ministers to the new member of the clergy. What is specially distinctive among Congregationalists is their admission of women to ecclesiastical office. Referring to the rites of ordination and liturgical functions, the official Manual declares that, "although the masculine pronoun is used . . . women are eligible to all stages of the ministry in Congregational Christian Churches." [54]

As in other denominations organized along similar lines, ordination to the Congregational ministry does not take place until after a person has "received a call to become the minister of a local church, or to serve a mission board or other church-related body. It is the general principle of our fellowship that ordination is given only for service in a local church or church related organization requiring ordination." [55] This is in accordance with the Cambridge Platform, adopted by the Congregational Synod held at Cambridge, Massachusetts, in 1648, which reduced the ordained ministry to mere functionalism. "Ordination," it stated, "we account as nothing else but the solemn putting a man into his place and office in the church." [56] And though ordination and installation are now ritually distinct, in principle the ordination does not confer essentially higher powers than those possessed by the unordained lay-preacher who may, if necessary, perform the duties of ministers, including the rite of the Lord's Supper.

ORGANIZATIONAL STRUCTURE

The structure of the Congregational Christian Churches is remarkably well organized along quasi-hierarchical lines, beginning with the local congregations and terminating in the General Council.

Local Churches are individually responsible for the doctrine, ministry and ritual of their own congregation. They appoint delegates (one or more) to the Associations and Conferences.

The *Associations* have authority to recognize local churches, promote cooperation, exercise discipline, license, ordain, install and dismiss ministers.

The *Conferences* are generally organized to correspond to state territories, with additional units in Hawaii and Porto Rico. Heading each Conference is a superintendent. Conferences recognize Associations, direct, and in many cases finance missionary activities within their territory. Basically a board of recommendation and counsel, the Conference specializes in promoting educational work among young people and women. Together with the Associations, Conferences elect the members of the General Council.

The *General Council* recognizes Conferences, elects the legal holding body of the Council, publishes the Congregational Yearbook which lists and rates the ministers, elects delegates to the National Council of the Churches of Christ, and collaborates with a variety of national organizations like the Board of Home Missions, the Council for Social Action, and the Annuity Fund for Congregational Ministers. Technically a voluntary society of Congregational Christian Churches, which meets every two years, the General Council's primary purpose is "to provide a gathering for useful discussion of questions of concern to the churches and to furnish inspiration for increased devotion and effectiveness." [57] It is therefore, "not a legislative body with ecclesiastical authority over the churches, the associations or the conferences." As part of its function, it may pass recommendations to the lower organizations, or bear "testimony to its faith through approved statements or resolutions on various topics." But all "these expressions carry with them no authority beyond the weight of their own wisdom." [58] In recent years, the General Council has been severely criticized by certain lay leaders in the church for its heavy clerical membership.

"In the General Council," they charge, "a minister has 250 times the voting power he has in the local church." [59] The movement for greater lay representation was occasioned by the General Council's approval of the Council for Social Action, a subsidiary of the Congregational Church, which, according to lay conservatives, "has openly advocated socialist doctrines . . . has at times presumed to speak for all Congregationalists . . . has expended nearly a million dollars that would otherwise have been used to further the missionary program of the churches." [60] Competent observers regard this as a symptom of the growing "anti-clericalism" developing in Protestant churches where the clergy have controlling influence.

CHURCH MERGERS

The principle of fellowship is not a dead-letter ideal in American Congregationalism. For almost a century it has found expression in a constant series of mergers, achieved or attempted, with other denominations. In 1866 an effort was made to re-unite the Free Baptists who had seceded from the Congregational churches a century before. But the proposed union never took place apparently because the Baptists rejected infant baptism. In 1892 the General Council admitted "into the fellowship" a group of Methodist churches from Georgia and Alabama. Between 1895 and 1923, serious attempts were made to join the Congregational and Episcopalian denominations. These were unsuccessful because of the intransigent position of the Episcopalians on the subject of orders. They interpreted the term "historic episcopate" so as to "require all other denominations to accept the order of bishops as officially superior to that of the ministry," and therefore, "to receive ordination through bishops who claim uninterrupted apostolic succession." Equivalently the Episcopalians refused "to recognize the clergy of other denominations either fraternally or officially as possessing a valid ministry." [61] Since Congregational ministers believed that "their ordination is valid . . . they would not accept re-ordination if it brought into question their Congregational ordination." [62] So the merger did not materialize. A projected union with the Disciples of Christ failed because the Disciples insisted on baptism by immersion. After years of negotiation, a merger with the United Brethren also foundered when the Congregationalists refused to give up the idea of local church autonomy.

In 1925 the Evangelical Protestant Churches, "noted for their liberal views and theology, and for their consciousness of need for social amelioration," were joined to the Congregationalists with a minimum of difficulty.[63] More trying and protracted over forty years was the merger of the Congregational and Christian bodies, finally completed in 1931. When originally proposed in 1895, there were difficulties on both sides. Some Congregational churchmen observed that the Christians' "rejection of all man-made formulas and creeds has sometimes led to the idea that they are Unitarians, because they will not adopt the word 'Trinity' which they do not find in the Bible." [64] On the other side, certain Christian leaders felt that "any merger with a church bearing a denominational name was departing from their principles. . . . They contended their churches could not become affiliated with a 'sect' which they considered the Congregationalists to be." [65] The matter was shelved until 1931, when the two joined to form a new body, the Congregational Christian Church, based upon "the acceptance of Christianity as primarily a way of life and not upon uniformity of theological opinion or any uniform practice of ordinances. . . . The autonomy of the local congregation and the right of each individual member to follow Christ according to his own conscience" was left undisturbed.[66]

For several years efforts were made to unite the Congregational Christian with the Evangelical and Reformed Church, and in June, 1955, at a joint meeting of the two church councils, it was decided that a formal merger should take place on June 25, 1957. The proposed name for the new amalgam is the *United Church of Christ,* which would mean the absorption of Congregationalism, at least nominally, after three centuries of relative autonomy in the United States. If the merger takes place, it will be only after the opposition of conservatives is overcome. They appealed to the civil courts to block the merger, but lost by a 4-2 decision of the New York state court of appeals, which decided in 1953 that the government has no jurisdiction over the proposed union. Undaunted, the minority sponsored a two-day conference of protest in Detroit (November, 1955), under the title of the Committee for the Continuation of Congregational Christian Churches, and the League to Uphold Congregational Principles. As reported by one of the delegates, "I am afraid I hadn't thought or known very much about Congregationalism before I went to Detroit. If I am critical of what went on there it is because I want desperately to believe that historic Congregationalism is a better, more Christian, more informed thing than I found there. There was in two days of discussion not one whisper of a suggestion that anyone there knew or cared about what the church of Christ is and/or ought to be." [67] Back of the agitation "that is stirring this denomination to its depths is the determination of some of its members, mainly laity with conservative social and political views, to destroy its claim to be a denomination and to establish that it can never be anything more than a loose congeries of autonomous local congregations." [68]

STATISTICS

Congregationalists, World Membership (1952)	1,838,108
Congregational Christian Church (U.S.A.)	
Membership	1,298,205
Churches	5,425
Ordained Clergy	5,764
Clergy with Charges	3,286
Colleges and Universities	51
Sunday Schools	4,783
Enrollment	730,931

REFERENCES

1. Douglas Horton, "What is a Congregationalist?", *A Guide to the Religions of America,* ed. by Leo Rosten (New York: Simon and Schuster, 1955), p. 37.
2. Oscar E. Maurer, ed., *Manual of the Congregational Christian Churches* (Boston: Pilgrim Press, 1951), p. 3.
3. Gaius G. Atkins and Frederick L. Fagley, *History of American Congregationalism* (Boston: Pilgrim Press, 1941), p. 60.
4. *Ibid.,* p. 77.
5. Maurer, *op. cit.,* p. 5.
6. Atkins and Fagley, *op. cit.,* p. 108.
7. *Ibid.,* p. 146.
8. *Ibid.,* p. 133.
9. Maurer, *op. cit.,* p. 29.
10. Atkins and Fagley, *op. cit.,* p. 404.
11. *Ibid.,* pp. 404-405.
12. *Ibid.,* p. 405.
13. *Assembly Work Book, World Council of Churches* (Geneva, 1954), pp. 98-99.
14. L. Wendell Fitfield, *What It Means to be a Member of the Congregational Church* (Boston: Pilgrim Press, n.d.), p. 2.
15. *Ibid.,* p. 3.
16. Maurer, *op. cit.,* p. 66.
17. Fitfield, *op. cit.,* p. 3.
18. Richard H. Bennet, *Christian Faith and Purpose, A Catechism* (Boston: Pilgrim Press, n.d.), p. 7.
19. Roy L. Minich, *What the Church Has to Offer* (Boston: Pilgrim Press, n.d.), p. 26.
20. *We Believe* (Boston: Pilgrim Press, n.d.), p. 10.
21. *Loc. cit.*
22. Fitfield, *op. cit.,* p. 5.
23. *Manual for Church Members* (Boston: Pilgrim Press, 1952), pp. 2-3.
24. *The Congregational Christian Churches, For What They Stand* (Boston: Beacon Press, n.d.), p. 2.
25. Minich, *op. cit.,* p. 13.
26. *Loc. cit.*
27. *Christian Teachings: A Manual for Those Preparing for Church Membership* (Boston: Pilgrim Press, n.d.), p. 9.
28. Bennet, *op. cit.,* p. 25.
29. *Loc. cit.*
30. *My Church: Pastor's Manual* (Boston: Pilgrim Press, n.d.), p. 89.
31. Albert W. Palmer, *I Believe in Baptism* (Boston: Pilgrim Press, n.d.), p. 8.

32. *Ibid.,* p. 7.

33. Luther was the first to popularize the historical anachronism that transubstantiation is a medieval innovation which the Church borrowed from Thomas Aquinas (1225-1274) and defined in the Fourth Lateran Council (1215 A.D.).

34. Palmer, *op. cit.,* pp. 8-9.

35. *Ibid.,* p. 9.

36. Bennet, *op. cit.,* p. 21.

37. Minich, *op. cit.,* p. 54.

38. *Ibid.,* pp. 54-55.

39. *Ibid.,* p. 52.

40. Bennet, *op. cit.,* p. 21.

41. *A Book of Worship* (New York: Oxford University Press, 1950), p. xiii.

42. *Ibid.,* p. xxii.

43. *Ibid.,* p. xvi.

44. *Loc. cit.*

45. *Ibid.,* p. xix.

46. *Ibid.,* p. xxi.

47. *Ibid.,* p. xxiii.

48. *Ibid.,* p. xxv.

49. *Ibid.,* p. 109.

50. Maurer, *op. cit.,* p. 210.

51. *Ibid.,* p. 214.

52. *Ibid.,* p. 215.

53. *Loc. cit.*

54. *Ibid.,* p. 101.

55. *The Congregational Christian Ministry: A Handbook of Standards, Procedures and Services* (New York: Department of the Ministry, 1953), p. 7.

56. Atkins and Fagley, *op. cit.,* p. 362. According to Catholic teaching, the priesthood imprints a permanent character on the soul and gives the power of offering Mass, forgiving sins in the name of Christ, and administering the other Sacraments. Only a bishop can ordain to the priesthood.

57. Maurer, *op. cit.,* p. 81.

58. *Ibid.,* pp. 80-81.

59. Ralph L. Roy, *Apostles of Discord* (Boston: Beacon Press, 1953), p. 344.

60. *Ibid.,* p. 342.

61. Atkins and Fagley, *op. cit.,* p. 348.

62. *Ibid.,* p. 349.

63. *Ibid.,* p. 355.

64. *Ibid.,* p. 351.

65. *Ibid.,* pp. 352-353.

66. *Ibid.,* p. 358.

67. "Movement or Machination?", *Christian Century,* LXXII (Nov. 23, 1955), 1359.

68. *Christian Century,* LXX (Dec. 16, 1953), 1444.

Evangelical and Reformed Church

Historians of the ecumenical movement point out that one measure of success in restoring unity to a fragmented Protestantism is the degree to which sects of different religious backgrounds finally unite in a single denomination. By this standard, the Evangelical and Reformed Church is the best large-scale example of progress in American ecumenism in modern times. Whereas the majority of church mergers take place between sects that were once united and came together again, the Evangelical and Reformed body was born of two religious groups which had only the remotest historical affinity to each other.

However while illustrating the strength of the ecumenical movement, the Evangelical and Reformed Church also betrays its fundamental weakness, which is the sacrifice of doctrinal convictions in the interests of greater organizational efficiency. The concessions made by the Reformed Church when it joined the Evangelicals will be further extended in the new merger with the Congregational Christians, whose "genius (in) subordinating ecclesiastical structure and creedal definition (has) made it peculiarly hospitable to far-reaching Christian fellowship." [1]

HISTORY

The Evangelical and Reformed Church was formed in 1934 by the merger of two sects of German and Swiss

274

origin, the Evangelical Synod of North America and the Reformed Church in the United States. Hailed as unique in American history, it was the first merger where the uniting denominations did not belong to the same religious family and were of approximately equal size and strength.

The larger and older of the parent bodies was the Reformed Church, which had its origin among the Dutch Calvinist immigrants of the early eighteenth century. October 25, 1725, is the traditional birthday of the denomination, when the first communion service was celebrated at Falkner Swamp, about forty miles north of Philadelphia. Ministers were scarce and the congregations were scattered along the Atlantic seaboard. In September, 1747, Michael Schlatter came to America as a delegate of the Synods of Holland, to organize the Coetus (Synod) of Philadelphia. Not until 1793 did the American branch declare its independence from Holland and become reorganized as the Synod of the German Reformed Church.

In its early history, the Reformed Church had no educational instituions, boards or established missionary work. As the church spread westward, pastors were sent to open mission stations. Membership grew until by 1819 the Synod divided into eight districts known as Classes. Five years later the Ohio Classis was made into a synod, with powers similar to those of the Mother Church in the East. A theological seminary was opened in 1825 at Carlisle, Pennsylvania, and later moved to Lancaster where it still stands. About the same time, the American Missionary Society was started in Frederick, Maryland, and a Board of Foreign Missions was established for work in the Orient. Competing with the eastern synod, the Ohio contingent built its own seminary at Canton, which was later transferred to Dayton, started an independent Mission Board, and published a separate denominational newspaper, the *Western Missionary*. Conscious of the inefficiency of this competition and stimulated by the tercentenary celebration of the Heidelberg Catechism (1563), the two synods combined in 1863 as the General Synod of the German Reformed Church. The word "German" was dropped in 1869. Comparable to the union of the Ohio and Eastern Synods was the split and reunion in 1837 of the pro-English and pro-German factions in the Reformed Church. Two Hungarian Classes were added in 1924 from the old Hungarian Reformed Church. On the eve of the 1934 merger there were about 350,000 members in the Reformed body, operating a dozen institutions of higher learning and concentrated in the States of Pennsylvania and Ohio.

The Evangelical Synod was an offshoot of the Evangelical United Church of Prussia, a hybrid of Lutheran and Reformed sectarians ordered into existence by the Prussian King, William III. Six ministers of the German society met at Gravois Settlement, near St. Louis, on October 15, 1840, to form the Evangelical Union of the West. Beginning as a ministerial association, the Union was permanently organized in 1849. Similar groups had sprung up in Ohio, the East and the Northwest. By 1872 they had all joined the original St. Louis union, and in 1877 adopted the name of the German Evangelical Synod.

Other congregations of German-speaking people, of Lutheran or Reformed background, and four synodical groups identified themselves with the nuclear body which in 1884 extended its work beyond the States through the Board of Foreign Missions. Gradually the word "German" was dropped from the title.

In the opinion of a Lutheran authority, the growing success of the Evangelicals in America and their eventual union with the Reformed is explained by the latitudinarianism and pietism which they inherited from their compromising Prussian forebears. Except for these factors the

Evangelicals would not have received the help from Europe which assured their continued existence as a distinct religious body. "Though there was at no time an organic union with the Evangelical Church of Prussia, the Evangelical Synod received moral and financial support from the State Churches of Germany, and especially from the Basel, the Berlin, and the Barmen Mission Societies. These societies espoused the unionistic and pietistic principles of the Prussian Union, and its emissaries implanted these trends upon the Evangelicals in America." [2] There were somewhat less than 300,000 members in the Evangelical Synod at the time of the merger in 1934.

The fusion of the Evangelicals and Reformed was directly occasioned by the Stockholm Ecumenical Conference of 1925, at which "the relationship of the (Reformed) Synod to other church bodies, both at home and abroad, had been strongly emphasized." [3] Merger relations were initiated by the Reformed Church and promoted, among others, by H. Richard Niebuhr, brother of Reinhold Niebuhr, and former President of Elmhurst College. When the new denomination was born, it was hailed as a model in the history of American ecumenism since the union "was entered upon in a spirit of complete mutual respect and confidence, the united body having been formed without even drafting a constitution or setting up a new doctrinal formula." [4]

DOCTRINE AND WORSHIP

The doctrinal position of the Evangelical and Reformed Church is summarized in the opening paragraphs of the Constitution adopted in 1936 and periodically amended by the General Synod:

> The Holy Scriptures of the Old and New Testaments are recognized as the Word of God and the ultimate rule of Christian faith and practice.

The doctrinal standards of the Evangelical and Reformed Church are the Heidelberg Catechism, Luther's Catechism and the Augsburg Confession. They are accepted as an authoritative interpretation of the essential truth taught in the Holy Scriptures.

Wherever these doctrinal standards differ, ministers, members and congregations, in accordance with the liberty of conscience inherent in the gospel, are allowed to adhere to the interpretation of one of these confessions. However, in each case the final norm is the Word of God.[5]

While the three standards of doctrine are theoretically of equal value, in practice the Heidelberg Catechism is given special prominence and generally featured as the distinctive possession of the Evangelical and Reformed Church. It was jointly written by two young theologians at the University of Heidelberg, Zacharias Ursinus (1534-1583), a pupil of Melancthon, and Casper Olevianus (1536-1587), a follower of John Calvin. Frederick III, Elector of the Palatinate, had ordered the Catechism in order to reconcile the warring factions among the Protestants. Frederick defended the Augsburg Confession as modified by Melancthon, but he inclined towards the "Reformed" point of view, as distinguished from the Lutheran, insisting on the self-sufficiency of Scripture and "repelled by the bigotry and intolerance of the 'ultra-Lutherans.'"[6] Published in 1563, the Heidelberg Catechism "combined in a remarkable manner the conciliatory spirit of Melancthon, the friend and assistant of Luther, and the practical spirit of Zwingli and Calvin."[7] Though still holding a place of honor in the Church's "sources of doctrine," the Heidelberg Catechism has been interpreted, sometimes beyond recognition, to suit the needs of a sect which "constantly endeavors to promote the unity of the Spirit in bond of peace (with) other Christian communions."[8]

Divinity of Christ and the Trinity. According to the Heidelberg Catechism, Christ is the only-begotten Son of God, "because Christ alone is the eternal and natural Son of God; but we are children adopted by God, by grace, for His sake." [9] Present-day teaching of the Evangelical and Reformed Church is less clear and more tendentious. A manual of instruction for Confirmation explains the title "Son of God" by quoting the words of Christ, "He who has seen me has seen the Father," remarking, "How near he must have felt to God to be able to say that. . . . All through the years Christians have called him 'Son of God.' To say it in another way, in Jesus God walked the earth as in no other person." [10]

Equally compromising is the Church's current teaching on the Trinity. When the early Christians used the word "person" relating to God, "a part at least of their meaning was that the one God had come to them in three different roles, just as an actor can play three different parts, or as one man can be a son, a husband, and a father at the same time." God meant so much to the followers of Christ that "they could not put all he did mean in one word or statement, but had to use three." [11]

Whatever dilution of doctrine is found in the manuals of instruction, it is mild compared with the liberalism tolerated among the ministers of the gospel. An outstanding example is Reinhold Niebuhr, professor of Christian Ethics at Union Theological Seminary and listed on the official Register of Ministers of the Evangelical and Reformed Church. Regarded by admirers as the most fearless theological critic of our age, Niebuhr is unalterably opposed to the dogma of the Incarnation. He characterized the Council of Chalcedon, which defined the union of two natures in Christ, as "wooden-headed literalism of orthodoxy." [12] For Niebuhr, the hypostatic union is not only non-existent, it is impossible. He argues that, "since the essence of the divine consists in its unconditional charac-

ter, and since the essence of the human lies in its conditional and contingent nature, it is not logically possible to
assert both qualities of the same person." [13]

The Church. In answer to the question, "What do you
believe concerning the Holy Catholic Church," the Heidelberg Catechism says: "That the Son of God, from age
to age, gathers and preserves unto Himself, by His Spirit
and word, a chosen communion, out of every race, agree-
ing in true faith." [14] Within the denomination, two types
of membership are recognized: communicant members
who have been baptized, confirmed, and made a profession of faith; and unconfirmed members who are only
baptized.

The Evangelical and Reformed Church is considered
one of the main branches of the Christian Church, along
with the Roman Catholic, Eastern Orthodox, Lutheran,
Anglican and similar bodies. One result of this feeling of
solidarity is a relative friendliness toward the Catholic
Church, judging by the manuals of church history and
doctrine. St. Anthony of Egypt is described as having gone
into the desert, "to live alone, fasting and spending much
time in prayer. Many other sincere Christians did likewise in the years that followed." St. Patrick appears as "a
missionary to Ireland in the fifth century and a real saint."
Also "one of the truest Christians of this age or any other
was Giovanni Bernadone, better known as Francis of
Assisi." The Dominicans were "great preachers and professors." Innocent III was a "great pope," Thomas Aquinas,
"the greatest thinker of the Roman Catholic Church." [15]
With the advent of Protestantism, "the Roman Catholic
Church increased its own efforts. It purified itself from
within. . . . It sent out missionaries into the far corners
of the earth. . . . It remains strong today in many lands." [16]
However, to balance these praises, the Catholic Church is
also said to have "persecuted the Protestants," and the Ref-

ormation was the fulness of time, when "God brought forward the men who were to expose the false principles, grave errors and serious corruption in the Church, and who would lead as many as would accept their leadership back again to the clear, bright light of Gospel truth." [17]

Sacraments and Rites. As stated in the Constitution, "The Sacraments of the Church, instituted by Christ, are Holy Baptism and the Lord's Supper. . . . The Rites of the Church are confirmation, ordination, consecration, marriage and burial." [18]

In the sacrament of baptism, God is said to impart "the gift of the new life unto man, receives him into his fellowship as a child, and admits him as a member of the Christian Church." [19] The accepted custom is to sprinkle a few drops of water three times on the head of the person being baptized, while pronouncing the Trinitarian formula. Sponsors are permitted but the parents of the child must be present to answer all the questions in the service. Unlike the Baptists, the Evangelical and Reformed Church "recognizes the Baptism of all Christian Churches." [20]

There is considerable ambiguity on the exact meaning of the Lord's Supper, partly the effect of a conflict between the Evangelical and Reformed segments of the denomination. On the Reformed side, as expressed by the Heidelberg Catechism, the communicant is told to pray, "may I receive, not only the bread and wine, but also become partaker of the Lord Himself by His Spirit." [21] The Evangelical version is less Zwinglian and states quite simply that, "The Lord's Supper is the sacrament by which we receive the body and blood of our Lord Jesus Christ as the nourishment of our new life." [22] Further evidence of a compromise attitude is the liberty of using either wine or unfermented grape juice in the communion service. Moreover, "members of other denominations," not only may but "should be invited to participate in the Church's administration of the Lord's Supper," regardless of what they believe about the Real Presence in the Eucharist.[23]

As prescribed by the *Book of Worship,* "the Sacrament of the Lord's Supper should be administered in every Congregation four times a year, and preferably more often." [24] The ritual follows the Roman Missal rather closely, and in sequence uses the Confession of Sins, Kyrie Eleison, Gloria in Excelsis Deo, Collect, Reading of Scripture, Creed (Apostles' or Nicene), Sermon, Offering, Preface, Sanctus, Intercession, Agnus Dei and Communion. A notable exception is the time when the words of institution are pronounced: "This is my body . . . my blood," is not said until the moment when the Minister is giving the bread and wine to the communicant.

Although children are baptized in infancy, it is understood that this does not make them full-fledged members of the Church. Quite unhistorically it is said that although in the early Church there were two parts to the rite of confirmation, anointing with oil and laying on of hands, "as the years went by confirmation was usually separated from baptism, *and* the first part of the rite was used less and less." [25] The Evangelical and Reformed Church "uses only the second part." After due instruction, the children make a public profession of "their faith in their Savior, Jesus Christ, promise obedience to him until death, and are received by the Church into active membership," in the ceremony of confirmation.[26]

In the rite of ordination of ministers, there is an imposition of hands and a declaration that, "we ordain, consecrate and appoint you to the office of the Christian Ministry." [27] But in special cases a man who has finished the prescribed theological studies may be temporarily licensed "to preach the gospel and administer the sacraments and rites of the Church," even before ordination.[28]

The rites of marriage and burial are practically the same as in other Protestant churches. But the rite of consecration is distinctive. Essentially it means the dedication of a lay member of the church, man or woman, to some auxiliary service like pastor's assistant, director of religious education, lay worker in the home or foreign missions, deaconness, or full-time worker in any other recognized department of the Evangelical and Reformed Church. After due promise is made by the kneeling candidate that he will labor with diligence in his vocation, the "Minister shall proceed to consecrate him, saying . . . We consecrate you a Commissioned Worker of the Church and appoint you to the office to which you have been called." [29] Consecrated persons are entitled to special privileges not granted to ordinary members, which are not forfeited by reason of illness or old age. Deaconnesses retain their family name but are called "Sisters," and are so designated in the *Yearbook* of the denomination.

ORGANIZATION AND MERGER PLANS

Evangelical and Reformed Church polity is modified Presbyterianism, wherein each local church is governed by a council elected from its own members. Above the local level and formed from the congregations is a synod. The thirty-four synods in the country are composed of a pastor and lay delegate from each parish; they meet twice a year and have considerable authority over the churches and pastors in their jurisdiction. Heading each synod is a president, generally full-time, and elected to his office. Full-time presidents must have been ministers for ten years, are elected for four years and may succeed themselves; part-time presidents must be ministers for five years, and after two terms of two years each are not eligible for re-election. For practical purposes, synod presidents are like the bishops in the Methodist Church, though with a wider range of authority and influence. They have the responsibility for the licensure and ordination of all candidates for the ministry, and enjoy the privilege of convening any of the church committees or councils, "and shall then do whatsoever may be advisable under the circumstances." [30]

Territorial synods are united into the General Synod, which is the highest governing body, consisting of equal representation of lay and clerical delegates. Elected by the General Synod and working under its supervision are denominational boards and commissions which take care of the church's social and educational activities: 20 homes for the aged, 12 hospitals and homes for the feeble-minded, 10 orphanages and homes for children, 14 colleges and seminaries in the States and 396 educational institutions in foreign countries, including 34 primary schools in India and 2 colleges in Japan.

In 1942 the Congregational Christian and Evangelical and Reformed Churches entered into negotiation with a view to organic merger. The final edition of the basis of union was drafted in 1947 and the name chosen, the United Church of Christ, "expresses a hope that in time soon to come, by further union between this Church and other bodies, there shall arise a more inclusive United Church." [31] As presently worded, the basis of union deliberately leaves many questions to be settled by the United Church itself. Following a declaration of faith which is Trinitarian, the plan of merger calls for a reorganization of the Church along Congregational lines, where "the liberty and independence of the local Church as the basic unit of the organization of the United Church of Christ is affirmed and safeguarded." [32] A like concession is made in favor of the Evangelical and Reformed party by providing for a General Synod which "shall carry on the general work of the church and shall meet the responsibilities of the Church for foreign missions, home missions, education and other activities." [33]

When in 1949 the General Council of the Congregational Church decided that a 72 per cent favorable vote of its churches was "sufficient to warrant consummation of the Union," it provoked a storm of protest that is still active. In 1950 the opposition Congregationalists won a decision from the Supreme Court of the State of New York, which declared that "the General Council of the Congregational Christian Churches was permanently restrained from entering into union with the General Synod of the Evangelical and Reformed Church." [34] This decision put an end to further negotiations. Meantime the Evangelical and Reformed group was invited to unite with the Presbyterian Churches, but turned down the invitation, since "we have made a promise to the Congregational Christian Churches, and because they are temporarily in trouble, we do not intend to go back on our promise." [35]

Three years later the New York State Court of Appeals reversed the 1950 decision of the lower court (nominally the Supreme Court of the State), "on the law and the facts, with costs, and complaint dismissed with costs." The judgment stated that, "in controversies such as this, ecclesiastical or doctrinal questions may be inquired into only in so far as it is necessary to do so to determine the civil or property rights of the parties." [36] Although a joint meeting of the two General Synods in 1955 decided that the merger will take place in June, 1957, there is still an organized counter-agitation among the Congregationalists, with the possibility of a further appeal to the New York State Supreme Court and, if necessary, the majority may have recourse to the Supreme Court of the United States.

STATISTICS (U.S.A.)

Communicant Membership	774,277
Churches	2,732
Pastors	1,874
Ministers without Charges	699
Sunday Schools	2,630
Enrollment	533,233

REFERENCES

1. Oscar E. Maurer (ed.), *Manual of the Congregational Christian Churches* (Boston: Pilgrim Press, 1951), p. 30.
2. F. E. Mayer, *The Religious Bodies of America* (St. Louis: Concordia Publishing House, 1954), p. 360.
3. Julius H. Horstmann and Herbert H. Wernecke, *Through Four Centuries: The Beginnings of the Evangelical and Reformed Church* (St. Louis: Eden Publishing House, 1938), p. 113.
4. *Ibid.*, p. 122.
5. *The Constitution and By-Laws of the Evangelical and Reformed Church*, p. 5.
6. Horstmann and Wernecke, *op. cit.*, p. 21.
7. *Ibid.*, p. 22.
8. *Constitution*, p. 6.
9. James I. Good, *Aid to the Heidelberg Catechism* (St. Louis: Eden Publishing House, n.d.), p. 20.
10. *My Confirmation* (Philadelphia: Christian Education Press, 1955), p. 38.
11. Oscar J. Rumpf, *Christian Faith and Life: The Meaning of Church Membership* (Philadelphia: Christian Education Press, 1952), p. 30.
12. Reinhold Niebuhr, *Beyond Tragedy* (New York: Scribner's, 1937), p. 28.
13. Reinhold Niebuhr, *Human Destiny* (New York: Scribner's, 1935), p. 70.
14. *Heidelberg Catechism*, p. 91.
15. *My Confirmation*, pp. 100-105.
16. *Ibid.*, p. 108.
17. Horstmann and Wernecke, *op. cit.*, p. 8.
18. *Constitution*, p. 6.
19. *Evangelical Catechism* (St. Louis: Eden Publishing House, 1929), p. 68.
20. Rumpf, *op. cit.*, p. 60.
21. *Heidelberg Catechism*, p. 278.
22. *Evangelical Catechism*, p. 71.
23. *Constitution*, p. 13.
24. *Book of Worship* (Approved by the General Synod of the Evangelical and Reformed Church), (St. Louis: Eden Publishing House, 1947), p. 65.
25. *My Confirmation*, p. 2. This statement is less than half true. Confirmation still follows immediately after Baptism in the Oriental Churches in union with Rome and in some Churches of the Latin Rite, *e.g.*, in Spain. Postponement of Confirmation until the age of reason began in the West about 1000 A.D. But the administration of Confirmation without anointing with chrism was an innovation of the Protestant Reformers.
26. *Evangelical Catechism*, p. 70.
27. *Book of Worship*, p. 316.
28. *Constitution*, p. 17.
29. *Book of Worship*, p. 326.
30. *Constitution*, p. 27.
31. Stephen Neill, *Towards Church Union* (Published on behalf of the Faith and Order Commission of the World Council of Churches), (London: Camelot Press, 1952), p. 63.
32. *Loc. cit.*
33. *Loc. cit.*
34. *Ibid.*, p. 64.
35. *Loc. cit.*
36. *Loc. cit.*

Part Two

MINOR PROTESTANT DENOMINATIONS

The Minor Sects

ANY ATTEMPT to classify Protestant denominations is bound to be inadequate. There is, first of all, a great deal of overlapping from one sect to another. Holiness bodies, for example, show many qualities of the Pentecostals, Legalistic churches may belong to the Reformed family, certain Anti-Trinitarian groups indulge in Spiritualistic practices. Also, within a given body, like the Healing cults, there are several characteristics: they are esoteric, pretend to be mystical and they are frequently called New Thought.

In spite of these inadequacies, however, the classification which has been adopted is not arbitrary. It is based on specific elements of historical origin and doctrinal emphasis which otherwise disparate bodies have in common, and which Protestant writers generally recognize as constituting an ecclesiastical family, made up of denominations, which are further divided into sects composed of the local churches.

ANTI-TRINITARIAN BODIES

The Unitarians were founded on the basic denial that there are three Persons in one God and that Christ is possessed of two natures, human and divine. Other religious bodies in America also deny the Trinity, but not all in the same way. Many respected churches, like the

Congregationalists, neutralize the doctrine by allowing quite unorthodox interpretations of its meaning. We are here concerned with still another class: those who may verbally profess the Trinity but officially teach that there is only one Person in God. They differ from the Unitarians in not having been organized originally on this negative principle.

The Swedenborgians, called the Churches of the New Jerusalem, are founded on the teachings of Emmanuel Swedenborg (1668-1772), a Swedish scientist turned theologian. In a series of spiritual experiences, Swedenborg claimed he had a vision of the other world, where he saw the last judgment of the Old Jerusalem and the descent of of the Holy City, or New Jerusalem, which inaugurated a new era in the religious life of nations. One of his disciples, the printer Robert Hindmarsh, started the New Church in London (1783) with a group of friends who used to meet for discussing the writings of Swedenborg. In 1792 the first Swedenborgian Society was founded in Baltimore, out of which two denominations have developed: the General Convention of the New Jerusalem, and the General Church of the New Jerusalem, totaling 6,000 members in the States and affiliated with like-minded bodies in France, Germany and Australia. Swedenborg said he had many conversations with angels and devils, with Luther, Melancthon and Calvin. Adding his own reflections, he concluded that the Incarnation is a myth: "that a son of God was born from eternity, descended and assumed the human may be compared to the fables of the ancients." [1] Without changing the doctrine, his followers have softened the wording. They admit "that there is one God, in whom there is a divine Trinity; and that He is the Lord Jesus Christ." [2] The Swedenborgian deity is a trinity of operations.

Christadelphians or Brethren of Christ were started in

1844 by Dr. John Thomas, an immigrant from England who had left the Disciples of Christ. A relatively small body of 3,000, they are Unitarian and Adventist, pacifist and interested in primitive Christianity, believing that the Kingdom of God will be established in Palestine on the personal return of Christ to the earth. Quasi-official head-quarters are at Waterloo, Iowa.

The Universalists, numbering 70,000 adherents, are the largest anti-trinitarian body in America after the Unitarians. For a theological system, they claim to go back to the third and fourth century Origenists who taught the universal salvation of mankind; but as a church body they were started in the United States in 1779, through the joint effort of George de Benneville, a French Calvinist, and John Murray, a Wesleyan evangelist from England.

Originally the primary emphasis was only a reaction to the harsh predestinarianism of John Calvin, and a claim that man is essentially good, that he has no need of redemption and without exception will attain to perfect happiness. But in denying man's sinfulness and its correlative of Christ's atonement, the Universalists were soon brought to deny also the divinity of Christ and the doctrine of the Trinity. Their own historians distinguish two stages in the development of Universalism. In the beginning they had only two doctrines on which they all agreed: "First, no hell. Second, no lost souls. All would be saved. Universal salvation! They had no question or doubt about these two things. Their protest was against the idea that (God's) purpose was to save some and condemn the rest." [3] They still profess this today, but under the solvent of rationalism their present *Avowal of Faith* is scarcely Christian and only by interpretation theistic. The omission of "traditional authority and uniqueness of Jesus, the name of the Bible, all reference to a future life, the salvation of souls" is deliberate. In the words of their recent president:

"Universalists today consider all religions, including Christianity, expressions of human spiritual aspirations; the Bible a marvelous work of man, not the miraculous handiwork of the gods; Jesus, a Spiritual Leader, not a Divine Savior; man's fate in human hands, not superhuman clutches; faith, the projection of known facts into the unknown, not blind creedal acceptance; the supernatural merely the natural beyond man's present understanding, not a violation of nature's laws." [4]

For many years the Universalists and Unitarians were aware that their objectives are basically the same. Collaboration in isolated projects led to their formal union in August, 1953. At a joint biennial convention of the American Unitarian Association and the Universalist Church of America, representatives of the two denominations formed the Council of Liberal Churches. The new federation coordinates their respective departments of education, publications and public relations, which is the limit to which these libertarian bodies can be united. Their combined membership now exceeds 160,000, with the prospect that "fifty years from now we may look upon it as . . . the first movement toward a wider federal union bringing together religious liberals from many different churches," whose number is already estimated at several million.[5]

HEALING CULTS

Among the healing religions, Christian Science is the best organized and certainly the most influential, but it represents only a fraction of the total membership in similar cults in America. Though widely different in the cultural levels on which they operate, they have enough in common to classify them under a few generic names. As New Thought movements, they believe in the immanence of the Divine in every human being; the power of God becomes universally accessible; with Mrs. Eddy, man is said to be the idea of his loving Father-Mother God; but unlike Christian Science, the existence of matter is not denied, yet evil and error are considered only products of mortal mind. As religions of Faith Healing, their radical principle is an absolute confidence in the power of the mind to cure any disease and solve any problem of human life. As egocentric sects, their main concern is to acquire or maintain bodily health and peace of mind by means of correct mental attitudes. Many groups like Psychiana and the Unity School of Christianity are too loosely organized to be considered denominations. Others like the Biosophical Institute and the Chapel of Truth are too small even to be listed in the *Yearbook of American Churches*. But their influence, especially on the millions of unchurched Americans, is considerable.

Christ Unity Science Church is the largest healing sect in the country, with a reported membership of more than a million. Formerly known as Unity Spiritual Science Church, it is an affiliation of local groups which profess "esoteric Christian ontology and divine healing." They distinguish between the Christ Spirit, indwelling in all men, which teaches Christian metaphysics, and the man Jesus, through whose physical mediation health of mind and body are achieved. In monistic fashion, they explain life and matter as a visible projection of the Spirit of God, with man as its highest expression.

The New Thought Alliance is a federation of twenty different sects which cooperate in the promotion of a common esoteric creed.[6] Similar to Christian Science in considering the visible world unreal, the Alliance shows many affinities with the Vedanta philosophy of India and the transcendentalism of William Channing, Ralph Waldo Emerson and Margaret Fuller. Its primary suppositions are contained in the *Affirmations,* which were adopted at St. Louis in 1917:

We affirm health, which is man's divine inheritance. Man's body is his holy temple. Every function of
it, every cell of it, is intelligent, and is shaped, ruled,
repaired, and controlled by mind. Spiritual healing has
existed among all races in all times. It has now become
a part of the higher science and art of living the life
more abundant. We affirm the divine supply.

We affirm the teaching of Christ that the Kingdom
of Heaven is within us, that we are one with the Father.

We affirm that Heaven is here and now, the life
everlasting that becomes conscious immortality, the
communion of mind with mind throughout the universe of thought, the nothingness of all error and negation, including death.[7]

Similar to New Thought on a lower social level is the
Peace Mission Movement of Father Divine, a crude mixture of theosophy and faith healing. Little is known of
Father Divine's early life except that, in his own words,
he "wasn't born." His followers, mostly Harlem Negroes,
address him as King of the Universe, Source of Salvation,
King of Peace, and the Almighty, although Father Divine
himself has never said he was God. Lacking organization
and without intelligible doctrine, "it is a chaotic surge of
unthinking and superstitious people about a sensational
leader." [8]

HOLINESS CHURCHES

The Holiness spirit in Protestantism stems from the
teaching of John Wesley, who believed there were two
stages in the process of justification: freedom from sin and
sanctification, or the "second blessing." In this Wesley departed from the doctrine of the earlier Reformers who
were too preoccupied with man's depravity to allow him
any chance of holiness or growth in Christian perfection.

With the decline of Wesleyan principles among American Methodists, there sprang up protest groups of various sizes, emphasizing sanctification as an essential part of the Methodist tradition. Popularly called the Holiness Movement, it gave birth to scores of religious bodies, juridically distinct, but united in professing the following tenets of Protestant perfectionism:

1. Besides justification, which is a sense of security that past sins are forgiven, there is a "second blessing" in which a person feels himself closely united with God.

2. There is an emotional experience produced in the heart by a direct action of the Holy Spirit. Although instantaneous, the "second blessing" may require years of preparation. It may be lost and regained, and may be increased in efficiency. But there is no mistaking the presence of the Spirit when He comes. More radical groups, called Pentecostals, will be discussed later. The milder Holiness churches identify the Spirit's coming and abiding presence by an exalted feeling, inner impression, bodily emotion and a deep sense of awareness of God's loving kindness.

3. As a group, Holiness sects depreciate the teachings and practices of the larger denominations for having abandoned the true faith and compromising with modernism. Their theology is fundamentalist and rigidly Biblical.

4. The favorite method of preaching is the popular revival—always for winning new converts, and in some cases revivalism is the essence of the denomination.

5. Most of the Holiness sects profess, without always stressing, the imminent second coming of Christ which is to inaugurate a millenium of earthly peace and happiness before the last day.

All told, there are probably half a million members in typical Holiness churches in America, scattered through about twenty sects. Some are microscopic in size, like the

Hephzibah Faith Missionary Association (700 members),
which derives its name from the prophecy of Isaias regarding the new Jerusalem, and Kodesh Church of Im-
manuel (560 members), organized in 1929 as an offshoot
of the African Methodist Episcopal Zion Church. In addition to several Methodist Holiness sects, three other groups
have a membership exceeding thirty thousand.

The Church of the Nazarene was established in 1908
by a merger of the Pentecostal, Nazarene and Holiness
Churches. In 1919 the word "Pentecostal" was dropped
from the name to disclaim any connection with the more
radical forms of the Holiness movement. For all practical
purposes a Methodist sect, the Church of the Nazarene is
becoming increasingly embarassed by the original reason
for its separation from the main body of Methodism,
namely, to preserve the vital sanctification of a converted
sinner preached by John Wesley. Nazarene schools have
eliminated the perfectionist label from their names. Accordingly, Texas Holiness University became Peniel College and Illinois Holiness University is now Olivet College.
None of six sectarian colleges and one seminary retains
the doctrinal "Holiness" name. Nazarene Publishing House
does an annual business approaching two million dollars.
The radio program, *Showers of Blessing,* is broadcast over
340 stations around the world. From 10,000 members in
1908, the church has grown to 260,551 in 1956, with 200
Americans and 1,000 native preachers doing missionary
work in 24 countries.

Church of God (Anderson, Indiana) was founded in
1880 by Daniel S. Warner as a protest against excessive
church organization. In his trial for heresy and expulsion
by the Winebrennerian Church of God, Warner claimed
to have discovered "one great spiritual principle, which
was the identification of the visible and invisible church
in a spiritual congregation of Christians from which no

Christian was excluded by any man-made rules or corporate forms of organization." [9] Baptism by immersion and foot washing are practiced. Church headquarters, an educational institution and a publishing house are all in Anderson, Indiana. The locality is part of the official name, to distinguish this sect from other Churches of God. Although formal records are not kept, 118,696 communicants were listed in 1956, with no creedal agreement but only a "spiritual experience" required for membership.

Pilgrim Holiness Church was organized in 1897 by a Methodist minister in Cincinnati, Martin Wells Knapp, in order to restore primitive Wesleyan doctrine on "apostolic practices, methods, power and success." Begun as the International Apostolic Holiness Church Union, it developed into a sect formed out of a dozen smaller bodies, and now has a membership of 31,480 in the United States with another 10,000 in Canada and the foreign missions. Its theology is conservative, with belief in the Trinity and the infallibility of Scripture. The government is a mixture of Episcopalian and Congregational polity. Two features are the admission of women to the ministry and a rigid examination on the creed by a church council before a candidate is received into the church. Headquarters are in Indianapolis, with 1,004 churches in 36 states.

JEHOVAH'S WITNESSES

An explanation is in order for including the Jehovah's Witnesses among the Protestant denominations. Though both sides would probably repudiate the identification, it is warranted for several reasons. Modern writers accept the term "Protestant" to mean everyone who calls himself a Christian, with the exception of members of the Eastern Churches, and is not in communion with Rome.[10] In common with traditionally Protestant sects, the Witnesses disclaim an infallible authority outside the Bible. And most

importantly, they consider themselves the spiritual heirs of
the Reformation. Martin Luther to them is "the successful
challenger who courageously defied the all-powerful domination of the popes of Rome (and) made possible the current four hundred year era of freedom, progress, enlighten-
ment, education and democracy of the western world." [11]

History. The Jehovah's Witnesses were founded in
Pittsburgh in 1872 by Charles Taze Russell, former Congregationalist and Alleghany haberdasher. They have
changed names three times: beginning as the Russellites,
they became the Millenial Dawnists, the International
Bible Students and, in 1931, the Jehovah's Witnesses. At
his death in 1916, Russell was succeeded by Judge J. F.
Rutherford, a Missouri lawyer who had defended Russell
in his several conflicts with the civil authorities. During
his thirty-six years of presidency, the Witnesses developed
their present hierarchical system and highly authoritarian
form of government. In 1942 Rutherford was succeeded by
Nathan Homer Knorr, of Allentown, Pennsylvania, formerly a member of the Reformed Church, who has been
associated full time with the Watch Tower Society since
his graduation from high school in 1923. His chief preoccupation is with foreign missions, and his most important contribution has been to shift the Society's emphasis
from the head to the members, which is exemplified in the
banishment of the portable phonograph (carrying Judge
Rutherford's voice) as standard equipment of the Witnesses in making house to house calls. The individual caller
is now privileged to give Jehovah's message personally.

Doctrine. A relative consistency in doctrine is maintained by means of a rigid authoritarianism, in which the
writings of Russell and Rutherford must be accepted without question. Russell's interpretation of Scripture is said
to be "far more extensive than the combined writings of
St. Paul, St. John, Arius, Waldo, Wyclif and Martin Lu-

ther—the six messengers of Christ who preceded him." In fact, "the place next to St. Paul in the gallery of fame as expounder of the Gospel of the Master will be occupied by Charles Taze Russell." [12] When Russell died, it was necessary to prove his divine mission. This was done by interpreting the prophecy of Ezechiel which foretells the coming of a seventh messenger of God to "mark Thau upon the foreheads of the men who sigh and mourn for all the abominations that are committed" (Ezechiel 9:4). Russell was this seventh man. He introduced the germinal concepts on which the present Watch Tower Society is founded, but the development of these notions into a doctrinal system was the work of Rutherford.

Theocracy, or the rule of God, is the foundation of the Bible Tract Society. According to Rutherford, when Lucifer rebelled he became ruler of the world, and from then on the human race has followed his lead. Satan remained in heaven until he was driven out by Christ in 1914, reflected on earth in the calamities of the First World War. But Lucifer is still master on earth, where he organized the visible part of his empire by founding churches, the great capitalistic organizations and civil societies. The great tragedy of history is that Satan has forced mankind to practice religion through this triple alliance of ecclesiastical, commercial and political powers. Since 1914 Christ has been fighting Satan invisibly, and will finally defeat him at Armageddon, annihilating the army of the devil with the help of a host of angels. This will usher in the millenium, a thousand years of earthly happiness for all the righteous who will be resurrected. The wicked will not rise from the dead. After the millenium, Satan will rise again for a short time, only to be utterly destroyed so that even his memory will disappear. At the same time the righteous begin to live forever in peace and blessedness.

The Trinity and Divinity of Christ are explicitly denied as "the Devil's doctrine, fraudulently imposed upon men to destroy their faith in Jehovah." [13] To admit Christ's divinity, Rutherford argued, would be inconsistent with the concept of a theocracy which requires that men obey only God, and never a human being. The Holy Spirit is denied to be either God or even a personality.

Immortality for the human soul is said to be an invention of the devil, propounded by earthly philosophers and become the corner-stone of Roman Catholicism. Jehovah alone is immortal; Christ received this gift as a reward for his virtue, to be earned by others if they are faithful to Jehovah in resisting the devil. Hell is denied as a place of eternal punishment by an appeal to divine mercy, since a "loving God could not torment any of his creatures." [14] Instead of going to hell, the wicked will be annihilated. On the other hand, a complicated theory of heaven provides for two kinds of paradise, one earthly and the other celestial. Only the 144,000 who were faithful followers of Jesus "will stand victorious with him on the heavenly Mount Zion," minus their bodies and living in spirit alone. "All the rest of mankind who take advantage of salvation to everlasting life through Jesus' sacrifice will remain on earth." [15]

Organization and Practices. Jehovah's Witnesses consider themselves a "Society of ministers," and accuse Protestant sectarians of watering down Luther's teaching on the universal priesthood of the laity. The public ceremony of water immersion sets one apart as a minister of Jehovah, with four classes of clergy to which a Witness may belong. On the lowest level are "Publishers" or part-time workers, who are expected to devote 60 hours a month to spreading the Society's literature; at the top level are "Pioneers" or full-time laborers; in between the "Special Pioneers" and "General Pioneers" who give 175 and 150 hours monthly to the Witness apostolate.

With all their opposition to ecclesiastical authority, the Witnesses have a closely-knit hierarchy consisting of the four hundred members of the Watch Tower Bible and Tract Society (New York), one of three legal corporations through which the Witnesses do their work. The other two are the Watch Tower Bible and Tract Society, Inc. (New York), and the International Bible Students Association (England). However, the principal officers of all three corporations are virtually the same. They elect a director who becomes international head of the Jehovah's Witnesses. Ministers working in administration or in the field get no pay. Officers get fourteen dollars a month plus room and board. To support themselves, most Witnesses do secular work.

Characteristic practices of the Witnesses flow naturally from their doctrines. They refuse to bear arms, salute the flag or participate in affairs of the secular government because they regard all civil authority as satanic. In the same way they exhaust the language of vituperation in attacking the Catholic Church as an emissary of the devil. They refuse blood transfusions as being against the Bible which says, "Whatsoever man . . . eats any manner of blood, I will cut him off from among his people" (Leviticus 17:10), since it makes no difference whether a person is "fed" blood through the mouth, or nose or intravenously.

Witnesses look upon the opposition they arouse as a sign of divine approval, quoting the words of St. Paul that, "all who will live godly in Christ Jesus shall suffer persecution" (2 Timothy 3:12). Their insistence on freedom to preach and proselytize, along with their refusal to do military service and salute the flag, has involved them in more legal suits than any other denomination in America. Between March, 1938, and April, 1955, there were forty-six United States Supreme Court cases involving the Jehovah's Witnesses, with the majority decided in their favor. Most of the litigations center around exemptions from military service and door-to-door propaganda work. In 1940 the Supreme Court ruled that a Connecticut conviction for breach of peace by playing a phonograph record which attacked the Catholic Church violated the freedom of speech and religion guaranteed by the First Amendment. Within three years, the Supreme Court reversed itself in another case and decided that compulsory saluting of the flag was unconstitutional. In delivering the majority opinion, Justice Robert Jackson declared: "If there is any fixed star in our constitutional constellation, it is that no official, high or petty, can prescribe what shall be orthodox in politics, nationalism, religion, or other matters of opinion or force citizens to confess by word or act their faith therein." [16]

Non-Catholic observers are willing to call the Witnesses "intolerant," but they also feel that these "simple, sincere" people are rendering a "service to the cause of religious freedom under our Constitution . . . as a result of their persistence." [17]

LEGALISTIC BODIES

Unlike the Holiness churches or even the Pentecostals which emphasize the operations of the Holy Spirit in man's relations with God, legalistic Protestant bodies stress the importance of certain human actions or external practices in the work of sanctification. Correlative with this legalism is a belief in the immediacy of the Holy Spirit's action on the human soul. Like the Quakers, they repudiate all formal creeds and rely on the Inner Light which requires no other illumination. They trace their origin to the wave of Pietism, especially in Germany, which rebelled against the crude formalism in public worship and the spiritual barrenness of continental Protestantism.

The Churches of the Brethren, also called the German

Baptists, number five sects in the United States. Substantially alike in doctrine and practice, only one is of considerable size. With 190,000 members, the Church of the Brethren (with no additional title) is sometimes described as the Conservative Dunkers, to distinguish it from the Progressive Dunkers (20,000 members) who are more liberal. The name Dunker is derived from the German *tunken*, "to dip or immerse," a characteristic Baptist requirement for receiving the first sacrament. They were first called Brethren when their society was founded in Schwarzenau, Germany, in 1708. Peter Becker led a company of Brethren to Germantown, Pennsylvania, in 1719. To this day they have remained largely a rural people. Their principal doctrines refer to peace, temperance, the simple life, brotherhood and obedience to Christ alone. Consistently, they are pacifists and refuse to go to war, they are required to abstain from all intoxicating drinks, their manner of life excludes worldly amusements and luxuries, they decry all class distinctions as unchristian and proclaim the unique importance of living a Christian life rather than subscribing to any particular creed. For years their women had to be veiled in church, but the custom is dying out.

Mennonites in the country number less than 200,000, yet they are divided into fourteen sects, ten of which have less than ten thousand members. As a world body, the Mennonites were organized at Zurich, Switzerland, in 1525, as the Swiss Brethren or Täufer who opposed Zwingli in his readiness to unite church and state. Denying the validity of infant baptism, they were also called Anabaptists because they demanded the rebaptism of all who were baptized in infancy. Their greatest leader was Menno Simons, an apostate priest (1496-1561) who was "rebaptized" in 1536 and after whom the denomination is named. The first group of Mennonites came to America from Crefeld, Germany, in 1683, and settled at Germantown,

now part of Philadelphia, which was also the haven of the
first Quaker, Dunker, Reformed, Lutheran, Moravian and
German Methodist congregations.

Mennonite theology is crystallized in the Confession
of Dortrecht (Holland), formulated in 1632 and generally
accepted by the American churches. Foot-washing is a
sacred ordinance or sacrament, which "the Lord Jesus
Christ" is said to have "instituted, enjoined and commanded." [18] Marriage is permitted only with another
Mennonite, so that husband and wife may become "united
with the church as one heart and soul . . . and stand in
one communion, faith, doctrine and practice." [19] Civil
authority should be respected and obeyed, except when it
comes to bearing arms. Following the example of Christ,
"we must not inflict pain, harm or sorrow upon anyone,
but seek the highest welfare and salvation of all men, and
even, if necessity require it, flee for the Lord's sake from
one city or country into another, and suffer the spoiling of
our goods . . . and when we are smitten, rather turn the
other cheek also, than take revenge or retaliate." [20] One
effect of this theory of non-resistance is the high number
of conscientious objectors the sect produces in war time.
About fifty per cent of the Mennonites drafted in World
War II chose civilian service instead of combat duty.

The most distinctive teaching of the Mennonites is
their ecclesiastical ban or separation from the church for
recalcitrant members. Once ostracized, the excommunicate
is to be "shunned, without distinction, by all the fellow
members of the church, especially those to whom it is
known, in eating, drinking, and other similar intercourse,
and no company be had with him." [21] Though interpreted
with varying degrees of severity, even at its mildest the
"shunning of the separated" is still an effective sanction.

Moravians, also called Unitas Fratrum and Unity of
the Brethren, trace their origin to John Hus, who was

burned at the stake as a Wyclifite heretic in 1415. Their immediate foundation is dated 1467 in Bohemia, when they established their own priesthood with the help of the Waldensians. The educator, John Amos Comenius (1592-1670), was the last bishop of the Czech-Moravian branch of the Unity. They came from Germany to America in 1734, first settling in Georgia. En route, they deeply affected John Wesley by their example of "simple, courageous piety." From a few thousand members in the eighteenth century, the Moravians have increased to 58,000 communicants, divided among four sects, of which the largest is the Moravian Church of America, with nine bishops, 145 churches and 52,000 members. Theoretically their main stress is on the love of God manifested in Christian conduct; but historically their predominant trait is Lutheran Pietism. In their teaching, the purpose of the church is to promote a "constant confidential intercourse with Christ." Great emphasis is placed on the believer's mystical union with the atoning Savior, which is to be achieved by a strict observance of the church's regulations and encouraged by attractive liturgical functions.

PENTECOSTAL CHURCHES

The extreme left wing of the Holiness movement developed into a group of sects commonly designated Pentecostal. They are similar to the Holiness churches in admitting the fundamentalist principles of Christ's divinity, the inerrancy of the Bible, the Virgin Birth and Resurrection, Christ's atonement and His imminent second coming. There is also an emphasis on sanctification as a separate work of grace which follows justification, but with an added feature which characterizes the Pentecostals and accounts for their distinctive name. When the Holy Spirit comes to perfect a soul, His advent is not merely invisible; it manifests itself by an external outpouring of spiritual gifts not unlike those bestowed on the Apostles at the first Pentecost, especially glossolalia or "speaking in foreign tongues, even as the Holy Spirit prompted them to speak" (Acts 2:4).

Normally the gift of tongues comes only after a long revivalist preparation, lasting up to several weeks, during which the evangelist preaches on the Holy Spirit, extols the great privilege of receiving the pentecostal graces, relates some graphic experiences and occasionally breaks out in an ecstatic muttering of strange phrases. A typical outpouring has been described by an eyewitness:

> At last conditions become right. Seekers come forward in anticipation of the gift. Confessions are made. Excitement runs high. Various blessings in the form of emotional reactions are secured. Some cry out, others fall in trances or wave their hands or bodies rhythmically in near ecstasy. One feels unduly blessed and rises to testify. He begins speaking, faster and faster, words fail, there is a muttering in the throat, and the subject breaks out in a flood of words that have no meaning to ordinary individuals. The pentecostal power has fallen, the blessing has been received, hallelujahs ring out, persons crowd about the favored saint, a familiar hymn is struck, and a wave of emotion, perceptible even to the unbelieving onlooker, sweeps the company like an electrical charge.[22]

On occasion, the preacher or someone in the congregation interprets the tongues, and the result is accepted as a prophecy from God. However, not all the churches which profess this doctrine are called Pentecostal. Some have added other charismata to the gift of tongues as marks of the "outpouring of the Latter Rain," *i.e.,* the second coming of the Holy Spirit since the original Pentecost.

The Assemblies of God, numbering 400,000 members,

are the largest Pentecostal association in America. They were organized in a constitutional convention at Hot Springs, Arkansas in 1914, which guaranteed the autonomy of the local churches and recognized the Bible as the only norm of faith and morals. In 1916 a supplementary creed was adopted. According to an official statement this body "considers it a serious disagreement with the Fundamentals, for any minister among us to teach contrary to our distinctive testimony that the baptism of the Holy Spirit is regularly accompanied by the initial physical sign of speaking in other tongues, as the Spirit of God gives the utterance." [23] Church organization is a combination of Presbyterian and Congregational. Besides the main English-speaking body, there are foreign-language branches for German, Polish, Ukrainian and Latin American Pentecostals—some imported and others native creations. More than six hundred missionaries are presently working outside the country on an annual subsidy of two million dollars.

The Churches of God which are strictly Pentecostal owe their origin to a small group of discontented Methodists and Baptists in eastern Tennessee and western North Carolina. Revivalist leaders were the two R. G. Spurlings, father and son, and W. F. Bryant, all Baptists. Starting as a Holiness church, in 1896 the society experienced an outbreak of "the baptism of the Holy Ghost." Itinerant preachers spread the movement to the southeastern states where it is presently concentrated, and out of the country to Jamaica and the Bahama Islands. Since 1908 the organization has maintained its headquarters in Cleveland, Tennessee, always adding the city and state as part of the denominational name. There are 138,000 members and 2,700 clergy, operating Lee College, several regional schools in North Dakota and California, and foreign mission stations in fifty-four countries.

The most colorful figure among the Churches of God
was A. J. Tomlinson, an American Bible Society salesman
from North Carolina, who was general overseer or bishop
from 1903 until his death in 1943. He was impeached in
1923 for his autocratic methods, and promptly set up a
church of his own, with the distinctive element of having
its officers appointed (by Tomlinson) instead of elected.
As first conceived by Tomlinson, "There are no creeds
connected with the Church of God, but only the Bible,
rightly divided, with the New Testament as the only rule
of faith and practice." [24] His insistence on the New Testament, instead of the whole Bible, as the only rule of faith
was something of an innovation. Tomlinson's death in 1943
was the signal for a chain of schisms that is still going on.
He had designated his son, Homer, to succeed him, but
the choice was opposed by a group of state overseers.
Homer placed his younger brother, Milton, a printer, in
charge. Shortly after, Homer was expelled from the church;
whereupon he formed a new sect, the *Church of God,
World Headquarters,* with himself as bishop, and moved
to Queens' Village, New York, where he now directs a society of 68,000 followers. Milton remained in Cleveland,
Tennessee, as head of the remnant of his father's flock,
first called *The Church of God Over Which M. A. Tomlinson Is General Overseer,* but now the Church of God
of Prophecy, with 32,000 members and 1,100 churches.

Pentecostal Churches which identify themselves by
name number about 300,000 adherents, most of whom belong to five sects. The largest is the United Pentecostal
Church with headquarters in St. Louis and 125,000 on the
roster in 1956. It was formed in 1945 by a union of two
previous groups: the Pentecostal Assemblies of Jesus
Christ which refused to enter the Assemblies of God, and
the Pentecostal Church, Inc., which consisted of the white

members of the Pentecostal Assemblies of the World. The latter denomination began in 1914 as an interracial body, but in 1924 the white section withdrew, leaving the Negroes to themselves. In addition to the usual Pentecostal tenets, they oppose secret societies, church festivals, jewelry, cosmetics and attractive clothing. The base of operations is Indianapolis, serving 60,000 members—an increase of 54,000 since 1936. The Pentecostal Church of God in America (43,000), the Pentecost Holiness Church (44,000) and the Calvary Pentecostal Church (20,000) are fairly static organizations, separated from the main bodies but adhering to the same belief that "the pentecostal experience is the crowning attestation of salvation."

The Apostolic Overcoming Holy Church of God is a Negro sect with 75,000 members which began in Alabama in 1919, under the aegis of W. T. Phillips, who is still the ruling bishop. "We believe," states the *Church Manual,* "in the baptism of the Holy Ghost as it was on the day of Pentecost." Revival services are "emotional affairs bordering on the bizarre, with the followers speaking in tongues and engaged in ecstatic dances." [25]

The International Church of the Foursquare Gospel is the creation of Mrs. (Sister) Aimee Semple McPherson, who at the age of seventeen was converted by her Baptist evangelist husband and became a preacher by divine revelation. A woman of striking appearance, dramatic ability, and adept in crowd psychology, Aimee McPherson managed to turn even alleged scandals to her own advantage. Thrice married, she used the names of her first and second husbands, omitting the third (David Hutton). After extensive travels in the Orient with Robert Semple, she settled in Los Angeles in 1918; three years later she founded the Echo Park Evangelistic Association and built the large Angus Temple. In 1927 she organized her thousands of

followers into the International Church of the Foursquare
Gospel. At her death the office of president passed on to
her son, Rolf. Though the church is less dramatic now
than it was during the lifetime of the foundress, it still
attracts a large following. Membership increased from
21,000 in 1936 to 87,000 in 1956. Rallies and assemblies
have replaced the pageants and lighting effects of Mrs.
McPherson. Young people are banded into Foursquare
Crusaders, and all are required to accept the Declaration
of Faith written by the first president. Foreign missions
and Bible colleges are established in ten countries, with a
concentration in Latin America. Fundamentalist in doctrine, the Declaration of Faith professes Spirit baptism
following conversion, the gift of tongues and their interpretation, eternal punishment for the wicked, and the
power to heal in answer to confident prayer. A radio sta-
tion, KFSG, broadcasts from Los Angeles.

REFORMED CHURCHES

At various times in the past centuries, the term "Reformed Church" has had a variety of meanings. Originally
it referred to all the Protestant sectarians who broke away
from Rome. Accordingly the Formula of Concord describes the Augustana Creed as "a common confession of
the Reformed Churches, whereby our Reformed Churches
are distinguished from the papists and other repudiated
and condemned sects and heresies." [26] Later on as doctrinal differences arose between Lutherans on the one
hand and Zwinglians and Calvinists on the other, the latter
appropriated the name as a domestic label and to this day
their churches on the continent are referred to as Reformed. In America the term is not so inclusive, since
Presbyterians, Baptists and others in the United States are
all Calvinist derivatives but are not called Reformed.

There are six Reformed sects, properly so-called, in this country, with an aggregate membership of about 450,000. Two of these bodies account for ninety per cent of the total.

The Reformed Church in America was a direct result of the business migration of Calvinists from Holland, sponsored by the Dutch East India Company. At first they were only scattered groups along the Hudson, but in 1628 they organized at New Amsterdam what has become the oldest church in America with an uninterrupted ministry. In 1792 they broke away from the parent body in Holland and held their first general synod two years later. Insistence on keeping the Dutch language in preaching and the liturgy retarded the church's growth and alienated many of its younger members. Efforts to unite with the German Reformed bodies failed because the Dutch were not satisfied with the Heidelberg Confession; they wanted to include the Dortrecht Articles (Mennonite) with their emphasis on God's primacy in human life and the Belgic Confession with its "mild and gentle spirit."

They recognize a three-fold ministry: bishops, elders and deacons. Technically "all ministers of the Gospel are bishops or overseers in the church; all are equal in rank and authority; and all are equal stewards of the mysteries of God." [27] Only they are allowed to officiate at the Lord's Supper. A significant emphasis, borrowed from Calvin, is the demand for a corporate worship of the whole congregation, instead of the "Medieval Roman custom" when "the actual act of worship was the duty of a special class of people, the priesthood. Everybody else enjoyed little more than the role of a spectator." [28] However, after three centuries of reformation, church authorities are asking themselves "how thoroughly this Reformed principle of corporate worship is understood today," and complain "how badly our practice falls short of our profession," when too many of their people "still think of worship as something which the minister does for them." [29]

The best known minister of the Reformed Church in America is Norman Vincent Peale, pastor of Marble Collegiate Church in New York City and author of the best-selling *The Power of Positive Thinking*. Peale exemplifies certain characteristics of his denomination. He studied at Ohio Wesleyan and until 1932 was minister exclusively in Methodist and Methodist Episcopal congregations. Recent figures show that in many areas less than twenty per cent of the communicants come from Reformed Church background. Also in line with a current tendency, Peale's church in New York is not called Reformed. To keep the name is considered a handicap, and efforts are being made "to develop community churches" instead. Most notable is the ecumenical spirit of the Reformed Church in America, which has long been a member of the Federal (now National) and World Councils of Churches, and which specializes in exchanging its ministers with other denominations. Current enrollment is 200,000 in 796 churches.

The Christian Reformed Church is an offshoot of the preceding denomination, organized in 1857 as the Holland Reformed Church, in protest against the doctrinal liberalism and anglicization of the parent body. After a decade the schismatic sect almost died out, until immigrants from Holland and anti-Masonic secessionists from the Reformed Church in America gave it new recruits. In time the name changed to its present form, and English gradually became the standard medium for preaching and the liturgy. Doctrinally the Christian Reformed Church has remained very conservative. For almost a century there has been little sign of relaxation in its rigid Calvinism, as interpreted in the Heidelberg, Dortrecht and Belgic Confessions. Most of the 156 day schools, elementary and secondary, sponsored by the Reformed churches and enrolling about 34,000 pupils, belong to the Christian Reformed Church. Membership in the Federal Council was maintained for only two years, and terminated on doctrinal grounds. "The strength of this denomination," says a church representative, "lies in its literal subscription and loyal adherence to its historic creeds; which serve both to stabilize its position and broaden its outlook."

SPIRITUALIST CHURCHES

Spiritualism is technically defined as a belief that the spirits of the dead in various ways communicate with the living through the agency of a person called a medium. It is also a religious movement which professes to be Christian and in recent years has been organized on a national scale into several denominations, with churches, schools and an ordained clergy.

The rise of American spiritualism is associated with the phenomena that took place at Hydesville and later at Rochester, New York, where the Fox sisters interpreted certain knockings in their home as signals from the spirit world. They worked out a system of communication. A year before, Andrew Jackson Davis had published *Nature's Divine Revelations,* which stated the basic principles that have since become the accepted philosophy of spiritualism.

At first spiritualist societies were small esoteric groups of interested persons who met regularly at seances and were united only by their common attachment to a particularly successful medium. A national society was organized in 1863, but it lasted only nine years. In 1893, the National Spiritualist Association was established in Chicago, and is today the largest autonomous sect among kindred bodies. Finally in 1936, an International General Assembly of Spiritualists was formed, with headquarters at Norfolk, Virginia, as a cooperative federation whose primary purpose is to charter Spiritualist churches throughout the world. Reported membership in 1952 was 157,000.

The doctrinal position is set forth in five propositions to which the National Spiritualist Association subscribes:

> We believe in Infinite Intelligence; and that the phenomena of nature, both physical and spiritual, are the expression of Infinite Intelligence.
>
> We affirm that a correct understanding of such expressions and living in accordance with them constitute the true religion; that the existence and personal identity of the individual continue after the change called death; and that communication with the so-called dead is a fact scientifically proved by the phenomena of Spiritualism.
>
> We believe that the highest morality is contained in the Golden Rule: "Whatsoever ye would that others should do unto you, do ye also unto them."
>
> We affirm the moral responsibility of the individual, and that he makes his own happiness or unhappiness as he obeys or disobeys Nature's physical and spiritual laws.
>
> We affirm that the doorway to reformation is never closed against any human soul, here or hereafter.[30]

In addition to the above, Spiritualists believe that Christ was a medium, that the Annunciation was a message from the spirit world and the Resurrection a proof that all men live on after death as disembodied spirits.

Religious services and seances are held in churches, in private homes or in rented halls. They follow the general pattern in Protestant churches, with prayer, singing, music, reading from the *Spiritualists Manual*, a sermon or lecture, and spirit messages from the departed. Communication with the spirit world is not limited to regular church services, nor even to public assemblies of professionals. "Making contact" with the dead is recommended at other times, even in the privacy of one's room and without the aid of a medium:

> Give a few minutes every day when you are quite peaceful and quite alone, to concentrate your mind on the one you wish to speak to. Think of him or her as simply as possible . . . call them by name . . . speak to them as if they were as close to you as I fully believe they are . . . if you persevere, some realization of the presence of the beloved one will come to you, so undeniable and so convincing to your own consciousness that a whole college of philosophers or scientists will not be able to persuade you that the one you loved and lost was not in close touch with you.[31]

Normally, however, spirit communications require a "highly psychic" person who acts as a medium between the mortal audience and the world beyond. Mediums are not the ministers in a congregation; they are not supported by free-will offerings but through the fees that are charged for classes and seances.

The National Spiritualist Association, with a current membership of 8,000 in 244 churches, is the largest independent spiritualist denomination in the country. It has a seminary in Milwaukee for the training of ministers, the Morris Pratt Institute, with many of its courses offered by correspondence. A national director of education, residing in Chicago, has charge of training for the three levels of ministry in the National Spiritualist Association: ordained clergymen or ministers, licentiates who teach, and mediums.

Besides the National Spiritualist Association, there are perhaps a dozen other sects in America that profess the same basic doctrines. They are generally short-lived, lasting a few years and then being absorbed by another society.

The Progressive Spiritual Church was founded in Chicago in 1907 by Rev. G. V. Cordingley, in order to "lift spiritualism above mere psychic research, to establish it upon a sound religious basis, and to secure its recognition among other Christian denominations." [32] Its confession of faith is substantially the same as that of the National Spiritualist Association, with some notable differences. Scriptures are recognized as the Word of God and the only necesary guide for spirit communication in the form of prophecy, palmistry, automatic writing, materialization and spiritual healing. Thus all the preternatural phenomena in revelation are reduced to a normal operation of the spirit world, given the proper conditions of time, place and receptive mediums. There are four sacraments: baptism, marriage, spiritual communion and burial.

The National Christian Spiritual Alliance is another, older group, organized in 1913, which emphasizes subnormal and impersonal spirit manifestations. Mediums are allowed to baptize, but only ministers may officiate at ordination and marriage ceremonies. Main offices are at Lake Pleasant, Massachusetts.

The Spiritualist Episcopal Church and the *Universal Psychic Science Church* have come into existence in the past fifteen years, occasioned by the desire of many persons to communicate with their husbands and sons who died in the last war. The first sect was started in 1941 by John W. Bunker, a former Methodist preacher from Grand Rapids, Michigan. Dissatisfied with the existing groups, he wanted to "provide a more churchly form of worship for spiritualism." Mr. and Mrs. J. Bertram Gerling founded the Psychic Science denomination at Rochester, New York, in 1942, where they capitalized on the city's long spiritualist tradition, going back to the Fox sisters in the last century. [33]

One evidence of the growing strength of spiritualism is the existence of an International Federation of

Spiritualists, composed of representatives from forty-one nations, with which the American sects are associated. Another sign is the number of current books by authors who may not be spiritualists themselves but who popularize the principles of spirit communication on a wide scale. Sherwood Eddy in *You Will Survive After Death,* James Crenshaw in *Telephone Between Worlds* and Horace Westwood in *There Is a Psychic World*—are all in support of intercommunication with the dead.

REFERENCES

1. B. F. Barrett, *The Question What Are the Doctrines of the New Church?* (Germantown, Pa: Swedenborg Publishing Association, 1909), pp. 23ff.
2. *Official Book of Worship* (Boston: General Convention of New Jerusalem, 1912), p. 673.
3. Robert Cummins, "Universalists," *Twentieth Century Encyclopedia of Religious Knowledge,* Vol. II (Grand Rapids: Baker Book House, 1955), p. 1141.
4. Brainerd Gibbons, quoted by F. E. Mayer, *The Religious Bodies of America* (St. Louis: Concordia, 1954), p. 511.
5. Harry B. Scholefield, *Guide to Unitarianism* (Boston: Beacon Press, 1955), p. 55.
6. The names of the affiliated sects illustrate their peculiar religious bias:
   Absolute Science Center
   Center of Religious Education
   Chapel of Truth
   Christian Assembly
   Christian Science Liberals
   Church of Advanced Thought
   Church of the Healing Christ
   Church of Truth
   Divine Science
   Fellowship of Divine Truth
   Fellowship of Universal Design
   Home of Truth
   Institute of Man
   Institute of Religious Thought
   Metaphysical School of Health
   New Thought
   New Thought Temple
   Radiant Life Fellowship
   Unity Church of Truth
   Unity Metaphysical Center
   Unity Truth Centers
7. G. G. Atkins, *Modern Religious Cults and Movements* (New York: Fleming H. Revell, 1923), p. 228.
8. Elmer T. Clark, *The Small Sects in America* (Nashville: Abingdon-Cokesbury, 1949), p. 124.
9. Charles E. Brown, *When the Trumpet Sounded: History of the Church of God* (Anderson, Ind.: Warner Press, 1951), p. 100.
10. Albert C. Knudson, "Cardinal Principles of Protestantism," *Protestantism,* ed. by William K. Anderson (Nashville: Parthenon Press, 1945), p. 125.
11. Marley Cole, *Jehovah's Witnesses: The New World Society* (New York: Vantage Press, 1955), p. 42.
12. Preface to Russell's *Sermons.*

318]

13. Joseph F. Rutherford, *Riches* (New York: Watch Tower and Bible Tract Society, 1936), p. 188.
14. Rutherford, *Salvation* (1939), p. 199.
15. Nathan H. Knorr, *Can You Live Forever in Happiness on Earth?* (Brooklyn: Watch Tower Bible and Tract Society, 1950), p. 15.
16. Anson P. Stokes, *Church and State in the United States*, Vol. II (New York: Harper, 1950), p. 615.
17. *Ibid.*, Vol. III, p. 546.
18. *Mennonite Church Polity* (Scottdale, Pa.: Mennonite Publishing House, 1952), p. 51.
19. *Ibid.*, p. 52.
20. *Ibid.*, p. 54.
21. *Ibid.*, pp. 56-57.
22. Clark, *op. cit.*, pp. 94-95.
23. J. R. Evans, General Secretary, quoted by Clark, *ibid.*, p. 107.
24. *Religious Bodies, Census of 1936*, Vol. II, Part 1 (Washington: 1951), p. 432.
25. Frank S. Mead, *Handbook of Denominations* (Nashville: Abingdon Press, 1951), p. 22.
26. Preface to the *Formula of Concord*, in Mayer, *op. cit.*, p. 191.
27. *Constitution of the Reformed Church in America* (New York-Grand Rapids: Department of Publication, 1955), p. 10.
28. Howard G. Hageman, *Our Reformed Church* (New York-Grand Rapids: Half Moon Press, 1952), p. 31.
29. *Ibid.*, p. 32.
30. *Religious Bodies, Census of 1936*, Vol. II, Part 2, p. 1600.
31. E. Katherine Bates, *Do the Dead Depart?* quoted by Marcus Bach, *The Will to Believe* (Englewood Cliffs, N. J.: Prentice-Hall, 1955), p. 162.
32. *Religious Bodies, Census of 1936*, p. 1605.
33. The first Spiritualist Church in Rochester, New York, is called the "International Shrine of Spiritualism." Next to it stands an obelisk with a commemorative plaque, "Erected by the Spiritualists of the World," concluding with the words: "There is no death. . . . There are no dead."

Part Three

STATISTICS ON RELIGIOUS BODIES
IN THE UNITED STATES

Statistics on Religious Bodies in the United States

NOTE: There is a slight difference between the statistical data in the body of the text and in the following tables. The latter were not available until the volume was already in print. In general, the current figures show a gain over the previous year. Quoted from the *Yearbook of American Churches 1957*. Copyright 1956 by the National Council of Churches. Used with permission.

I. Church Membership in the United States

THE figures here tabulated are based on reports from official statisticians of the various religious bodies.

In 1955 the total church membership for Continental United States was 100,162,529 persons in 258 bodies. This represents an increase of 2,679,918 from 1954. Protestants numbered 58,448,567 in 198 bodies; Catholics 33,396,647; Jews 5,500,000; Eastern Churches (18) had 2,386,945; Old Catholic and Polish National Catholic Churches 367,370; and Buddhists 63,000.

Unfortunately the churches are not uniform in computing members. Catholics count all baptized persons, including infants. The Jews regard as members all Jews in communities having congregations. The Eastern Churches include all persons in their nationality or cultural groups. Most Protestant bodies count all persons who have attained "full membership," and estimates indicate that all but a small minority of these are over 13 years of age. However, many Lutheran bodies and the Protestant Episcopal Church now report all baptized persons, and not only those confirmed.

The Church of Christ, Scientist, did not furnish membership figures because of a regulation of that body which forbids "the numbering of people and the reporting of such statistics for publication."

CHURCH MEMBERSHIP STATISTICS

Mainly for the Calendar Year 1955 or a Fiscal Year
Ending in 1955

Name of Religious Body	Year	No. of Churches Reported	Inclusive Church Membership
Adventist Bodies:			
Advent Christian Church	1954	410	30,585
Church of God (Abrahamic Faith)	1955	101	4,215
Life and Advent Union	1955	3	320
Primitive Advent Christian Church	1955	13	500
Seventh-day Adventists	1955	2,858	277,162
African Orthodox Church	1953	30	7,000
Amana Church Society	1955	7	814
American Evangelical Christian Churches	No statistics available		
American Rescue Workers	1952	23	1,240
Apostolic Overcoming Holy Church of God	1951	300	75,000
Assemblies of God	1955	7,320	400,047
Associated Gospel Churches	No report		
Baha'i Faith	No report		
Baptist Bodies:			
American Baptist Convention	1955	6,490	1,513,697
Southern Baptist Convention	1955	30,340	8,467,439
National Baptist Convention, U.S.A., Inc.	1954	25,603	4,557,416
National Baptist Convention of America	1955	11,291	2,610,774
American Baptist Association	1951	2,105	286,691
Baptist General Conference of America	1955	425	54,000
Christian Unity Baptist Association	1955	11	630
Conservative Baptist Association of America	1955	998	250,000
Duck River (and Kindred) Associations of Baptists	1952	326	9,720
Evangelical Baptist Church, Inc., Gen. Conf.	1952	31	2,200
Free Will Baptists	1955	1,947	159,831
General Association of Regular Baptist Churches	1955	726	124,039
General Baptists	1955	710	53,893
General Six-Principle Baptists	1955	5	324
Independent Baptist Church of America	1954	2	50('52)
National Baptist Evangelical Life and Soul Saving Assembly of U.S.A.	1951	264	57,674
National Primitive Baptist Convention of the U.S.A.	1952	1,019	80,000
North American Baptist Association	1955	1,688	251,062
North American Baptist General Conference	1955	288	47,319
Primitive Baptists	1950	1,000	72,000
Regular Baptists	1936	266	17,186

Name of Religious Body	Year	No. of Churches Reported	Inclusive Church Membership
Separate Baptists	1955	87	7,065
Seventh Day Baptist General Conference	1955	62	6,095
Seventh Day Baptists (German 1728)	1951	3	150
Two-Seed-In-The-Spirit Predestinarian Baptists	1945	16	201
United Baptists	1955	568	63,641
United Free Will Baptist Church	1952	836	100,000
Bible Protestant Church	1955	39	2,300

Brethren (German Baptists):

Brethren Church (Ashland, Ohio)	1955	107	18,672
Brethren Church (Progressive)	1953	141	20,819
Church of the Brethren	1955	1,049	195,609
Church of God (New Dunkards)	1953	8	611
Old German Baptist Brethren	1955	55	3,953
Plymouth Brethren	1936	664	25,806

Brethren (River):

Brethren in Christ	1955	114	6,017
Old Order, or Yorker, River Brethren	1936	7	591
United Zion Church	1955	17	976
Buddhist Churches of America	1955	48	63,000('54)
Catholic Apostolic Church	1936	7	2,577
Christ Unity Science Church	1953	4,481	1,581,286
Christadelphians	1954	250	3,000
Christian and Missionary Alliance	1955	954	57,109('54)
Christian Catholic Church	1955	5	No data
Christian Nation Church	1955	30	500
Christian Union	1938	220	15,400
Christ's Sanctified Holy Church	1955	28	500
Church of Christ (Holiness), U.S.A.	1955	130	7,952
Church of Christ, Scientist	No statistics furnished		
Church of Eternal Life	1940	2	113

Churches of God:

Church of God (Cleveland, Tenn.)	1955	2,803	142,668
Church of God (Anderson, Ind.)	1955	2,146	123,523
Church of God (Seventh Day)	1951	15	2,000
The (Original) Church of God, Inc.	1952	75	6,000
The Church of God	1955	1,818	70,941
The Church of God (Seventh Day), Denver, Colo. ..	1955	124	3,750
The Church of God of Prophecy	1955	1,105	33,119
Evangelistic Church of God	1953	12	774
Church of God and Saints of Christ	1955	216	36,041
Church of God in Christ	1955	3,500	343,928
Church of Illumination	1945	7	5,000
Church of Our Lord Jesus Christ of the Apostolic Faith, Inc.	1954	155	45,000
Church of the Gospel	1955	5	46
Church of the Nazarene	1955	4,090	270,576
The Church of Revelation	1954	10	3,490('53)
Churches of Christ	1955	16,500	1,600,000
Churches of Christ in Christian Union	1955	197	10,900
Churches of God, Holiness	1954	36	23,500
Churches of God in N.A. (General Eldership)	1955	398	36,882

Churches of the Living God:

Church of the Living God (Christian Workers for Fellowship)	1952	5	65
House of God, Which is the Church of the Living God, the Pillar and the Ground of the Truth, Inc.	1936	119	4,838

Name of Religious Body	Year	No. of Churches Reported	Inclusive Church Membership
Churches of the New Jerusalem:			
General Convention of the New Jerusalem in the U.S.A.	1955	55	4,273
General Church of the New Jerusalem	1954	8	1,707
Congregational Christian Churches	1955	5,561	1,342,045
Congregational Holiness Church	1955	138	4,121
Disciples of Christ, International Convention	1955	7,951	1,897,736
Divine Science Church and College, Inc.	No report		
Eastern Churches:			
Albanian Orthodox Church in America	1955	14	13,500
American Carpatho-Russian Orthodox Greek Catholic Church	1955	70	100,000
American Catholic Church (Syro-Antiochean)	1955	36	4,280
The American Holy Orthodox Catholic			
Apostolic Eastern Church	1955	25	2,800
The American Orthodox Church	No report		
Apostolic Episcopal Church	1947	46	7,086
Armenian Apostolic Church of America	1955	50	75,000
Assyrian Orthodox Church	1951	4	3,300
Bulgarian Eastern Orthodox Church	1955	20	5,300
Church of the East and of the Assyrians	1952	10	3,200
Eastern Orthodox Catholic Church in America	1955	1	39
Greek Archdiocese of North and South America	1955	353	1,000,000
Holy Orthodox Church in America (Eastern Catholic and Apostolic)	1955	4	1,300 ('44)
Romanian Orthodox Episcopate of America	1955	51	50,000
The Russian Orthodox Catholic Church, Archdiocese of the Aleutian Islands and North America	No report		
The Russian Orthodox Church Outside Russia	1951	91	55,000
The Russian Orthodox Greek Catholic Church of America	1955	350	750,000
Serbian Eastern Orthodox Church	1955	53	100,000
Syrian Antiochian Orthodox Church	1955	80	100,000
Ukrainian Orthodox Church of America	1954	34	44,200
Ukrainian Orthodox Church of U.S.A.	1955	93	71,940
Ethical Culture Movement	1955	23	5,678
Evangelical and Reformed Church	1955	2,732	774,277
Evangelical Congregational Church	1955	167	28,546
Evangelical Free Church of America	1955	312	24,353
Evangelical Mission Covenant Church of America	1954	488	53,388
Evangelical United Brethren Church	1955	4,370	737,489
Evangelistic Associations:			
Apostolic Christian Church (Nazarean)	1954	25	1,650
Apostolic Christian Church of America	1954	58	7,669
Apostolic Faith Mission	1936	17	2,288
The Christian Congregation	1955	138	12,860
Church of Daniel's Band	1951	4	200
Church of God (Apostolic)	1954	22	600
Church of God as Organized by Christ	1938	14	2,192
Metropolitan Church Association	1955	26	435 ('54)
Missionary Bands of the World, Inc.	1955	11	236
Missionary Church Association	1954	95	6,673
Pillar of Fire	1948	61	5,100
Federated Churches	1936	508	88,411
Fire-Baptized Holiness Church	1940	300	6,000
Fire-Baptized Holiness Church (Wesleyan)	1955	52	974
Free Christian Zion Church of Christ	1952	734	18,975
Friends:			
Central Yearly Meeting of Friends	1955	10	552
Five Years Meeting of Friends	1955	516	70,245

Name of Religious Body	Year	No. of Churches Reported	Inclusive Church Membership
Ohio Yearly Meeting of Friends Church (Independent)	1955	85	6,454
Oregon Yearly Meeting of Friends Church	1955	57	4,972
Pacific Yearly Meeting of Friends	1955	20	855
Philadelphia Yearly Meeting of the Religious Society of Friends		Statistics included in statistics for the Religious Society of Friends (General Conference)	
Religious Society of Friends (Conservative)	1955	25	2,223
Religious Society of Friends (General Conference) .	1955	217	27,829
Religious Society of Friends (Kansas Yearly Meeting)	1955	85	8,338
Religious Society of Friends (Philadelphia and Vicinity)		This group (Arch Street Yearly Meeting) united in 1955 with the Race Street Yearly Meeting, to become Philadelphia Yearly Meeting of the Religious Society of Friends, see above.	
Holiness Church of God, Inc.	1955	25	550
House of David	1955	1	150
Independent Churches	1936	384	40,276
Independent Fundamental Churches of America	1946	650	65,000
Independent Negro Churches	1936	50	12,337
International Church of the Foursquare Gospel	1955	650	94,571

Italian:

Christian Church of North America	1955	200	18,000
Jehovah's Witnesses	1955	3,484	187,120
Jewish Congregations	1954	4,079	5,500,000
Kodesh Church of Immanuel	1936	9	562

Latter-Day Saints:

Church of Christ, Temple Lot	1951	25	2,275
Church of Jesus Christ (Bickertonites)	1955	40	2,272
Church of Jesus Christ (Cutlerites)	1953	1	16
Church of Jesus Christ of Latter Day Saints	1955	2,624	1,230,021
Church of Jesus Christ of Latter Day Saints (Strangites)	1952	6	200
Reorganized Church of Jesus Christ of Latter Day Saints	1955	808	137,856
Liberal Catholic Church	1955	7	4,000
Lithuanian National Catholic Church	1954	3	5,672

Lutheran:
Lutheran Synodical Conference of N.A.

Lutheran Church—Missouri Synod	1955	4,805	2,004,110
Evangelical Lutheran Joint Synod of Wisconsin and Other States	1954	850	328,969
Norwegian Synod of the American Evangelical Lutheran Church	1955	80	12,872
Slovak Evangelical Lutheran Church	1952	59	20,562
Negro Missions	1955	50	6,460
American Evangelical Lutheran Church	1955	86	21,800
American Lutheran Church	1954	1,919	836,485
Augustana Evangelical Lutheran Church	1955	1,169	629,602
Church of the Lutheran Brethren of America	1955	39	4,150
Evangelical Lutheran Church	1954	2,444	940,580
Evangelical Lutheran Church in America (Eielsen Synod)	1955	12	1,575
Finnish Apostolic Lutheran Church of America	1953	57	6,567
Finnish Evangelical Lutheran Church (Suomi Synod)	1955	163	33,314
Independent Lutheran Churches	1953	1	53

Name of Religious Body	Year	No. of Churches Reported	Inclusive Church Membership
Lutheran Free Church	1955	358	72,135
National Evangelical Lutheran Church	1955	58	7,282
Protestant Conference (Lutheran)	1955	7	3,253('47)
United Evangelical Lutheran Church	1955	168	54,098
United Lutheran Church in America	1955	4,050	2,175,726

Mennonite Bodies:

Church of God in Christ (Mennonite)	1954	32	3,870
Conference of the Evangelical Mennonite Church ..	1955	22	2,182
Conservative Mennonite Conference	1955	60	5,459
Evangelical Mennonite Brethren	1955	20	2,348
General Conference Mennonite Church	1955	180	34,589
Hutterian Brethren	1955	29	2,850
Krimmer Mennonite Brethren Conf.	1955	10	1,600
Mennonite Brethren Church of N.A.	1954	75	11,930
Mennonite Church	1955	440	70,283
Old Order Amish Mennonite Church	1955	222	16,471
Old Order (Wisler) Mennonite Church	1955	31	4,004
Reformed Mennonite Church	1955	16	670
Unaffiliated Conservative Amish Mennonite Church .	1955	23	2,145
United Missionary Church	1955	206	10,223

Methodist Bodies:

African Methodist Episcopal Church	1951	5,878	1,166,301
African Methodist Episcopal Zion Church	1955	3,080	760,000
African Union First Colored Methodist Protestant Church, Inc.	1953	33	5,000
Christian Methodist Episcopal Church	1951	2,469	392,167
Congregational Methodist Church	1953	190	12,448
Congregational Methodist Church of U.S.A.	1954	100	7,500
Cumberland Methodist Church	1954	4	65
Evangelical Methodist Church	1955	90	4,125
Free Methodist Church of N.A.	1955	1,215	51,437
Holiness Methodist Church	1955	28	825
Independent A.M.E. Denomination	1940	12	1,000
Independent Fundamental Methodist Church	1955	14	575
Lumber River Annual Conference of the Holiness Methodist Church	1955	7	534
The Methodist Church	1955	39,854	9,292,046
New Congregational Methodist Church	1936	25	1,449
Primitive Methodist Union Episcopal Church ...	1955	92	12,166
Reformed Methodist Union Episcopal Church	1954	33	11,000
Reformed New Congregational Methodist Church ..	1936	8	329
Reformed Zion Union Apostolic Church	1955	52	15,000
Southern Methodist Church	1955	52	4,724
Union American Methodist Episcopal Church	1936	71	9,369
Wesleyan Methodist Church of America	1955	988	36,000

Moravian Bodies:

Bohemian and Moravian Brethren	Statistics included in those for the Presbyterian Church in the U.S.A.		
Evangelical Unity of the Czech-Moravian Brethren in N.A.	1954	32	5,276
Moravian Church in America (Unitas Fratrum)	1955	158	55,524
Muslims	No report		
National David Spiritual Temple of Christ Church Union (Inc.), U.S.A.	1955	66	40,675
New Apostolic Church of N.A., Inc.	1955	174	12,600

Old Catholic Churches:

American Catholic Church, Archdiocese of N.Y. ...	1947	20	8,435
North American Old Roman Catholic Church	1955	64	84,564
Old Catholic Church in America	1940	28	6,274
The Reformed Catholic Church (Utrecht Confession), Province of North America	1955	20	2,217

Name of Religious Body	Year	No. of Churches Reported	Inclusive Church Membership
Open Bible Standard Churches, Inc.	1955	249	26,000
Pentecostal Assemblies:			
Calvary Pentecostal Church, Inc.	1944	35	20,000
Emmanuel Holiness Church	1955	56	1,200
International Pentecostal Assemblies	1952	96	5,000
Pentecostal Assemblies of the World, Inc.	1954	395	60,000
Pentecostal Church of Christ	1955	35	937
Pentecostal Church of America, Inc.	1955	850	60,000
Pentecostal Fire-Baptized Holiness Church	1955	48	812
The Pentecostal Holiness Church, Inc.	1955	1,112	46,827
United Pentecostal Church	1955	1,500	125,000
Pilgrim Holiness Church	1955	948	31,625
Polish National Catholic Church of America	1954	156	265,879
Presbyterian Bodies:			
Associate Presbyterian Church of N.A.	1955	7	470
Associate Reformed Presbyterian Church (General Synod)	1955	147	27,116
Bible Presbyterian Church	No report		
Colored Cumberland Presbyterian Church	1944	121	30,000
Cumberland Presbyterian Church	1955	1,007	84,990
Orthodox Presbyterian Church	1955	72	8,754
Presbyterian Church in the U.S.	1955	3,852	810,917
Presbyterian Church in the U.S.A.	1955	8,282	2,645,745
Reformed Presbyterian Church in N.A. (General Synod)	1953	11	1,729
Reformed Presbyterian Church of N.A. (Old School)	1954	74	6,442
United Presbyterian Church of N.A.	1955	833	244,973
Protestant Episcopal Church	1954	7,271	2,757,944
Reformed Bodies:			
Christian Reformed Church	1955	481	204,621
Free Magyar Reformed Church in America	1955	27	9,000
Netherlands Reformed Congregations	1955	22	5,408
Protestant Reformed Churches of America	1955	18	2,385
Reformed Church in America	1955	804	205,323
Reformed Episcopal Church	1955	74	8,015
Roman Catholic Church	1955	21,086	33,396,647
Salvation Army	1955	1,323	249,641
The Schwenkfelder Church	1950	5	2,400
Social Brethren	1955	25	1,470
Spiritualists:			
International General Assembly of Spiritualists ..	1955	201	163,000
National Spiritual Alliance of the U.S.A.	1955	30	2,873
National Spiritualist Association of Churches	1955	245	7,990
Triumph the Church and Kingdom of God in Christ ..	1953	500	5,000 ('52)
Unitarian Churches	1955	378	96,715
United Brethren Bodies:			
United Brethren in Christ	1955	314	19,971
United Christian Church	1955	14	595
United Holy Church of America, Inc.	1953	376	26,500
Universalist Church of America	1955	386	40,977
Vedanta Society	1955	11	1,000
Volunteers of America	1955	194	26,506
Totals: (268 bodies; 258 reporting)		305,449	100,162,529

II. Sunday or Sabbath Church Schools

AT THE beginning of 1956 there were 264,726 Sunday or Sabbath schools in all religious bodies, with 3,029,386 teachers and officers, and a total enrollment of 38,921,033 persons.

A year earlier there was reported a total enrollment of 37,623,530. Thus the increase was 1,297,503, or 3.4 per cent; compared with an increase of 2,234,064 persons, or 6.3 per cent, for the previous year.

The figure of 2,277,948 persons, furnished by the publishers of the *Official Catholic Directory*, corresponds to the number of public school children attending special religious instruction classes. This is in addition to 672,299 students in 2,383 Catholic high schools, and 3,544,598 pupils in 9,568 Catholic elementary schools.

		Sunday or Sabbath Church Schools		
Name of Religious Body	*Year*	*No. of Sunday or Sabbath Schools*	*Officers and Teachers Enrolled*	*Total Enroll-ment**
Adventist Bodies:				
Advent Christian Church	1954	368	3,500 ('47)	28,938
Church of God (Abrahamic Faith) ..	1955	96	363 ('54)	3,856
Life and Advent Union	1955	3	19	128
Primitive Advent Christian Church ..	1950	7	12	155
Seventh-day Adventists	1955	2,980	38,314	273,823
African Orthodox Church	1953	30	120	2,400
Amana Church Society	1955	4	13	175
American Evangelical Christian Churches	No statistics available			
American Rescue Workers	1952	23	40	1,020
Apostolic Overcoming Holy Church of God	1942	180	131 ('36)	698 ('36)
Assemblies of God	1955	7,063	84,756	805,182
Associated Gospel Churches	No report			
Baha'i Faith	No report			
Baptist Bodies:				
American Baptist Convention	1955	6,317 ('53)	112,565 ('36)	969,007
Southern Baptist Convention	1955	29,461	684,653	6,632,418
National Baptist Convention, U.S.A., Inc.	1954	22,004	143,079 ('50)	2,407,348
National Baptist Convention of America	1944	10,100	No data	1,000,100

* Includes pupils, officers, and teachers enrolled.

Name of Religious Body	Sunday or Sabbath Church Schools			
	Year	No. of Sunday or Sabbath Schools	Officers and Teachers Enrolled	Total Enroll-ment*
American Baptist Association	1952	1,147	8,000	146,000
Baptist General Conference of America	1955	481	5,082 ('53)	70,621
Christian Unity Baptist Association ..	1955	5	8 ('52)	162
Conservative Baptist Association of America	1955	998	No data	No data
Duck River (and Kindred) Associations of Baptists	1949	60	300	2,100
Evangelical Baptist Church, Inc., Gen. Conf.	1952	31	178	3,100
Free Will Baptists	1955	1,843	No data	140,000
General Association of Regular Baptist Churches	1955	No data	No data	No data
General Baptists	1955	700	3,250 ('52)	70,000
General Six-Principle Baptists	1955	5	29 ('49)	402
Independent Baptist Church of America	1954	1	2	14
National Baptist Evangelical Life and Soul Saving Assembly of U.S.A. .	1949	447	1,777	46,021
National Primitive Baptist Convention of the U.S.A.	1952	500	3,462	42,308
North American Baptist Association .	1955	1,688	16,736	273,281
North American Baptist General Conference	1955	304	4,913	45,292
Primitive Baptists	1936	41	312	40,360
Regular Baptists	1936	54	402	3,754
Separate Baptists	1955	87	487 ('36)	3,419 ('36)
Seventh Day Baptist General Conference	1955	56	612	3,595
Seventh Day Baptists (German 1728) .	1951	2	20	120
Two-Seed-In-The-Spirit Predestinarian Baptists	No report			
United Baptists	1955	210	1,160	15,385
United Free Will Baptist Church	1952	654	1,950	31,500
Bible Protestant Church	1955	39	484	4,140
Brethren (German Baptists):				
Brethren Church (Ashland, Ohio)	1955	109	1,354	16,410
Brethren Church (Progressive)	1953	141	1,000 ('44)	26,897
Church of the Brethren	1955	1,064	14,775	154,275
Church of God (New Dunkards)	1953	8	84	728
Old German Baptist Brethren	1955	None	None	None
Plymouth Brethren	1952	550	3,840	35,240
Brethren (River):				
Brethren in Christ	1955	142	2,048 ('54)	15,302
Old Order, or Yorker, River Brethren	No report			
United Zion Church	1955	13	183 ('51)	1,443
Buddhist Churches of America	1954	84	650 ('48)	15,450
Catholic Apostolic Church	1936	2	7	2,577
Christ Unity Science Church	1953	3,726	5,711	548,990
Christadelphians	1936	65	299	1,875
Christian and Missionary Alliance	1955	943	5,570 ('36)	123,470
Christian Catholic Church	1955	4	150	1,250
Christian Nation Church	1955	30	100	700
Christian Union	1936	79	895	5,597
Christ's Sanctified Holy Church	1955	27	149	719
Church of Christ (Holiness), U.S.A.	1955	130	910	8,668
Church of Christ, Scientist	No statistics furnished			
Church of Eternal Life	No report			

* Includes pupils, officers, and teachers enrolled.

Name of Religious Body	Year	Sunday or Sabbath Church Schools		
		No. of Sunday or Sabbath Schools	Officers and Teachers Enrolled	Total Enroll-ment*

Churches of God:

Church of God (Cleveland, Tenn.) ...	1955	2,926	26,804	263,419
Church of God (Anderson, Ind.)	1955	2,146	21,000	218,880
Church of God (Seventh Day)	1951	25	100	3,000
The (Original) Church of God, Inc. ..	1952	75	400('49)	10,000
The Church of God	1955	1,767	13,982	105,783
The Church of God (Seventh Day), Denver, Colo.	1955	124	720	3,750
The Church of God of Prophecy	1955	1,000	No data	41,000
Evangelistic Church of God	1953	9	47	706
Church of God and Saints of Christ ...	1955	216	1,306('54)	36,041
Church of God in Christ	1955	3,200	16,349	78,569
Church of Illumination	1952	8	11	900
Church of Our Lord Jesus Christ of The Apostolic Faith, Inc.	1954	155	1,628('52)	16,000
Church of the Gospel	1955	5	6	65
Church of the Nazarene	1955	4,068	47,257	582,475
The Church of Revelation	1954	6	14	264
Churches of Christ	1936	2,935	18,465	209,615
Churches of Christ in Christian Union .	1955	197	1,975	19,275
Churches of God, Holiness	1954	58	425	42,925
Churches of God in N.A. (General Eldership)	1955	394	4,970	38,275

Churches of the Living God:

Church of the Living God (Christian Workers for Fellowship)	1951	5	10	36('44)
House of God, Which is the Church of the Living God, the Pillar and the Ground of the Truth, Inc.	1949	71	625	975

Churches of the New Jerusalem:

General Convention of the New Jerusalem in the U.S.A.	1955	43	208	1,723
General Church of the New Jerusalem	1949	3	13	71
Congregational Christian Churches	1955	4,861	70,345('36)	773,235
Congregational Holiness Church	1955	138	690	7,172('54)
Disciples of Christ, International Convention	1955	7,966	66,551('54)	1,248,495
Divine Science Church and College, Inc.	No report			

Eastern Churches:

Albanian Orthodox Church in America	1955	14	42	2,842
American Carpatho-Russian Orthodox Greek Catholic Church	1955	52	180	2,480
American Catholic Church (Syro-Antiochean)	1955	38	123	2,602
The American Holy Orthodox Catholic Apostolic Eastern Church	1955	15	50	800
The American Orthodox Church	No report			
Apostolic Episcopal Church	1944	53	115	1,135
Armenian Apostolic Church of America	1955	49	228	2,883
Assyrian Orthodox Church	1951	3	15	100
Bulgarian Eastern Orthodox Church ..	1955	9	41	690
Eastern Orthodox Catholic Church in America	1955	None	None	None

* Includes pupils, officers, and teachers enrolled.

Name of Religious Body	Sunday or Sabbath Church Schools			
	Year	*No. of Sunday or Sabbath Schools*	*Officers and Teachers Enrolled*	*Total Enrollment**
Greek Archdiocese of North and South America	1955	355	4,500('54)	25,000
Holy Orthodox Church in America (Eastern Catholic and Apostolic) .	No report			
Romanian Orthodox Episcopate of America	1955	25	121	771
The Russian Orthodox Catholic Church, Archdiocese of the Aleutian Islands and North America	No report			
The Russian Orthodox Church Outside Russia	1951	96	No data	No data
The Russian Orthodox Greek Catholic Church of America	1955	200	800	10,800
Serbian Eastern Orthodox Church ..	1955	50	80	3,080
Syrian Antiochian Orthodox Church ..	1955	100	750	5,750
Ukrainian Orthodox Church of America	1955	34	34	1,894
Ukrainian Orthodox Church of U.S.A.	1955	82	214	3,963
Ethical Culture Movement	1955	20	157	1,487
Evangelical and Reformed Church	1955	2,634	No data	545,512
Evangelical Congregational Church ..	1955	165	3,610	34,150
Evangelical Free Church of America ...	1955	317	5,790('53)	42,391
Evangelical Mission Covenant Church of America	1954	510	7,282	76,407
Evangelical United Brethren Church	1955	4,391 ('54)	63,184	687,713
Evangelistic Associations:				
Apostolic Christian Church (Nazarean)	1954	25	75('51)	550('51)
Apostolic Christian Church of America	1954	58	348	5,649
Apostolic Faith Mission	1936	13	122	1,005
The Christian Congregation	1955	150	412	13,312
Church of Daniel's Band	1951	2	10	100
Church of God (Apostolic)	1954	20	88	463
Church of God as Organized by Christ	1936	1	2	22
Metropolitan Church Association	1955	26	82('54)	921 ('54)
Missionary Bands of the World, Inc. .	1954	11	73	673
Missionary Church Association	1954	95	No data	15,622
Pillar of Fire	1949	42	173	1,480
Federated Churches	1936	484	8,126	69,628
Fire-Baptized Holiness Church	1949	42	298	2,098
Fire-Baptized Holiness Church (Wesleyan)	1954	52	No data	No data
Free Christian Zion Church of Christ ..	1952	734	938	11,174('51)
Friends:				
Central Yearly Meeting of Friends ..	1955	10	60('52)	481
Five Years Meeting of Friends	1955	436	595	27,476
Ohio Yearly Meeting of Friends Church (Independent)	1955	85	No data	10,810
Oregon Yearly Meeting of Friends Church	1955	57	665	7,230
Pacific Yearly Meeting of Friends ...	1955	15	No data	No data
Philadelphia Yearly Meeting of the Religious Society of Friends	Statistics included in statistics for the Religious Society of Friends (General Conference).			
Religious Society of Friends (Conservative)	1955	9	27	457
Religious Society of Friends (General Conference)	1955	159	660('50)	6,469('50)
Religious Society of Friends (Kansas Yearly Meeting)	1947	84	840	6,447

* Includes pupils, officers, and teachers enrolled.

Name of Religious Body	Year	Sunday or Sabbath Church Schools		
		No. of Sunday or Sabbath Schools	Officers and Teachers Enrolled	Total Enrollment*
Religious Society of Friends (Philadelphia and Vicinity)		This group (Arch Street Yearly Meeting) united in 1955 with the Race Street Yearly Meeting, to become Philadelphia Yearly Meeting of the Religious Society of Friends, see above.		
Holiness Church of God, Inc.	1955	25	101 ('53)	725
House of David	1955	None	None	None
Independent Churches	No report			
Independent Fundamental Churches of America	No report			
Independent Negro Churches	No report			
International Church of the Foursquare Gospel	1955	638	5,025('53)	62,567
Italian:				
Christian Church of North America .	1955	141	No data	No data
Jehovah's Witnesses	No statistics furnished			
Jewish Congregations	1954	2,840	13,000	412,818
Kodesh Church of Immanuel	1950	12	115	1,515
Latter-Day Saints:				
Church of Christ, Temple Lot	1936	10	76	319
Church of Jesus Christ (Bickertonites)	1955	37	280	1,420
Church of Jesus Christ (Cutlerites) ..	1953	None	None	None
Church of Jesus Christ of Latter Day Saints	1955	2,921	63,391	1,232,493
Church of Jesus Christ of Latter Day Saints (Strangites)	No report			
Reorganized Church of Jesus Christ of Latter Day Saints	1955	845	7,123	80,623
Liberal Catholic Church	1955	6	15('51)	350
Lithuanian National Catholic Church ..	1951	3	6	85 ('44)
Lutheran:				
Lutheran Synodical Conference of N.A.				
Lutheran Church—Missouri Synod ..	1955	4,639	61,180	678,156
Evangelical Lutheran Joint Synod of Wisconsin and Other States ..	1954	821	4,071 ('36)	49,067
Norwegian Synod of the American Evangelical Lutheran Church .	1955	69	438	3,527
Slovak Evangelical Lutheran Church	1952	45	432	4,501
Negro Missions	1955	50	175	3,172
American Evangelical Lutheran Church	1955	74	707	5,259
American Lutheran Church	1954	1,908	28,432	362,107
Augustana Evangelical Lutheran Church	1955	1,130	21,422	218,105
Church of the Lutheran Brethren of America	1955	45	339('52)	2,775('54)
Evangelical Lutheran Church	1954	2,248	36,864	313,310
Evangelical Lutheran Church in America (Eielsen Synod)	1955	6	20	225
Finnish Apostolic Lutheran Church of America	1953	32	234	1,760
Finnish Evangelical Lutheran Church (Suomi Synod)	1955	110	1,244	12,205
Independent Lutheran Churches	1955	None	None	None
Lutheran Free Church	1955	316	3,698	32,257
National Evangelical Lutheran Church	1955	48	369	2,808
Protestant Conference (Lutheran) ...	1955	3	6	175
United Evangelical Lutheran Church .	1955	165	2,472	23,749
United Lutheran Church in America .	1955	4,191	98,701	987,496

* Includes pupils, officers, and teachers enrolled.

		Sunday or Sabbath Church Schools		
Name of Religious Body	*Year*	*No. of Sunday or Sabbath Schools*	*Officers and Teachers Enrolled*	*Total Enroll-ment**

Mennonite Bodies:

Church of God in Christ (Mennonite)	1954	32	150('44)	5,043
Conference of the Evangelical Mennonite Church	1955	22	185('53)	2,465
Conservative Mennonite Conference .	1955	60	802	7,675
Evangelical Mennonite Brethren	1953	25	112('44)	1,612('44)
General Conference Mennonite Church	1955	180	3,859	32,362
Hutterian Brethren	1955	18	40('54)	738
Krimmer Mennonite Brethren Conf. .	1955	18	200	2,286
Mennonite Brethren Church of N.A. .	1954	75	980	14,698
Mennonite Church	1955	674	11,575	105,153
Old Order Amish Mennonite Church .	1955	None	None	None
Old Order (Wisler) Mennonite Church	1955	None	None	None
Reformed Mennonite Church	1955	None	None	None
Unaffiliated Conservative Amish Mennonite Church	1955	None	None	None
United Missionary Church	1955	195	2,927	24,802

Methodist Bodies:

African Methodist Episcopal Church .	1951	6,472	38,832	363,432
African Methodist Episcopal Zion Church	1955	3,000	25,650('52)	400,000
African Union First Colored Methodist Protestant Church, Inc.	1953	33	82	1,302
Christian Methodist Episcopal Church	1949	1,932	8,614	125,382
Congregational Methodist Church ...	1953	147	655('49)	8,022
Congregational Methodist Church of U.S.A.	1952	100	100	3,250
Cumberland Methodist Church	1954	2	10	130
Evangelical Methodist Church	1955	90	610	6,215
Free Methodist Church of N.A.	1955	1,096	16,661	150,479
Holiness Methodist Church	1955	28	124	1,496
Independent A.M.E. Denomination ..	1936	17	126	535
Independent Fundamental Methodist Church	1955	14	50('54)	650
Lumber River Annual Conference of the Holiness Methodist Church .	1955	7	126	1,207
The Methodist Church	1955	37,798	561,469	6,810,661
New Congregational Methodist Church	1936	10	59	540
Primitive Methodist Church, U.S.A. .	1955	76	1,355	10,940
Reformed Methodist Union Episcopal Church	1954	33	42('52)	684('52)
Reformed New Congregational Methodist Church	No report			
Reformed Zion Union Apostolic Church	1955	50	200	5,200
Southern Methodist Church	1955	50	420	4,420
Union American Methodist Episcopal Church	1936	66	679	5,465
Wesleyan Methodist Church of America	1955	1,045	11,361	129,879

Moravian Bodies:

Bohemian and Moravian Brethren ..	Statistics included in those for the Presbyterian Church in the U.S.A.			
Evangelical Unity of the Czech-Moravian Brethren in N.A.	1954	24	362	2,529
Moravian Church in America (Unitas Fratrum)	1955	156	2,983	30,253

Muslims	No report			
National David Spiritual Temple of Christ Church Union (Inc.), U.S.A.	1955	65	44	1,232
New Apostolic Church of N.A., Inc. ..	1955	179	562	3,130

* Includes pupils, officers, and teachers enrolled.

Name of Religious Body	Sunday or Sabbath Church Schools			
	Year	No. of Sunday or Sabbath Schools	Officers and Teachers Enrolled	Total Enrollment*

Old Catholic Churches:

American Catholic Church, Archdiocese of N.Y.	1949	3	30	489
North American Old Roman Catholic Church	1955	63	500('53)	30,709
Old Catholic Church in America	1936	11	36	295
The Reformed Catholic Church (Utrecht Confession), Province of North America	1955	11	No data	No data
Open Bible Standard Churches, Inc. ..	1955	249	2,000	22,000

Pentecostal Assemblies:

Calvary Pentecostal Church, Inc. ...	1947	55	200	8,200
Emmanuel Holiness Church	1955	56	224	2,424
International Pentecostal Assemblies	1947	60	621('36)	5,736('36)
Pentecostal Assemblies of the World, Inc.	1951	500	7,500	40,000
Pentecostal Church of Christ	1955	30	177	2,220
Pentecostal Church of God of America, Inc.	1955	850	2,200('52)	63,000
Pentecostal Fire-Baptized Holiness Church	1955	46	410('49)	5,710('49)
The Pentecostal Holiness Church, Inc.	1955	1,101	7,500	114,135
United Pentecostal Church	1955	1,500	8,000('52)	130,000('52)
Pilgrim Holiness Church	1955	1,050	10,750	130,750
Polish National Catholic Church of America	1951	216	265	23,543

Presbyterian Bodies:

Associate Presbyterian Church of N.A.	1955	4	25	370
Associate Reformed Presbyterian Church (General Synod)	1955	142	1,322('50)	20,149
Bible Presbyterian Church	1951	70	936	9,146
Colored Cumberland Presbyterian Church	1944	121	605	10,605
Cumberland Presbyterian Church	1955	891	6,500	69,034
Orthodox Presbyterian Church	1955	82	391('36)	8,102
Presbyterian Church in the U.S. ...	1955	3,599	57,727	677,875
Presbyterian Church in the U.S.A. ..	1955	8,261	155,629	1,619,262
Reformed Presbyterian Church in N.A. (General Synod)	1953	11	110	1,117
Reformed Presbyterian Church of N.A. (Old School)	1954	70	No data	4,821
United Presbyterian Church of N.A. .	1955	852	16,869	192,986
Protestant Episcopal Church	1954	5,619('51)	80,819	776,847

Reformed Bodies:

Christian Reformed Church	1955	481	3,273('47)	51,417
Free Magyar Reformed Church in America	1955	22	45('52)	2,750
Netherlands Reformed Congregations	1955	10	45('54)	2,460
Reformed Episcopal Church	1955	74	515	5,925
Roman Catholic Church	1955	17,639('49)	30,000('49)	2,277,948
Salvation Army	1955	1,104	8,144	161,748
The Schwenkfelder Church	1950	6	150('42)	2,200
Social Brethren	1955	20	57('36)	1,144

* Includes pupils, officers, and teachers enrolled.

Name of Religious Body	Year	Sunday or Sabbath Church Schools		
		No. of Sunday or Sabbath Schools	Officers and Teachers Enrolled	Total Enrollment*
Spiritualists:				
International General Assembly of Spiritualists	1955	268	381	4,635 ('52)
National Spiritual Alliance of the U.S.A.	1955	None	None	None
National Spiritualist Association of Churches	1955	52	183	1,766
Triumph the Church and Kingdom of God in Christ	1953	800	2,400	30,400
Unitarian Churches	1955	310	5,597	47,561
United Brethren Bodies:				
United Brethren in Christ	1955	315	3,924	34,957
United Christian Church	1955	9	183 ('53)	1,161
United Holy Church of America, Inc. ..	1953	347	1,802	12,929
Universalist Church of America	1955	290 ('52)	2,305	21,275
Vedanta Society	1953	None	None	None
Volunteers of America	1955	151	1,632	9,556
Totals (268 bodies; 243 reporting total enrollment)		264,726	3,029,386	38,921,033

III. Number of Clergy

THE inquiry to statisticians of religious bodies asked for information on two questions: The number of pastors having charges (parishes or congregations) and the total number of ordained persons, whether in active service or retired.

Name of Religious Body	Year	Number of Pastors having Charges	Total Number of Ordained Persons
Adventist Bodies:			
Advent Christian Church	1954	308	459
Church of God (Abrahamic Faith)	1955	61	67
Life and Advent Union	1955	3	8
Primitive Advent Christian Church	1955	9	18
Seventh-day Adventists	1955	2,196	2,106
African Orthodox Church	1953	30	90
Amana Church Society	1955	22	None
American Evangelical Christian Churches	No report		

* Includes pupils, officers, and teachers enrolled.

Name of Religious Body	Year	Number of Pastors having Charges	Total Number of Ordained Persons
American Rescue Workers	1952	23	30
Apostolic Overcoming Holy Church of God	1951	850	No data
Assemblies of God	1955	7,320	8,502
Associated Gospel Churches	No report		
Baha'i Faith	No report		

Baptist Bodies:

American Baptist Convention	1955	5,305	8,000
Southern Baptist Convention	1955	24,130	27,600
National Baptist Convention, U.S.A., Inc.	1954	18,964('52)	30,251
National Baptist Convention of America	1955	No data	28,499
American Baptist Association	No report		
Baptist General Conference of America	1955	405	521
Christian Unity Baptist Association	1955	6	12
Conservative Baptist Association of America	1955	970	1,600
Duck River (and Kindred) Associations of Baptists .	1952	No data	151
Evangelical Baptist Church, Inc., Gen. Conf.	1952	22	37
Free Will Baptists	1955	1,543	2,567
General Association of Regular Baptist Churches .	1955	675	1,025('53)
General Baptists	1955	300	1,145
General Six-Principle Baptists	1955	4	5
Independent Baptist Church of America	1954	2	4('52)
National Baptist Evangelical Life and Soul Saving Assembly of U.S.A.	1951	128	137
National Primitive Baptist Convention of the U.S.A.	1952	600	750
North American Baptist Association	1955	1,547	1,547
North American Baptist General Conference	1955	283	426
Primitive Baptists	No report		
Regular Baptists	No report		
Separate Baptists	1955	60('54)	98
Seventh Day Baptist General Conference	1955	45	76
Seventh Day Baptists (German 1728)	1951	2	4
Two-Seed-In-The-Spirit Predestinarian Baptists ...	No report		
United Baptists	1955	415	1,110
United Free Will Baptist Church	1952	915	784
Bible Protestant Church	1955	24	28

Brethren (German Baptists):

Brethren Church (Ashland, Ohio)	1955	93	160
Brethren Church (Progressive)	1953	141	249('51)
Church of the Brethren	1955	876	2,366
Church of God (New Dunkards)	1953	8	5
Old German Baptist Brethren	1955	55	124
Plymouth Brethren	No report		

Brethren (River):

Brethren in Christ	1955	114	224
Old Order, or Yorker, River Brethren	No report		
United Zion Church	1955	19	49
Buddhist Churches of America	1955	59	67
Catholic Apostolic Church	No report		
Christ Unity Science Church	1953	4,971	5,019
Christadelphians	1955	None	None
Christian and Missionary Alliance	1955	922	1,026
Christian Catholic Church	1955	No data	17
Christian Nation Church	1955	34	19
Christian Union	No report		
Christ's Sanctified Holy Church	1955	14	25
Church of Christ (Holiness), U.S.A.	1955	97	265
Church of Christ, Scientist	No statistics furnished		
Church of Eternal Life	No report		

Name of Religious Body	Year	Number of Pastors having Charges	Total Number of Ordained Persons
Churches of God:			
Church of God (Cleveland, Tenn.)	1955	2,779	4,243
Church of God (Anderson, Ind.)	1955	1,776	2,702
Church of God (Seventh Day)	No report		
The (Original) Church of God, Inc.	1952	50	155
The Church of God	1955	1,519	2,131
The Church of God (Seventh Day), Denver, Colo. ..	1955	61	48('54)
The Church of God of Prophecy	1955	1,050	730
Evangelistic Church of God	1953	7	17
Church of God and Saints of Christ	1955	No data	No data
Church of Illumination	No report		
Church of God in Christ	1955	3,260	4,760
Church of Our Lord Jesus Christ of the Apostolic Faith, Inc.	1954	150	165
Church of the Gospel	1955	3	3
Church of the Nazarene	1955	3,979	5,188
The Church of Revelation	1954	10	37
Churches of Christ	1955	14,000('54)	15,500
Churches of Christ in Christian Union	1955	192	287
Churches of God, Holiness	1954	32	45
Churches of God in N.A. (General Eldership)	1955	340	389
Churches of the Living God:			
Church of the Living God (Christian Workers for Fellowship)	1952	7	10
House of God, Which is the Church of the Living God, the Pillar and the Ground of the Truth, Inc.	No report		
Churches of the New Jerusalem:			
General Convention of the New Jerusalem in the U.S.A.	1955	36	56
General Church of the New Jerusalem	1954	12	24
Congregational Christian Churches	1955	3,486	5,938
Congregational Holiness Church	1955	138	274
Disciples of Christ, International Convention	1955	4,033	7,339
Divine Science Church and College, Inc.	No report		
Eastern Churches:			
Albanian Orthodox Church in America	1955	14	14
American Carpatho-Russian Orthodox Greek Catholic Church	1955	50	59
American Catholic Church (Syro-Antiochean)	1955	61	67
The American Holy Orthodox Catholic Apostolic Eastern Church	1955	21	21
The American Orthodox Church	No report		
Apostolic Episcopal Church	No report		
Armenian Apostolic Church of America	1955	42	42
Assyrian Orthodox Church	1951	4	4
Bulgarian Eastern Orthodox Church	1955	6('54)	9
Church of the East and of the Assyrians	1952	8	38
Eastern Orthodox Catholic Church in America	1955	1	7
Greek Archdiocese of North and South America ..	1955	405	410('54)
Holy Orthodox Church in America (Eastern Catholic and Apostolic)	1955	4	10
Romanian Orthodox Episcopate of America	1955	35	35
The Russian Orthodox Catholic Church, Archdiocese of the Aleutian Islands and North America ..	No report		
The Russian Orthodox Church Outside Russia	1951	150	224
The Russian Orthodox Greek Catholic Church of America	1955	345	410
Serbian Eastern Orthodox Church	1955	59	60

Name of Religious Body	Year	Number of Pastors having Charges	Total Number of Ordained Persons
Syrian Antiochian Orthodox Church	1955	90	105
Ukrainian Orthodox Church of America	1955	34	52
Ukrainian Orthodox Church of U.S.A.	1955	86	104
Ethical Culture Movement	1955	14	21
Evangelical and Reformed Church	1955	1,874	2,573
Evangelical Congregational Church	1955	161	129
Evangelical Free Church of America	1955	381	298
Evangelical Mission Covenant Church of America ...	1954	394	519
Evangelical United Brethren Church	1955	2,934	3,473

Evangelistic Associations:

Apostolic Christian Church (Nazarean)	1954	40	9
Apostolic Christian Church of America	1954	163	25
Apostolic Faith Mission	1952	2	2
The Christian Congregation	1955	136	138
Church of Daniel's Band	1951	4	10
Church of God (Apostolic)	1954	20	50
Church of God as Organized by Christ	No report		
Metropolitan Church Association	1955	26	61
Missionary Bands of the World, Inc.	1954	11	26
Missionary Church Association	1954	95	145
Pillar of Fire	No report		
Federated Churches	No report		
Fire-Baptized Holiness Church	No report		
Fire-Baptized Holiness Church (Wesleyan)	1955	50	75
Free Christian Zion Church of Christ	1952	624	698

Friends:

Central Yearly Meeting of Friends	1955	10	39
Five Years Meeting of Friends	1955	317	553
Ohio Yearly Meeting of Friends Church (Independent)	1955	83	172
Oregon Yearly Meeting of Friends Church	1955	57	150
Pacific Yearly Meeting of Friends	1955	None	None
Philadelphia Yearly Meeting of the Religious Society of Friends	Statistics included in statistics for the Religious Society of Friends (General Conference).		
Religious Society of Friends (Conservative)	1955	None	15
Religious Society of Friends (General Conference) .	1955	13	None
Religious Society of Friends (Kansas Yearly Meeting)	No report		
Religious Society of Friends (Philadelphia and Vicinity)	This group (Arch Street Yearly Meeting) united in 1955 with the Race Street Yearly Meeting, to become Philadelphia Yearly Meeting of the Religious Society of Friends, see above.		
Holiness Church of God, Inc.	1955	24	40
House of David	1955	12	10
Independent Churches	No report		
Independent Fundamental Churches of America	No report		
Independent Negro Churches	No report		
International Church of the Foursquare Gospel	1955	650	1,277

Italian:

Christian Church of North America	1955	172	226
Jehovah's Witnesses	No statistics furnished		
Jewish Congregations	1954	2,902	3,965
Kodesh Church of Immanuel	No report		

Name of Religious Body	Year	Number of Pastors having Charges	Total Number of Ordained Persons
Latter-Day Saints:			
Church of Christ, Temple Lot	No report		
Church of Jesus Christ (Bickertonites)	1955	40	304
Church of Jesus Christ (Cutlerites)	1953	None	3
Church of Jesus Christ of Latter Day Saints	1954	2,619	No data
Church of Jesus Christ of Latter Day Saints (Strangites)	No report		
Reorganized Church of Jesus Christ of Latter Day Saints	1955	808	9,657
Liberal Catholic Church	1955	7	28
Lithuanian National Catholic Church	1954	3	3
Lutheran:			
Lutheran Synodical Conference of N.A.			
Lutheran Church—Missouri Synod	1955	3,871	5,020
Evangelical Lutheran Joint Synod of Wisconsin and Other States	1954	659	741
Norwegian Synod of the American Evangelical Lutheran Church	1955	52	71
Slovak Evangelical Lutheran Church	1952	47	7
Negro Missions	1955	25	27
American Evangelical Lutheran Church	1955	67	90
American Lutheran Church	1954	1,500	1,897
Augustana Evangelical Lutheran Church	1955	868	1,157
Church of the Lutheran Brethren of America	1955	39	110
Evangelical Lutheran Church	1954	1,310	1,924
Evangelical Lutheran Church in America (Eielsen Synod)	1955	4	5
Finnish Apostolic Lutheran Church of America	1953	17	22
Finnish Evangelical Lutheran Church (Suomi Synod)	1955	81	92
Independent Lutheran Churches	1953	1	1
Lutheran Free Church	1955	162	245
National Evangelical Lutheran Church	1955	25	26
Protestant Conference (Lutheran)	1955	7	17
United Evangelical Lutheran Church	1955	129	198
United Lutheran Church in America	1955	3,021	4,154
Mennonite Bodies:			
Church of God in Christ (Mennonite)	1954	31	125
Conference of the Evangelical Mennonite Church	1955	19	24
Conservative Mennonite Conference	1955	106	109
Evangelical Mennonite Brethren	1955	28	40
General Conference Mennonite Church	1955	163	200
Hutterian Brethren	1955	46	33
Krimmer Mennonite Brethren Conf.	1955	10	40
Mennonite Brethren Church of N.A.	1954	70	252
Mennonite Church	1955	1,073	1,515
Old Order Amish Mennonite Church	1955	610	775
Old Order (Wisler) Mennonite Church	1955	45	65
Reformed Mennonite Church	1955	21	23
Unaffiliated Conservative Amish Mennonite Church	1955	61	74
United Missionary Church	1955	181	213
Methodist Bodies:			
African Methodist Episcopal Church	1951	5,878	7,089
African Methodist Episcopal Zion Church	1955	2,400	2,370
African Union First Colored Methodist Protestant Church, Inc.	1953	33	40
Christian Methodist Episcopal Church	1951	1,820	1,631
Congregational Methodist Church	1953	160('49)	262
Congregational Methodist Church of U.S.A.	1954	100	120
Cumberland Methodist Church	1954	2	6

Name of Religious Body	Year	Number of Pastors having Charges	Total Number of Ordained Persons
Evangelical Methodist Church	1955	91	134
Free Methodist Church of N.A.	1955	1,066('54)	1,986
Holiness Methodist Church	1955	26	38
Independent A.M.E. Denomination	No report		
Independent Fundamental Methodist Church	1955	14	17
Lumber River Annual Conference of the Holiness Methodist Church	1955	4	6
The Methodist Church	1955	23,665	26,649
New Congregational Methodist Church	No report		
Primitive Methodist Church, U.S.A.	1955	74	70
Reformed Methodist Union Episcopal Church	1954	33	37
Reformed New Congregational Methodist Church ..	No report		
Reformed Zion Union Apostolic Church	1955	40	50
Southern Methodist Church	1955	25	21
Union American Methodist Episcopal Church	No report		
Wesleyan Methodist Church of America	1955	942	1,385

Moravian Bodies:

Bohemian and Moravian Brethren	Statistics included in those for the Presbyterian Church in the U.S.A.		
Evangelical Unity of the Czech-Moravian Brethren in N.A.	1954	8	8
Moravian Church in America (Unitas Fratrum)	1955	131	151

Muslims	No report		
National David Spiritual Temple of Christ Church Union (Inc.), U.S.A.	1955	66	265
New Apostolic Church of N.A., Inc.	1955	174	572

Old Catholic Churches:

American Catholic Church, Archdiocese of N.Y. ...	No report		
North American Old Roman Catholic Church	1955	64	79
The Old Catholic Church in America	No report		
The Reformed Catholic Church (Utrecht Confession), Province of North America	1955	18	21

Open Bible Standard Churches, Inc.	1955	249	530

Pentecostal Assemblies:

Calvary Pentecostal Church, Inc.	No report		
Emmanuel Holiness Church	1955	55	90
International Pentecostal Assemblies	1952	85	137
Pentecostal Assemblies of the World, Inc.	1954	384	258
Pentecostal Church of Christ	1955	34	73
Pentecostal Church of God of America, Inc.	1955	850	954
Pentecostal Fire-Baptized Holiness Church	1955	45	67
The Pentecostal Holiness Church, Inc.	1955	1,034	1,581
United Pentecostal Church	1955	1,500	1,400

Pilgrim Holiness Church	1955	923	1,607
Polish National Catholic Church of America	1954	136	141

Presbyterian Bodies:

Associate Presbyterian Church of N.A.	1955	6	6
Associate Reformed Presbyterian Church (General Synod)	1955	100	102
Bible Presbyterian Church	No report		
Colored Cumberland Presbyterian Church	No report		
Cumberland Presbyterian Church	1955	618	732
Orthodox Presbyterian Church	1955	68	110
Presbyterian Church in the U.S.	1955	2,371	3,292
Presbyterian Church in the U.S.A.	1955	6,372	9,871
Reformed Presbyterian Church in N.A. (General Synod)	1953	5	8

Name of Religious Body	Year	Number of Pastors having Charges	Total Number of Ordained Persons
Reformed Presbyterian Church of N.A. (Old School)	1954	56	416
United Presbyterian Church of N.A.	1955	665	967
Protestant Episcopal Church	1954	4,963('51)	7,193

Reformed Bodies:

Christian Reformed Church	1955	386	541
Free Magyar Reformed Church in America	1955	18	21
Netherlands Reformed Congregations	1955	7	8
Protestant Reformed Churches of America	1955	18	19
Reformed Church in America	1955	689	996
Reformed Episcopal Church	1955	54	73
Roman Catholic Church	1955	16,108	48,165
Salvation Army	1955	3,181	5,159
The Schwenkfelder Church	1950	5	5
Social Brethren	1955	18	34

Spiritualists:

International General Assembly of Spiritualists ...	1955	215	183
National Spiritual Alliance of the U.S.A.	1955	37	37
National Spiritualist Association of Churches	1955	150	227
Triumph the Church and Kingdom of God in Christ ..	1953	387	900
Unitarian Churches	1955	343	525

United Brethren Bodies:

United Brethren in Christ	1955	245	247
United Christian Church	1955	10	11
United Holy Church of America, Inc.	1953	353	382
Universalist Church of America	1955	237	446
Vedanta Society	1955	13	13
Volunteers of America	1955	291	291
Totals: (268 bodies; 222 reporting pastors with charges)		222,018	353,695

IV. *Groups of Religious Bodies*

THE following tabulation gives the religious bodies which have more than one sect in the denomination. In the parenthesis after the name of the "family" is the number of sects reporting.

Number of Churches and Inclusive Church Membership, by Groups of Religious Bodies, According to Most Recently Reported Figures, Mainly for the Year Ending December 31, 1954.

	Number of Churches	Inclusive Membership
Adventist Bodies (5)	3,385	312,782
Baptist Bodies (27)	87,107	18,793,097
Brethren (German Baptists) (5)	1,360	239,664
Brethren (River) (3)	138	7,284
Churches of God (8)	8,098	382,775
Churches of the Living God (2)	124	4,903
Churches of the New Jerusalem (2)	63	5,980
Eastern Churches (19) [1]	1,385	2,386,945
Evangelistic Associations (11)	471	39,903
Friends (8)	1,015	121,468
Latter Day Saints (6)	3,504	1,372,640
Lutheran Bodies (19)	16,375	7,059,593
Mennonite Bodies (14)	1,366	168,624
Methodist Bodies (22)	54,295	11,784,060
Moravian Bodies (2)	190	60,800
Old Catholic Churches (4)	132	101,491
Pentecostal Assemblies (9)	4,127	319,776
Presbyterian Bodies (10) [2]	14,406	3,860,686
Reformed Bodies (5)	1,352	426,737
Spiritualists (3)	476	173,863
United Brethren Bodies (3)	328	20,566
All Other Bodies (70) [3]	105,752	52,518,892
Total—256 Bodies Reporting	305,449	100,162,529

[1] There are two additional bodies for which figures are not available.
[2] There is one additional body for which figures are not available.
[3] There are 6 additional bodies for which neither number of churches nor church membership was reported and one additional body that reported number of churches but not membership.

The Larger Bodies

There are 82 religious bodies with over 50,000 members each, and these reported 98.4 per cent of the total number of members, or 98,571,528 persons.

Fifty-three bodies report over 100,000 members each, and these had a combined membership of 96,607,968 persons, or 96.4 per cent of the total membership.

V. Constituency of the National Council of Churches

BESIDES the constituent members listed below, the National Council of the Churches of Christ in the U.S.A. also includes a number of agencies as consultative bodies, notably the American Bible Society, the National Council of the Young Men's Christian Associations, the National Board of the Young Women's Christian Association and the U.S.A. Conference of the World Council of Churches. These agencies are only advisory members of the National Council of Churches, without voting power.

Constituent Bodies of the National Council of Churches in Continental United States

Constituent Body	Year	Number of Churches	Inclusive Membership	Pastors Having Charges
African Methodist Episcopal Church	1951	5,878	1,166,301	5,878
African Methodist Episcopal Zion Church	1955	3,080	760,000	2,400
American Baptist Convention	1955	6,490	1,513,697	5,305
American Evangelical Lutheran Church	1955	86	21,800	67
Augustana Evangelical Lutheran Church	1955	1,169	529,602	868
Church of the Brethren	1955	1,049	195,609	876
Christian Methodist Episcopal Church	1951	2,469	392,167	1,820
Congregational Christian Churches	1955	5,561	1,342,045	3,486
Disciples of Christ, International Conv.	1955	7,951	1,897,736	4,033
Evangelical and Reformed Church	1955	2,732	774,277	1,874
Evangelical United Brethren Church	1955	4,370	737,489	2,934
Evangelical Unity of the Czech-Moravian Brethren in North America	1954	32	5,276	8
Greek Archdiocese of North and South America	1955	353	1,000,000	405

Constituent Body	Year	Number of Churches	Inclusive Member-ship	Pastors Having Charges
Moravian Church in America (Unitas Fratrum) .	1955	158	55,524	131
National Baptist Convention of America	1955	11,291	2,610,774	28,499*
National Baptist Convention, U.S.A., Inc.	1954	25,603	4,557,416	18,964
Presbyterian Church in the U.S.	1955	3,852	810,917	2,371
Presbyterian Church in the U.S.A.	1955	8,282	2,645,745	6,372
Protestant Episcopal Church	1954	7,271	2,757,944	4,963
Reformed Church in America	1955	804	205,323	689
** Religious Society of Friends (Philadelphia and Vicinity)	1954	51	6,859	......
Romanian Orthodox Episcopate of America	1955	51	50,000	35
Seventh Day Baptist General Conference	1955	62	6,095	45
Syrian Antiochian Orthodox Church	1955	80	100,000	90
The Five Years Meeting of Friends	1955	516	70,245	317
The Methodist Church	1955	39,854	9,292,046	23,665
The Russian Orthodox Greek Catholic Church of America	1955	350	750,000	345
Ukrainian Orthodox Church of America	1954	34	44,200	34
United Lutheran Church in America	1955	4,050	2,175,726	3,021
United Presbyterian Church of N.A.	1955	833	244,973	665
Total		144,362	36,719,786	120,160

* This is the total number of ordained persons. The number of pastors having charges is not known.

** Merged in 1955, with another Friends body—see directory for data.

VI. Church Giving

THE financial data are for only a portion of the religious bodies in the United States. But they represent all the larger non-Catholic denominations. Statistics were furnished by national officials of the churches reporting.

Total Benevolences are the sum of:

Budget benevolence, which includes contributions from living donors to the benevolent budget of the denomination as determined by the proper authority.

Denominational benevolence, which includes all the budget benevolences and such other contributions for the work of the denomination as may be reported to its national headquarters.

Other benevolences, which are contributions for various causes not in the denominational list, and include only a small part of what is actually contributed because only what is reported to denominational headquarters is given in the following tables.

Congregational Expenses include contributions to the expenses of the local parish or church, such as building funds, repairs, fuel, minister's salary and anything that is for the immediate benefit of the congregation.

Total Contributions are the sum of total benevolences and congregational expenses.

Foreign Missions are included under the total contributions.

Total Contributions from Living Donors

Religious Body	Total Benevolences	Congregational Expenses	Total Contributions
1. Adventists: Seventh Day	$ 40,118,187	$ 9,591,739	$ 49,709,926
2. Baptist: *American Convention	10,199,362[1]	55,154,822	65,354,184[1]
3. *National Convention U.S.A., Inc. .	....	....	....
4. North American General Conference	876,982	2,497,400	3,374,382
5. Seventh Day General Conference .	59,196	151,500	210,696
6. Southern Convention	52,926,157	252,647,497	305,573,654
7. Brethren: Progressive (National Fellowship)	411,197	961,921	1,373,118
8. *Church of the Brethren	2,249,999	5,562,807	7,812,806
9. *The Brethren Church (Ashland, Ohio)	156,182	662,008	818,190
10. Brethren in Christ	373,382	393,824	767,206
11. *Church of the Nazarene	6,259,669	27,351,377	33,611,046
12. Church of God, Anderson, Indiana ..	1,559,428	9,200,000	10,759,428
13. Churches of God in N.A. (General Eldership)	193,295	1,249,165	1,442,460
14. *Congregational Christian	8,419,252	63,367,582	71,786,834
15. *Disciples of Christ	10,236,405	55,688,759	65,925,164
16. Eastern: American Catholic (Syro-Antiochean)	18,972	13,566	32,538
17. Ukrainian Orthodox Church of America	7,000	10,000	17,000
18. *Evangelical and Reformed	5,884,673	30,376,594	36,261,267
19. Evangelical Mission Covenant Church of America	1,730,718	4,940,688	6,671,406
20. *Evangelical United Brethren	7,549,027	29,060,571	36,609,598
21. *Friends: Ohio Yearly Meeting	236,943	296,969	533,912
22. International Foursquare Gospel ...	867,155	3,812,541	4,679,696
23. Lutheran: *American	5,810,262	28,392,725	34,202,987
24. *Augustana	5,989,965	16,304,133	22,203,098
25. Evangelical	6,704,769	26,608,157	33,312,926
26. Free Church[2]	501,025	1,600,001	2,101,026
27. Finish Evangelical (Suomi Synod) .	111,372	563,182	674,554
28. Missouri Synod	17,379,086	71,243,515	88,622,601
29. Norwegian	67,648	309,973	377,621
30. *United	15,454,575	60,849,769	76,304,344
31. United Evangelical	397,841	1,870,359	2,268,200
32. Wisconsin and Other States	2,376,926	8,568,690	10,945,616
33. Mennonite: Conference of Evangelical	138,901	88,076	226,977
34. General Conference	1,260,421	1,483,085	2,743,506
35. Mennonite Church	1,950,077	1,480,194	3,430,271
36. Methodist: Free	2,226,163	5,818,431	8,044,594
37. *Methodist Church	52,481,949	292,934,499	345,416,448

Religious Body	Total Benevolences	Congregational Expenses	Total Contributions
38. Wesleyan	$ 1,198,403	$ 5,177,174	$ 6,375,577
39. Moravian: Evangelical Unity Czech-Moravian Brethren	25,355	73,551	98,906
40. Moravian Church (Northern Province)	233,027	1,228,631	1,461,658
41. Presbyterian: Associate Reformed (General Synod)	289,272	1,020,878³	1,310,160
42. Cumberland	393,410	2,687,955	3,081,365
43. Orthodox	152,196	487,043	639,239
44. *U.S.	13,686,412	45,536,571	59,222,983
45. *U.S.A.	26,259,698	131,850,915	158,110,613
46. *United	3,199,345	11,598,008	14,797,353
47. *Protestant Episcopal	22,731,304	69,348,364	92,079,668
48. *Reformed Church in America	2,636,625	12,103,650	14,740,275
49. United Brethren in Christ	470,153	1,334,499	1,804,652
Total U.S., 1955	$334,368,371	$1,353,553,358	$1,687,921,729
Total U.S., 1954⁴	308,874,662	1,233,766,530⁴	1,542,641,192⁴
50. Baptist: *Convention of Ontario and Quebec	$ 817,262	$ 2,598,660	$ 3,415,922
51. *Union of Western Canada	192,649	929,196	1,121,845
52. *United Convention of Maritime Provinces	319,734	1,263,037	1,582,771
53. *The Angelican Church of Canada⁵ ..	3,510,163	14,662,477	18,172,640
54. *Presbyterian in Canada	1,333,631	6,274,974	7,608,605
55. *United Church of Canada	7,027,130	29,881,649	36,908,779
Total Canada, 1955	$ 13,200,569	$ 55,609,993	$ 68,710,562
Total Canada, 1954	10,737,629	45,416,497	56,154,126
Grand Total, U.S. and Canada, 1955	$347,568,940	$1,409,163,351	$1,756,732,291
Grand Total, U.S. and Canada, 1954⁴	319,612,291	1,279,183,027	1,598,795,318

Source: Reports from officials of religious bodies.

* Member of Joint Department of Stewardship and Benevolence.

1 The above figures do not include $2,082,300 received during the fiscal year 1954-55 in a building fund campaign. They are, therefore, not entirely comparable with the figures in last year's Statistics of Giving which figures by mistake included $805,135 received during the fiscal year 1953-54 in the building fund campaign.

2 Reported for the first time.

3 This figure represents contributions for Congregational Expenses in 1953.

4 Congregational expenses and total contributions have been revised to include an additional $5,508,883 reported by the Disciples of Christ after publication of last year's report.

5 This body was formerly known as the Church of England in Canada. The large increase in Congregational Expenses is due to the inclusion of parish capital expenditures this year for the first time.

Per Member Contributions from Living Donors

Religious Body	Total Benevolences	Congregational Expenses	Total Contributions	Foreign Missions
1. Adventists: Seventh Day	$140.38	$ 33.58	$173.94	$ 32.78
2. Baptist: *American Convention	6.73	36.43	43.17	1.16
3. *National Convention U.S.A., Inc. .	......	......	......	.05
4. North American General Conference	20.51	58.42	78.93	4.14
5. Seventh Day General Conference .	9.70	24.84	34.54	1.92
6. Southern Convention	7.30	34.87	42.17	1.44
7. Brethren: Progressive (National Fellowship)	21.65	50.66	72.31	......
8. *Church of the Brethren	13.21	32.67	45.88	1.83
9. *The Brethren Church (Ashland, Ohio)	8.36	34.45	43.82	1.77
10. Brethren in Christ	62.04	65.45	127.51	12.13
11. *Church of the Nazarene	23.23	101.48	124.71	7.27
12. Church of God, Anderson, Indiana ..	14.87	87.72	102.58	3.83
13. Churches of God in N.A. (General Eldership)	5.68	36.74	42.42	1.42
14. *Congregational Christian	6.42	48.35	54.76	1.40
15. *Disciples of Christ	5.39	29.37	34.77	1.17
16. Eastern: American Catholic (Syro-Antiochean)	3.10	2.22	5.31	.32
17. Ukrainian Orthodox Church of America	......	......	......	......
18. *Evangelical and Reformed	7.60	39.23	46.83	.88
19. Evangelical Mission Covenant Church of America	32.28	90.30	124.45	9.69
20. *Evangelical United Brethren	10.40	40.03	50.43	1.81
21. *Friends: Ohio Yearly Meeting	39.22	49.15	88.37	12.36
22. International Foursquare Gospel ...	9.94	43.72	53.66	5.13
23. Lutheran: *American	9.99	48.83	58.83	1.06
24. *Augustana	16.51	45.63	62.14	4.72
25. Evangelical	10.39	41.24	51.64	1.26
26. Free Church[1]	10.61	33.90	44.51	2.71
27. Finish Evangelical (Suomi Synod) .	4.86	24.60	20.47	1.30
28. Missouri Synod	13.31	54.52	67.82	1.03
29. Norwegian	8.39	38.46	46.85	.35
30. *United	10.17	40.07	50.25	1.62
31. United Evangelical	11.38	53.49	64.86	1.69
32. Wisconsin and Other States	10.67	38.45	49.11	.49
33. Mennonite: Conference of Evangelical	63.66	40.36	104.02	28.09
34. General Conference	35.30	41.54	76.84	9.62
35. Mennonite Church	29.13	22.11	51.24	......
36. Methodist: Free	53.90	140.89	194.79	12.77
37. *Methodist Church	5.70	31.83	37.53	1.23
38. Wesleyan	33.25	143.66	176.91	6.93
39. Moravian: Evangelical Unity Czech-Moravian Brethren	5.85	16.96	22.81	.46
40. Moravian Church (Northern Province)	9.49	50.02	59.51	3.96
41. Presbyterian: Associate Reformed (General Synod)	10.67	37.65	48.32	2.09
42. Cumberland	4.64	31.71	36.35	1.25
43. Orthodox	25.37	81.19	106.56	10.69
44. *U.S.	17.45	58.07	75.54	3.36
45. *U.S.A.	10.21	51.26	61.47	2.28
46. *United	13.49	48.88	62.37	3.98
47. *Protestant Episcopal	12.79	39.04	51.84	1.53
48. *Reformed Church in America	12.86	59.01	71.87	4.03
49. United Brethren in Christ	23.25	66.00	89.25	8.58
Total U.S., 1955	$ 9.70	$ 39.25	$ 48.95	$ 1.67[2]
Total U.S., 1954[3]	9.17	36.63[3]	45.80[3]	1.57[2]
50. Baptist: *Convention of Ontario and Quebec	$ 15.93	$ 50.66	$ 66.59	$ 4.50
51. *Union of Western Canada	11.37	54.82	66.19	2.72
52. *United Convention of Maritime Provinces	4.79	18.93	23.72	1.53

Religious Body	Total Benevolences	Congregational Expenses	Total Contributions	Foreign Missions
53. *The Anglican Church of Canada ...	$ 6.48	$ 27.04	$ 33.52	$ .23
54. *Presbyterian in Canada	7.27	34.23	41.50	1.50
55. *United Church of Canada	7.86	33.40	41.25	1.60
Total Canada, 1955	$ 7.52	$ 31.69	$ 39.21	$ 1.26
Total Canada, 1954	6.40	27.09	33.49	1.73
Grand Total, U.S. and Canada, 1955	$ 9.59	$ 38.88	$ 48.48	$ 1.65[2]
Grand Total, U.S. and Canada, 1954	9.04	36.18	45.22	1.58[2]

Source: Reports from officials of religious bodies.

* Member of Joint Department of Stewardship and Benevolence.

[1] Reporting for the first time.

[2] The 4,526,478 membership of the National Baptist Convention U.S.A. Inc. has been included in the membership figure for the purpose of calculating the per member contribution to foreign missions.

[3] Revised by inclusion of an additional amount reported by Disciples of Christ after publication of the previous year's report.

VII. Christian Day Schools
Under Protestant Auspices

THE following report was prepared by John L. Cowan, Assistant in Christian Education Research, Bureau of Research and Survey, Division of Christian Education, National Council of the Churches of Christ. It is here quoted with permission.

In most cases, figures are explicitly for elementary and high schools only. However, some kindergartens, mission schools, or boarding schools may be included.

Denomination	Schools	Enrollment
Adventists, Seventh Day	919	29,724
Baptists	15	1,364
Lutherans: Synodical Conference of North America		
Missouri Synod	1,171	112,712
Norwegian Synod	13	602
Slovak Synod	3	100
Wisconsin Synod	202	20,484
Colored Missions of foregoing Synods	38	2,210
Other Lutherans		
American Lutheran Church	38	2,743
Augustana Evangelical Lutheran Church	2	
United Lutheran Church	3	
Mennonites	64	9,064
Presbyterian, United States	125	
Protestant Episcopal	100	
Reformed Persuasion, Churches of the	156	33,377
Other	122	7,323
Total	2,971	219,703

Index

A NOTE ON THE TYPE

IN WHICH THIS BOOK IS SET

This book is set in Baskerville, a Linotype face, created from the original types used by John Baskerville, the eighteenth-century typefounder and printer. This type has long been considered one of the finest book types ever developed. The letters are wide and open and have a businesslike approach. The finer hairlines give exquisite delicacy. The heavier strokes give color and strength. The relation of the two in combination gives a brilliant effect and makes for easy reading. The book was composed and printed by the Wickersham Printing Company of Lancaster, Pa., and bound by Moore and Company of Baltimore. The typography and design are by Howard N. King.